Gender, Justice and Legal Feminism

Volume 5

The Series Gender, Justice and Legal Feminism seeks to harness the diverse and innovative work within and across the boundaries of jurisprudence and gender studies, with a specific attention to approaches inspired both by traditional and more recent feminist movements (e.g., both by difference feminism and LGBTQ+ streams – with their different conceptualizations of identity and neutrality). Sexual difference can be considered as one of the characteristics that differentiate individuals (like for instance age, or ethnic belonging) and such difference plays a focal function in issues of equality, justice, discrimination, as the philosophical concept of "différence" as properly shown. Such difference is indeed linguistic, logica, theoretical and must be studied in all its aspects. Through the lense of the difference, the series aim to publish works engaging with the intrinsic bond between justice and gender studies (through language and psychoanalysis), encouraging perspectives that can be defined as feminist according to the various meanings attributed to such term. For example, like in the meaning attributed to the term by the project of Feminist Legal Judgments, which demonstrated that legal practice can be "rewritten" and re-imagined from a point of view that includes diverse subjectivities and does not consider the male subject as the dominant and principal subject of the law. The main objective of the series is to build on theories on gender and feminism in order to propose a different perspective on legal science and method. In pursuing these tasks, the series aims to engage with the connections between gender identity, gender relations and political systems, and with all the societal aspects interacting in the construction and depiction of gender through language and human action. Such type of inquiries challenges the positivist view of law and constitutes a privileged critical point of observation. The series welcomes proposals – be they edited collections or single-authored monographs – emphasizing the conflicts and connections between justice, gender, and law, proposing critical approaches to law and feminist studies, offering analyses in areas such as jurisprudence, legal theory, gender studies, legal semiotics, law and language.

Keywords: Justice, Law, Feminism, Gender Studies, Jurisprudence, Equality, Language, Symbolic Order, Difference Feminism, Abuse, Violence, Stereotypes, Neglection, Vulnerability, Welfare, Mental health and Social Care, Anti-Discriminatory/Affirmative Actions, Human Rights, Freedom of Expression and Choice, Resilience, Queer studies, LGBTQ+ studies

Unique Selling Points:

- Challenges traditional approaches to gender and law through the unique lense of feminist discourses
- Combines the insights from legal theory, legal feminist, semiotics of law, law and language and is strongly interdisciplinary
- Proposes a new interdisciplinary field bringing together well established and young, innovative research

Tameshnie Deane

Gender-Based Violence and Femicide in South Africa

Springer

Tameshnie Deane
University of the Free State
Bloemfontein, South Africa

ISSN 2948-1651 ISSN 2948-166X (electronic)
Gender, Justice and Legal Feminism
ISBN 978-3-031-61052-3 ISBN 978-3-031-61053-0 (eBook)
https://doi.org/10.1007/978-3-031-61053-0

This Springer imprint is published by the registered company Springer Nature Switzerland AG
The registered company address is: Gewerbestrasse 11, 6330 Cham, Switzerland

To
Ryan Deane (KumuranRaja), Aedon Deane (Chellakuty), Gregory Deane, and Santhayagie Thirumudu.

For being at the root of every blessing in my life!

Om Gam Ganapathaye Namaha

Preface

South Africa (SA) is a country that is currently struggling to balance one of the most inclusive and progressive constitutions in the world, with its largely patriarchal and culture driven society. Gender-based violence (GBV), specifically femicide (GBVF) within the South African context is occurring on such a large scale that it appears to be socially normalized, legitimized, and accompanied by a culture of acceptance. Its enormous scale is indicative that society's beliefs of what does and does not constitute violence against women may be legitimizing acts of violence or providing a space for these crimes to occur. Regardless of the increased attention to women's rights in SA, there has been little progress in reducing violence against women. The question therefore remains that despite these gains, why is the rate of violence against women so unacceptably high?

By looking at the current situation and statistics around GBV, the South African government's responses, and the conditions that exacerbate GBV leading to femicide, this book adds to the knowledge base and knowledge gap on GBVF in the country. This book is unique as through a focus on real-life cases and a situational analysis of GBVF in South Africa, it highlights the failings of the government and its branches in its response efforts. This is done with the aim of using evidence for action and providing a solution on how to effectively manage the high rates of GBV leading to femicide.

Despite focusing on GBVF in SA, this book will have a wide appeal and is aimed at researchers, practitioners, students, professionals, and advocates in the field of GBV. Each chapter builds on and contributes to existing global and national concerns about GBV.

Bloemfontein, South Africa　　　　Tameshnie Deane

Contents

List of Abbreviations

ACRWC	African Charter on the Rights and Welfare of the Child
AU	African Union
CC	Constitutional Court
CEDAW	Convention on the Elimination of All Forms of Discrimination against Women
CET	Community Education and Training
CGE	Commission for Gender Equality
CJS	Criminal Justice System
CPA	Criminal Procedure Act
CRC	Convention on the Rights of the Child
DEVAW	Declaration on the Elimination of Violence against Women
DHET	Department of Higher Education and Training
DVA	Domestic Violence Act
DVAA	Domestic Violence Amendment Act
EEA	Employment Equity Act
FGM	Female Genital Mutilation
GBH	Grievous Bodily Harm
GBV	Gender-Based Violence
GBVCC	Gender-Based Violence Command Centre
GBVF	Gender-Based Violence and Femicide
GDP	Gross Domestic Product
GHRU	Gender & Health Research Unit
HEI	Higher education institution
HSRC	Human Sciences Research Council
ICCPR	International Covenant on Civil and Political Rights
ICESCR	International Covenant on Economic, Social and Cultural Rights
ICCS	International Classification of Crime for Statistical Purposes
IACtHR	Inter-American Court of Human Rights
IPID	Independent Police Investigative Directorate
ISS	Institute for Security Studies

KPMG	Klynveld Peat Marwick Goerdeler
LGBTQ+	Lesbian, Gay, Bisexual, Transgender, Intersex, Queer/Questioning, Asexual and Many Other Terms (Such as Non-Binary and Pansexual)
MATTSO	Ministerial Advisory Task Team on the Adjudication of Sexual Offences Matters
MDGs	Millenium Development Goals
MRC	Medical Research Council
NDP	National Development Plan
NPA	National Prosecuting Authority
NSP	National Strategic Plan
PEP	Post Exposure Prophylaxis
PEPUDA	Promotion of Equality and Prevention of Unfair Discrimination Act
PSET	Post School Education and Training System
RCMA	Recognition of Customary Marriages Act
RISDP	Regional Indicative Strategic Development Plan
SA	South Africa
SADC	Southern African Development Community
SAHRC	South African Human Rights Commission
SAPS	South African Police Service
SC	Supreme Court
SCA	Supreme Court of Appeal
SDGs	Sustainable Development Goals
SOA	Sexual Offences Act
SOCA	Sexual Offences and Community Affairs Unit
SRHR	Strategy for Sexual and Reproductive Health and Rights
Stats SA	Statistics South Africa
TCC	Thuthuzela Care Centers
TVET	Technical and Vocational Educational Training
UDHR	Universal Declaration of Human Rights
UK	United Kingdom
UN	United Nations
UNGA	United Nations General Assembly
UNODC	United Nations Office on Drugs and Crime
UNSC	United Nations Security Council
US	United States
VoCS	Victims of Crime Survey
WCDCS	Western Cape Department of Community Safety
WHO	World Health Organization
ZAR	South African Rand

Chapter 1
An Introduction to Gender-Based Violence and Femicide in South Africa

1.1 Introduction

1.1.1 Background and Rationale

Violence against women is a serious human rights violation and a public health problem of global proportions.[1] For many years, South Africa has been in the midst of a chronic gender-based violence (GBV) crisis arising in part from a dehumanizing and vicious apartheid history, a widespread acceptance of violence as being the norm which is further entrenched by gender and other related social and economic inequalities.[2] Traditions of gender inequality are built into the history and culture of South Africa, and the inextricable cultural link between power, dominance, and maleness manifests itself in GBV that is highly normalized in South African society.

In 1994, the first democratic elections were conducted. This brought with it an end to the decades-long struggle against the apartheid system, a system that was rooted in the hegemonic European colonization of South Africa. A key element of the new dispensation in South Africa was a formal commitment to gender as well as racial equality. This was primarily because prior to the abolishment of apartheid, violence by the dominant group against the disempowered was legitimized by both cultural and legal practices.[3] One of the many injustices of the apartheid regime included racist policies that gave white South Africans rights and status that their Black peers were deliberately deprived of.[4] These methods of exclusion, discrimination, dominance, and inequalities experienced by the minority[5] extended

[1]Deane (2019), p. 129.

[2]Deane (2018), p. 84.

[3]Moffett (2006), p. 129.

[4]Lacey (2020), para 3–4.

[5]For example, Black men were commonly hanged for rapes, but only if the victim was a white woman. See Sigsworth (2009), p. 2. Under apartheid, no white man was sentenced to death for rape.

T. Deane, *Gender-Based Violence and Femicide in South Africa*, Gender, Justice and Legal Feminism 5, https://doi.org/10.1007/978-3-031-61053-0_1

ubiquitously across all social minorities, including women. Under apartheid, citizenship was granted only to men, and women were classified exclusively as dependents.[6] Remnants of this standard persisted in the post-apartheid law that restricted protections for women,[7] particularly in cases of GBV.[8]

Apartheid policies and ideologies have provided men with a "legitimate" foundation for having a higher status in the country.[9] The legacy of racism and patriarchal indigenous laws interlinked "to spawn a particular kind of South African masculinity, which left women in a particularly vulnerable position."[10] This has resulted in the persistent belief that it is a cultural entitlement for men to control and own women which justifies their violence against them. This "power" or "authority" consequently alluded to social status and is further determined by position and income. Educational inequalities[11] and high unemployment rates among South African women or earning lower salaries than men[12] perpetuate a cycle of subordination and poverty. These factors, along with the traditional/cultural practices of men's rights over women's rights, have negated the social status of women in South Africa resulting in them lacking social and economic freedom and authority. This leaves women and girls even more vulnerable to experiencing violence in its various forms.

In addition, to date the male identity is still strongly tied to ownership of or stewardship over a woman and their children. The ideology or belief that without a wife and children, an adult man is still considered a boy is still very much socially engrained today. This cultural prerequisite to manhood conditions men to view women as something to be obtained and controlled rather than autonomous individuals, which emphasizes the idea that women are weaker and should be subordinate. The conflation of power and violence against women exacerbates and normalizes the idea that women are inferior to their male counterparts and that there should be no consequences to men exerting physical, emotional, and mental dominance over women. This is evident in how women especially are experiencing a general lack of safety and respect for their human dignity and autonomy in both their private and public lives. These feelings encompass the extent and brutality of rapes and murders of women and girls and the degree to which there is impunity and a lack of

---

Both facts reveal the racism of the legal system at the time and that is only crimes committed by Black men or against white women were worthy of legal action. See also Hirschauer (2014), p. 84.

[6]Lalloo (1998), pp. 439–459.

[7]For example, marital rape was not recognized as a criminal offense in South Africa until the creation of the *Prevention of Family Violence Act of 1993*, which stated that "a husband may be convicted of the rape of his wife." See South African Parliament (1993), pp. 1–4.

[8]Gouws (2016), p. 400.

[9]Jewkes et al. (2005), pp. 1809–1820.

[10]Maphosa (2022), pp. 87–106; Deane (2018), p. 88.

[11]Chapin and Warne (2020), p. 14.

[12]Bluedorn et al. (2021), p. 5.

individual, state, and societal accountability for the scourge.[13] Whilst the various forms and conceptualizations of GBV will be discussed in depth in the next chapters, it suffices to mention herein that violence against women or GBV is wide in scope and pervasive in its multidimensionality, the most brutal of this being femicide, which is the lethal end point of a continuum of multiple, overlapping and interconnected forms of GBV.

The enormous scale of gender-based violence and femicide (GBVF) is indicative that society's beliefs of what does and does not constitute violence against women may be legitimizing acts of violence or providing a space for these crimes to occur. The persistent systemic discrimination against South African women has been addressed by many government and social ventures, but cultural, gender and other inequalities persists, which is evident by the rates of GBV that is prolific throughout South Africa. Furthermore, the lack of effective support offered to survivors of GBV, the inadequate response to this scourge and the subsequent failure to, inter alia, integrate the issue into the wider human development agenda, contributes towards an overall lack of understanding of the issue. It also impacts a holistic understanding towards an experience that results in secondary traumatization of survivors, ultimately leading to an inadequate focus on preventing GBV.

In addressing the various concerns mentioned herein, the overall research question guiding this book is why despite the increased attention to women's rights and the significant social progress that has been made in South Africa since 1994, does the country find itself struggling to balance one of the most inclusive and progressive constitutions in the world. To answer this question this book interrogates why GBV persists in South Africa, and what factors need to be considered to effectively address it.

This rationale for this research is founded on South Africa's regional, national, and international obligations to eradicate violence and achieve women's equality. The continued and escalating levels of violence against women in South Africa, goes against well-established national and international principles. South Africa is a signatory to various international human rights instruments which means that the state and all its organs are obliged to respect, protect, promote, and fulfil their obligation to protect women and girls. The universal human rights framework, on which *the South African Constitution, 1996* (*Constitution*) is based, regards GBV as one of the most serious crimes that violates the right to life, equality, human dignity, freedom, and security of the person. Based on the principles in the *Constitution*, the government has enacted a fairly progressive legislative framework and has adopted policies, programs and plans of action aimed at ending sexual violence, including various sexual offenses legislation, specialized sexual offenses courts and a comprehensive National Policy Guidelines for Victims of Sexual Offences.

Specifically, South Africa has committed itself to the realization of the 2030 Agenda for Sustainable Development. Adopted by United Nations Member States in

[13] Deane (2018).

2015,[14] the Agenda and its 17 Sustainable Development Goals (SDGs) and 169 targets encompasses a set of hugely ambitious targets that build on the progress of the Millennium Development Goals (MDGs),[15] which concluded in 2015.[16] It calls on the world's countries to achieve peaceful and inclusive societies and to significantly reduce all forms of violence everywhere.

Specifically, and more relevant to this book, SDG 5, which addresses gender equality and the empowerment of women and girls, is comprehensive and equally ambitious. Embedded in SDG 5 is the need to break down barriers to gender equality, including by transforming the underlying norms, structures, and practices that prevent women and girls from enjoying their rights. Recognized as a core tenet of the 2030 Agenda, gender equality is both a stand-alone goal of sustainable development and a cross-cutting priority for achieving all the SDGs. Therefore, whilst women's equality and empowerment are one of the 17 SDGs, it is integral to all dimensions of inclusive and sustainable development. In short, all the SDGs depend on the achievement of Goal 5.[17]

The SDGs have highlighted interpersonal violence and violence against women and girls as impediments to development globally. South Africa is particularly and adversely affected by GBV. Achieving gender equality and the empowerment of women and girls will require more vigorous efforts to counter deeply rooted gender-based discrimination.

1.1.2 Aims, Object, and Purpose of the Book

This book is one of those efforts towards raising awareness of GBV and is a call for action towards its elimination. This book presents various new and differing perspectives on GBVF in South Africa where the subject remains taboo in everyday discourse. It focuses on understandings of the phenomenon of GBV in South Africa and the reasons for its persistence despite legislative and other efforts to combat it. Since the perceptions and experiences of women in general, and of survivors of GBV particularly, are founded in both the construction and analysis of data, this book incorporates various statistics and findings from fieldwork in South Africa to inform the examination of the present character of violence against women as understood and experienced and of the interventions in South Africa.

[14] United Nations (2015).

[15] World Health Organization (2018, February 19).

[16] The SDGs build on the Millennium Development Goals (MDGs) that were in place during 2000–2015.

[17] Goal 5 of the SDG addresses gender equality, as one of its targets, the elimination of all forms of violence against all women and girls in the public and private spheres, including trafficking and sexual and other types of exploitation.

Additionally, this book makes a valuable contribution towards explaining the high prevalence of violence against women in South Africa. It presents an opportunity to develop a broader understanding of the causes of GBVF and does this by highlighting how the various forms of violence against women acts as barriers to inequalities, informing interventions by all stakeholders including men, women, government departments, and wider society to address this scourge.

The book is a domestic rather than comparative evaluation of GBV in South Africa which assesses the status of women in South Africa and considers the importance of effective data in the elimination of all forms of violence against women. Despite only focusing on South Africa, this book nevertheless provides insight for comparative scholars considering the value of different constitutional articulations of human rights and how these support (or fail to support) efforts to address GBVF. By assessing recent incidences and responses to GBVF, the book also provides a view of not only the societal but jurisprudential opportunities and pitfalls in this area that may be applicable elsewhere. Gender equality and central to this, the right of women to live lives free of violence, is a precondition for full democratic participation and is a universal goal. The South African experience contributes to a wider understanding of the possibilities, societal limitations, and laws in challenging the ubiquity of violence against women. It is aimed at researchers, practitioners, students, professionals, and advocates in the field of GBVF. Each chapter builds on and contributes to existing global and national concerns about GBVF.

1.1.3 Hypothesis and Structure

The main hypothesis guiding this book's research question is that GBV is a manifestation of unequal gender relations and harmful manifestations of hegemonic masculinity governed by patriarchal beliefs, institutions, and systems, adversely impacting ones' mental health, damaging one's sense of self-worth, leads to lower educational attainment and reduced economic opportunities.

In addressing the research questions the structure of this book contains ten chapters of quantitative research. The various chapters assess not only the levels and determinants of violence against women, but it also examines, amongst others, men's attitudes toward GBV, perceptions of violence, the legislative and other frameworks governing violence against women, and the current cases and jurisprudence relating to this scourge. This chapter starts by providing a brief introduction and background into an understanding of GBVF in South Africa. It paves the way for an in-depth understanding into the rationale for the book and delves into what the research questions are.

Chapter 2 starts by providing the reader with the definitions of GBVF as well as pursuing an analysis around the conceptualizations of GBVF in the country. By defining various terminologies associated with this phenomenon, the aim is to provide a solid foundation towards a more in-depth understanding and conceptualization of GBVF. The chapter concludes by looking at some of the most prevalent forms of GBVF specific to the South African context.

Chapter 3 is important as it provides the reader with reasons why it is important for a country like South Africa to focus on the elimination of GBVF. By specifically referring to the 2030 SDG Agenda, it highlights how the Agenda presents a potentially transformative framework for urgent change, not only in South Africa, but throughout the world. It also highlights the economic costs associated with GBV thereby providing strong arguments for why preventing and responding to such violence should be a priority for governments, donors, and the private sector.

This is followed by Chap. 4 which includes a situational analysis of GBVF. It presents data that examines the nature, scope, and extent of GBVF in South Africa. This chapter also presents statistics for some types of crimes perpetrated against women in South Africa to provide an assessment of the trends, extent, and prevalence of victimization of women. This evidence is an important aspect to work towards achieving the SDGs target of eliminating all forms of violence against women. In addition, an understanding of what crime statistics reveal remains a vital starting point towards any protection and prevention measures. Statistics are therefore valuable tools for developing evidence-based policies and interventions to end violence against women and girls.

Chapter 5 presents a theoretical framework for understanding the high rates of GBVF in the country. By analyzing some feminist and alternative theories, the aim is to explore and provide a better understanding of the context of GBVF in the country. This chapter seeks to address a fraction of the many complex questions that arise when studying an issue like GBVF.

Chapter 6 looks at the perceptions and fear of crime. This is a crucial analysis as the perceptions and fear of crime is a very important phenomenon. It constrains behavior and lifestyles, increases anxiety, decreases social engagement, and increases the cost of criminal justice and security measures. It consequently impacts the quality of a person's life. The statistical and other evidence provided in this chapter will potentially assist policymakers, law enforcement agencies and civil society to gauge progress and plan interventions for protecting women and girls and end GBVF.

Chapter 7 examines the progressive steps taken to address GBVF in South Africa. This discussion is situated within an aim to explore, specifically, the countries legal and policy responses to GBVF in various sectors. While the law may not be the only panacea for what is now termed "a second pandemic" in the country it is the best place to start. The chapter analyzes and provides a broad understanding of the policy and legislative frameworks regarding GBVF. This chapter also investigates South Africa's human rights obligations towards the elimination of GBVF.

Chapter 8 presents a discussion on practical cases and responses to GBVF. It analyzes and contributes to the understanding of GBVF by looking at the judicial responses to the issue. It does so by providing a survey of the jurisprudence on GBV in assessing the Court's record in this area. Examples of such cases, albeit not an exhaustive list, will provide illustrations of some of the most horrendous crimes that were committed against women in the country.

Chapter 9 specifically analyzes GBVF in institutions of higher learning (HEIs). It looks at how HEIs hold the potential to address societal problems and consequently provides recommendations on how to tackle gender equality whilst at the same time empowering women and reducing GBVF. In addition, this chapter looks at how perceptions of crime, expressions of outrage, and media reporting is impacting the quality of life of women and girls. The consequence of GBV in HEIs translates to lost potential, inequality in education and a failure to achieve a country's development goals. This is especially serious for a developing country like South Africa who has international, national, and regional obligations to eliminate discrimination and violence and commitments towards development goals. This chapter therefore looks at GBV in HEIs as a specific challenge that needs to be addressed.

The concluding chapter provides suggestions for further research, and concludes by advocating for the reframing of conversations and initiatives on GBVF from individual actions to the broader context in which GBVF is allowed to persist.

1.1.4 Methodology and Limitations

The methodology utilized herein includes various meta-analysis literature reviews of relevant accredited articles, books, legal policies, and national strategies/action plans as well as programs and interventions related to GBVF specifically within South Africa. The evidence base around GBVF varies a great deal in terms of design (both qualitative and quantitative) and academic strength. For this study multiple databases were reviewed to identify relevant academic publications (whether published or not), books, journal articles, program evaluations, survey data, and other influential sources, including data from peer-reviewed journals, grey literature, and other sources.[18] Many resources included in this review consist of grey literature publications such as program documents, reports, and evaluations by, inter alia, the World Health Organization (WHO), newspaper reports, Statistics South Africa (Stats SA), Institute for Security Studies (ISS), and Amnesty International. To meet the aims and objectives of this study the main results of the literature reviews will include an analysis of the collected facts, data, and other information, whereafter logical inferences will be drawn. The results from the reviews will then be included to develop a better understanding of and strengthen recommendations toward GBVF prevention in the country.

This book aims to achieve its objectives through a multi-dimensional sociological,[19] and criminological[20] approach, which will also involve some international observations. Whilst this may seem somewhat complicated, any solutions towards

[18] Deane (2023), p. 2.

[19] This approach focuses on the examination of the features specific to the killing of women that make it a phenomenon, per se.

[20] This approach aims to distinguish femicide as a unique sector in "homicide" studies.

the elimination of GBVF is indeed complex and requires different approaches. To this end this book also, where appropriate, discusses an additional perspective, namely, a feminist[21] discourse towards a better understanding of GBVF. This discourse is not presented as a matter of methodology, as "... alternatives to ... other methods ..."[22] It serves as an instrument for a better understanding of and emphasizing difficulties and disparities in behavior with the aim of incentivizing an effective implementation strategy for more robust interventions towards the elimination of GBVF. Importantly, this book does not seek to replace or apply the feminist discourse as an alternative method to the laws and regulations rather, the aim is to locate interventions within the broader feminist discourse, whilst acknowledging the fundamental importance of rules, regulations, and policies. It is also worth mentioning that the feminist discourse, or theory, is not portrayed as one single entity. Rather, "... feminist explorations can be likened to an archaeological dig"[23] where the outcome is not to homogenize feminist theory, but to utilize the various layers of feminist discourse in ways that render it useful for a particular purpose. Consequently and, albeit aware of the fact that many different forms of feminist theory exist, the approach is to focus on only theories in a manner of engagement deemed useful to this book's research aims and objectives.

However, seeing that not all research on femicide refers to a common defining framework, Corradi suggests that future research on femicide should refer to the ecological framework of violence against women, a complex and multilayered interdisciplinary framework that understands and analyses femicide as a social phenomenon and as a "violent act" based on "the micro, meso and macro levels."[24] This book accordingly advocates for a similar approach in dealing with GBVF. However, it is acknowledged that this model has its own challenges. For example, it has been suggested that "the inherently functionalist view of society and social relationships embedded within the ecological framework results in a fundamental inability to see power relationships. It cannot 'see' patriarchy, and patriarchal social relationships are central to the work emanating from the feminist movement on femicide."[25] What is important to note though is the importance of the contribution of feminist movement actors to defining femicide in specific contexts, as well as to processes of data collection.[26]

Referring to data, the literature reviews highlight that the lack of data and adequate forms of data collection is a grave concern towards the elimination of GBVF. The concerns around the limitations of data availability and comparability have been attributed to an absence of common definitions, standards, and parameters

---

[21] This approach confronts patriarchal domination at the same time as it investigates the killing of women.

[22] Charlesworth (2005), p. 5.

[23] Charlesworth (2002), p. 99.

[24] Corradi et al. (2016), p. 988.

[25] The European Institute for Gender Equality (2021), p. 8.

[26] Sheehy (2017).

to count and document specifically, femicide. In March 2022, the United Nations Statistical Commission at its 53rd session approved a statistical framework that guides countries in the development of such a granular system.[27] It stresses the need to improve data on GBV on the characteristics of victims and perpetrators, and to measure and monitor the effectiveness of State responses to this phenomenon.[28] However to date, estimating the global number of gender-related killings of women and girls remains challenging. Some challenges can be attributed to a lack of reporting mechanisms between sub-national, national, and international data producers. In other cases, femicides are simply not recorded by or reported to the police or other competent authorities due to strong traditional and religious beliefs and an overall resistance and failure to acknowledge femicides as a criminal offense.[29]

In addition, whilst there is a plethora of articles on risk assessment of intimate partner femicides for example, many of the articles reviewed are restrictive and do not always contribute to identifying variables to define and distinguish different types of femicide. Consequently, this book refers to various grey literature where appropriate.

1.1.5 Concluding Remarks

This chapter provides a brief background into an understanding of GBVF in South Africa and aims to pave the way for an in-depth understanding to the rationale for the book. The research questions that it aims to answer is why despite the strides made by the country does GBVF remain unacceptably high. This chapter goes on to discuss the book's aims, methodology, and structure. This study remains uniquely positioned to shed light on the complex issues of sex, gender, race, power, politics, and their intersections with GBV. The next chapter will consequently provide a more in-depth analysis on the conceptualization of GBVF and its various forms.

---

[27] United Nations Statistical Commission (2022).

[28] The Statistical Framework aims to assist national statistical offices, institutions within the criminal justice and public health systems, mechanisms for the advancement of women and gender equality, civil society organizations and academia in harmonizing data collection within countries, and across countries and regions. UNODC and UN Women have started working together to support Member States in implementing the Statistical Framework, through outreach and advocacy, supporting the creation of national coordination mechanisms and by providing technical assistance to strengthen national capacities for collecting and integrating harmonized and complete data on gender-related killings. UNODC is expected to report back to the UN Statistical Commission in 2025 on the results of implementing the Statistical Framework. See United Nations Office on Drugs and Crime (2022), p. 14.

[29] Hamel and Russell (2022), p. 8.

References

Bluedorn J et al. (2021) Gender and employment in the COVID-19 recession: evidence on "She-cessions." International Monetary Fund Research Department

Chapin J, Warne V (2020) Gender responsive pedagogy in higher education: a framework. International Network for International Network for Advancing Science and Policy (INASP), London

Charlesworth H (2002) The hidden gender of international law temp. Int Comp Law J 16(93): 98–100

Charlesworth H (2005) Feminist ambivalence about international law. Int Leg Theory 11(1):5–6

Corradi C et al (2016) Theories of femicide and their significance for social research. Curr Sociol 64(7):975–995

Deane T (2018) Sexual violence and the limits of laws' powers to alter behaviour: the case of South Africa. J Int Women's Stud 19(2):84–103

Deane T (2019) Using theory to understand and reduce the high rates of sexual violence in South Africa. In: Sengupta PP (ed) Women empowerment and development - challenges & issues, pp. 129–138

Deane T (2023) A proposed national strategy for suicide prevention in South Africa. Australasian Rev Afr Stud J 44(1):1–37

Gouws A (2016) Women's activism around gender-based violence in South Africa: recognition, redistribution and representation. Rev Afr Polit Econ 43(149):400–415. https://doi.org/10.1080/03056244.2016.1217838

Hamel J, Russell B (eds) (2022) Gender and domestic violence: contemporary legal practice and intervention reforms. Oxford University Press, London

Hirschauer S (2014) Rape and the state, sexual violence and its political narrative and othering in 21st century South Africa. Afr Insight 44(1):84–102. https://doi.org/10.4314/AI.V44I1

Jewkes R et al (2005) 'If they rape me, I can't blame them': reflections on gender in the social context of child rape in South Africa and Namibia. Soc Sci Med 61(8):1809–1820. https://doi.org/10.1016/j.socscimed.2005.03.022

Lacey G (2020) Gender-based violence against women in South Africa. Ballard Brief 1:1–10

Lalloo K (1998) Citizenship and place: spatial definitions of oppression and agency in South Africa. Afr Today 45(3/4):439–459

Maphosa R (2022) Tackling the "shadow pandemic": the development of a positive duty on adults to report domestic violence. De Jure Law J 55:87–106

Moffett H (2006) These women, they force us to rape them: rape as narrative of social control in post-apartheid South Africa. J South Afr Stud 32(1):129–144. https://doi.org/10.1080/03057070500493845

Sheehy E (2017) A feminist reflection on domestic violence death reviews. In: Dawson M (ed) Domestic homicides and death reviews: an international perspective. Palgrave Macmillan, London, pp 373–402

Sigsworth R (2009) Anyone can be a rapist: an overview of sexual violence in South Africa. Center for the Study of Violence and Reconciliation, Johannesburg

South African Parliament (1993) Prevention of Family Violence Act of 1993. https://www.gov.za/sites/default/files/gcis_document/201409/act133of1993.pdf. Accessed 24 Nov 2023

The European Institute for Gender Equality (2021) Defining and identifying femicide: a literature review. Publications Office of the European Union, Luxembourg

United Nations (2015) Transforming our world: the 2030 agenda for sustainable development. https://sdgs.un.org/2030agenda. Accessed 2 Apr 2023

United Nations Office on Drugs and Crime (2022) Statistical framework for measuring the gender-related killing of women and girls. https://www.unodc.org/documents/data-and-analysis/statistics/Statistical_framework_femicide_2022.pdf. Accessed 6 Aug 2023

United Nations Statistical Commission (2022) Report on the fifty-third session (28 February–2 March and 4 March 2022). https://unstats.un.org/unsd/statcom/53rd-session/documents/2022-41-FinalReport-E.pdf. Accessed 5 Dec 2023

World Health Organization (2018, February 19) Millennium Development Goals (MDGs). https://www.who.int/news-room/fact-sheets/detail/millennium-development-goals-(mdgs)#:~:text=The%20United%20Nations%20Millennium%20Declaration. Accessed 19 Jan 2023

Chapter 2
Conceptualizing Gender-Based Violence and Femicide in South Africa

2.1 Overview

Violence against women and girls is now widely acknowledged as a global pandemic affecting millions worldwide.[1] An estimated 736 million women and girls have been subjected to various forms[2] of violence[3] ranging from approximately 640 million women aged 15 and older being subjected to intimate partner violence, 81,000 women and girls being victims of femicide and approximately 47,000 women and girls dying at the hands of an intimate partner or a family member.[4] Whilst violence takes many forms and occurs in different contexts, settings, circumstances and relationships, two of the most prevalent types of violence that women experience are intimate partner violence and non-partner sexual violence[5] where one in three women across the world have experienced one[6] or both of these forms of violence at least once in their lifetime.[7]

Violence against women and girls is any act of *violence or harmful act that is directed against a person because of their gender*, the most serious of which leads to femicide. Violence against women and girls is therefore any act of gender-based

---

[1] Bows and Fileborn (2020), p. 300.

[2] Violence against women includes such violence including but not limited to physical, sexual, emotional, financial, structural, and psychological. These different forms are not mutually exclusive and multiple incidences of violence can be happening at once and reinforcing each other. Inequalities experienced by a person related to their race, (dis)ability, age, social class, religion, sexual orientation, or gender identity can also drive acts of violence. This means that while women face violence and discrimination based on gender, some women experience multiple and interlocking forms of violence. See United Nations (2013), para 5.

[3] World Health Organization (2021a), p. 2; World Bank (2023).

[4] United Nations Office on Drugs and Crime (2021).

[5] World Health Organization (2021a).

[6] World Bank (2019).

[7] World Health Organization (2021b).

T. Deane, *Gender-Based Violence and Femicide in South Africa*, Gender, Justice and Legal Feminism 5, https://doi.org/10.1007/978-3-031-61053-0_2

violence (GBV)[8] that results in, or is likely to result in physical, sexual or psychological harm or suffering, including threats of such acts, coercion or arbitrary deprivation of liberty, whether occurring in public or private life.[9] This would include violence comprising of non-partner sexual violence.[10] It also includes those acts once considered a private or a family matter and historically overlooked and condoned like, intimate partner sexual violence and domestic violence.[11] This book clarifies that States are responsible for femicide when they tolerate and facilitate a system in which perpetrators can act with impunity.

A significant characteristic of GBV is that it transcends all social or economic boundaries and affects women and girls of all socio-economic backgrounds. In addition, violence against women has been recognized as a form of gender discrimination, which results from the historically unequal power relations between women and men,[12] and "seriously inhibits women's ability to enjoy rights and freedoms on a basis of equality with men."[13] It is therefore considered one of the most fundamental social, political and economic means by which the subordinate position of women with respect to men and their stereotyped roles are perpetuated.[14] Violence against women has both short and long-term adverse consequences on their health, psychosocial, and developmental outcomes[15] It severely impacts the full enjoyment of their basic human rights.[16] It is consequently acknowledged as a gross human rights violation rooted not only in unjust and unequal power and gender relations but includes structures contributing to this inequality in societies. The framing of GBV as a human rights violation is deliberate and implies an important conceptual shift. It means recognizing that women are not exposed to violence by accident, or because of an in-born vulnerability. Instead, violence is the result of structural, deep-rooted discrimination, which remains obligatory to address. Any attempt at addressing and preventing GBV must acknowledge and identify those complexities that enable such

[8] Gender-based violence against women is violence that is directed against a woman because she is a woman or violence that affects women disproportionately. See Council of Europe (2011).

[9] United Nations (1993).

The United Nations *Declaration on the Elimination of Violence Against Women* (DEVAW) defines GBV as "any act of gender-based violence that results in or is likely to result in physical, sexual or psychological harm or suffering to women, including threats of such acts, coercion or arbitrary deprivations of liberty, whether occurring in public or private life."

[10] Garcia-Vergara et al. (2022).

[11] Domestic violence includes violence between adults who are or have been an intimate partner but is broader than intimate partner violence and includes any family member. See Karystianis et al. (2019).

Intimate partner violence is restricted to that violence or abuse that occurs from a pre-existing or past intimate or romantic relationship. See National Center for Injury Prevention and Control, Division of Violence Prevention (2022).

[12] African Union (2003).

[13] UN Committee on the Elimination of Discrimination Against Women (CEDAW) (1992).

[14] United Nations (2017).

[15] Wirtz et al. (2018).

[16] United Nations (2013).

violence to continue. All legislative, administrative, and institutional measures and reforms, including the eradication of gender stereotypes, must form the foundations for any efforts and initiatives. GBV has consequently become increasingly visible on the global health and development agenda[17] as a matter of social justice and equality for women and as a public health priority.[18] GBV is a specific form of discrimination that affects women and girls' welfare, health, their families, and communities.[19] Specifically the costs[20] associated with GBV burdens both households and economies.[21]

Various studies suggest that the African region has some of the highest rates of GBV and femicide (GBVF) including physical and sexual intimate partner violence in the world.[22] Whilst violence against women is endemic in the world and Africa, it has reached extreme and crisis proportions in South Africa.[23] The country has been described as a "deeply violent and continues to wrestle with the impact of decades of institutionalised racism, exclusion, structural violence and other factors that have continued to undermine human development and positive social cohesion."[24] Furthermore, the Global Peace Index has consistently identified South Africa as one of the most violent places in the world, ranked 123 out of 163 countries in 2020[25] and 118 in 2022.[26] Despite the marginally better position in 2022, South Africa still has one of the highest murder rates found globally outside of a country at war or a conflict-ridden zone.[27] The country is also considered to be the country with one of the world's highest rates of GBV, including femicide, rape[28] and intimate partner violence.[29] GBVF is described as being "rampant" in the country[30] and despite

[17] Ellsberg et al. (2015).

[18] Temmerman (2015).

[19] Ellsberg et al. (2008).

[20] GBV costs South Africa between R28.4-billion and R42.4-billion per year, which amounts to 0.9% to 1.3% of its GDP annually. To give this some context, this is equivalent to employing an additional 200,000 primary school teachers for a year or providing National Health Insurance to a quarter of the South African population. See Africa Health Organisation (2021).

[21] World Bank Group (2014). In some countries, violence against women is estimated to cost countries up to 3.7% of their GDP—more than double what most governments spend on education.

[22] Corradi (2021); see also Mpani and Nsibande (2015).

[23] In Africa, South Africa has the highest prevalence rate of femicide of approximately 9.46 per 100,000 female population. See United Nations Office on Drugs and Crime (2019).

[24] Government of South Africa (2020), p. 23.

[25] News24 (2020), para 4.

[26] Mail & Guardian (2022), para 3.

Despite the slight increase in the index, this ranking still puts South Africa on the lower end of the scale (in the lowest quartile), but still some way off war-torn regions like Syria and Afghanistan.

[27] South African Human Rights Commission (2021).

[28] Deane (2018).

[29] Oram et al. (2022).

[30] South African Government (2022a).

various efforts by the government GBVF continues seemingly unabated in the country.[31]

An overview of a 2018 statistical analysis of prevalence data from 2000–2018 across 161 countries found that worldwide, nearly one in three, or 30%, of women have been subjected to physical and/or sexual violence by an intimate partner or non-intimate partner or both.[32] A 2022 report[33] found that intimate partner violence is the most common form of violence worldwide, including in South Africa, and contributes substantially to the global burden of mental health problems. Indeed, approximately 50% of women in South Africa have experienced physical or intimate partner sexual violence.[34] South Africa is also one of the top countries for femicides. Femicide is five times higher in South Africa than the global average, with South Africa having the fourth-highest female interpersonal violence death rate out of the 183 countries listed by the World Health Organization (WHO).[35] This translates to the issue being more serious in South Africa than in most countries and leads to perceptions of it being normalized in the country.

Unsurprisingly, this is a major cause for concern. If one looks at gender inequality in South Africa, one can argue that South Africans find themselves confronted with a somewhat conflicting situation. On the one hand South Africa has one of the most inclusive and progressive *Constitutions*[36] in the world with regards to the legal protection of gender rights and the explicit provision for a democratic state based on, amongst others, the value of "non-sexism."[37] On the other hand South Africa finds itself struggling to balance this with its largely patriarchal and culture driven society.[38] It therefore begs the question of why regardless of the increased attention to women's rights in the country,[39] there has been little progress in reducing GBVF.

---

[31] South African Government (2022b).

[32] World Health Organization (2021a).

[33] Oram et al. (2022).

[34] Daily Maverick (2022).

[35] Africa Health Organisation (2021).

[36] The *Constitution of the Republic of South Africa, 1996* (*Constitution*).

[37] *Constitution*, section(1)(b).

[38] Deane (2018).

[39] The end of Apartheid brought a major shift in attitudes and policies towards gender equality in South Africa. The issue of achieving gender equality and advancing the rights of women became a key policy commitment in the new democratic dispensation. Specifically, the 1996 *Constitution* went on to provide women with a full range of rights including the right to equality, dignity, the right not to be discriminated against based on one's gender or race and the right to be free from violence. A range of measures were set up that was aimed at the protection of women which included, inter alia, the National Gender Machinery through establishing an Office on the Status of Women (African Development Fund (2009); the Commission on Gender Equality and an *ad-hoc* Committee on the Quality of Life and Status of Women. In addition, there was an overhaul of legislation and policies specifically recognizing the equal status of women such as the *Employment Equity Act 55 of 1998*, the *Labour Relations Act 66 of 1995*; the *Domestic Violence Act No 116 of 1998*, new legislation for sexual offenses; as well as ratifying various international treaties such as the *Convention on the Elimination of all forms of Discrimination against Women*, 1992; *UN*

This situation calls for an explanation of why women's gains in the "public" sphere have coincided with a deterioration of their physical security. To answer this, one needs to first gain a conceptual understanding of GBVF.

2.2 Conceptualizing Gender-Based Violence and Femicide

2.2.1 Gender-Based Violence

GBV and violence against women are terms used to explain, describe, and define "... one of the most pronounced expressions of the unequal power relations between women and men."[40] These types of violence are deeply rooted in the social and cultural structures, norms and values that govern society, and is often perpetuated by a culture of denial and silence. It is consequently based upon the imbalance of, and inequality in access to, power, where the violence is perpetrated with the intent of subjugation and/or humiliation and where the outcome is aimed towards asserting superiority.[41] Additionally, it is important to mention that GBV or violence against women include many different forms of violence, spanning from verbal abuse to gender-motivated killings of women, an aspect raised in this book as "femicide."

GBV is not a new phenomenon. Throughout history, the relations between males and females have involved various forms of discrimination based on gender.[42] However, the term "gender-based violence" itself has only been well-defined within the last few decades. This was because of the continued fight of activists and advocates of gender equality to reduce discrimination and harmful practices against women. A major achievement in this regard is the 1993 *United Nations Declaration on the Elimination of Violence against Women (DEVAW)*.[43] *DEVAW* adopted the same principles as the 1979 *Convention on the Elimination of All Forms of Discrimination against Women (CEDAW)*[44] committee's *General Recommendation 19*,[45] which recommendation identified the need for "a clear and comprehensive definition of violence against women, a clear statement of the rights to be applied to ensure the elimination of violence against women in all its forms, a commitment by

Declaration on Violence against Women, 1993; *UN Human Rights Summit Vienna, 1993*; *International Conference on Population and Development Cairo, 1994*; *Fourth World Conference on Women, Beijing 1995*, etc., all aimed at the eradication of violence against women.

[40] Pandea et al. (2019), p. 21.

[41] Pandea et al. (2019), p. 18.

[42] Carpenter (2006).

[43] UN General Assembly, *Declaration on the Elimination of Violence against Women*, 20 December 1993, A/RES/48/104.

[44] Adopted by the United Nations General Assembly and entered into force as an international treaty on 3 September 1981.

[45] General Recommendation No 19: Violence Against Women, CEDAW/A/47/38 (1993).

States in respect of their responsibilities, and a commitment by the international community at large to the elimination of violence against women."[46]

The UN Committee on the Elimination of Discrimination Against Women, established under *CEDAW*, clearly acknowledged that "gender-based violence is a form of discrimination which seriously inhibits women's ability to enjoy rights and freedoms on a basis of equality with men."[47] The committee further states that the general prohibition of gender discrimination includes GBV and that GBV is violence that is directed against a woman because she is a woman, or which affects women disproportionately.[48] In recognition thereof, *General Recommendation 19* laid the framework for conceptualizing GBV, wherein it broadened the definition of violence against women to include physical, sexual and psychological harm, including "threats of such acts, coercion or arbitrary deprivation of liberty, whether occurring in public or private life."[49] Moreover, it demonstrated that violence between intimates affects women disproportionately, demarcating women as a group in need of proactive state protection. To this end, it recommended that states take specific steps to reduce domestic violence, namely, by improving the legal protection of women, through legislative amendments and gender-sensitive training for the judiciary;[50] gathering statistics in order to identify the nature and extent of the problem;[51] and, creating complaint mechanisms and places of refuge for women escaping violent circumstances.[52] Finally, it incorporated reference to the so-called "due diligence" standard to determine what diligent states should do to fulfil the objectives contained

[46] Preamble to *DEVAW.*

[47] Article 1 of *DEVAW* defines violence against women as "any act of gender-based violence that results in, or is likely to result in, physical, sexual or psychological harm or suffering to women, including threats of such acts, coercion or arbitrary deprivation of liberty, whether occurring in public or private life." Pursuant to Article 2 of *DEVAW*, the definition further includes, but is not limited to: "a. Physical, sexual and psychological violence occurring in the family, including battering, sexual abuse of female children in the household, dowry-related violence, martial rape, female genital mutilation and other traditional practices harmful to women, non-spousal violence and violence related to exploitation; b. Physical, sexual and psychological violence occurring within the general community, including rape, sexual abuse, sexual harassment and intimidation at work, in education institutions and elsewhere, trafficking in women and forced prostitution. c. Physical, sexual and psychological violence perpetrated or condoned by the State, wherever it occurs."

[48] Similarly, Article 34 of the 1989 *Convention on the Rights of the Child* (*CRC*) requires state parties to undertake to protect the child from all forms of sexual exploitation and sexual abuse. UN General Assembly, *Convention on the Rights of the Child*, 20 November 1989, United Nations, Treaty Series, vol. 1577.

[49] General Recommendation 19, para 6.

[50] General Recommendation 19, para 24(b).

[51] General Recommendation 19, para 24(c).

[52] General Recommendation 19, paras 24(i), (k) and r.

in *General Recommendation 19*.[53] The definition of GBV has evolved in different international legal sources over the years.[54]

In its adoption thereof, *DEVAW* however offered the first official definition of GBV which defined it as:[55]

> any act of gender-based violence that results in, or is likely to result in, physical, sexual or psychological harm or suffering to women, including threats of such acts, coercion or arbitrary deprivations of liberty, whether occurring in public or private life ... Violence against women shall be understood to encompass, but not be limited to, the following: physical, sexual and psychological violence occurring in the family [and in the community], including battery, sexual abuse of female children ..., dowry-related violence, marital rape, female genital mutilation and other traditional practices harmful to women, non-spousal violence and violence related to exploitation ... sexual harassment and intimidation at work, in educational institutions and elsewhere, trafficking in women and forced prostitution ... and violence ... perpetrated or condoned by the State.

There have been some criticisms around this definition. Some argue that because *DEVAW* articulates violence against women as "gender-based" violence (rather than the reverse), then there may be "other types" of GBV that are not violence against women. Such an interpretation has been argued to rest on a certain logic or literalness that overlooks how "gender" was understood and used by many women's rights activists at the time *DEVAW* was drafted (and up to the present), i.e., as a word to describe the socially imposed hierarchy between males and females.[56] Importantly, the *DEVAW* definition recognizes that GBV and the violence directed against women is a cause and consequence of gender inequality and patriarchy. This is especially relevant to the South African context. For example, GBV in South Africa can be understood against its history of apartheid.[57] This apartheid-era was dominated by deeply entrenched patriarchal norms and attitudes towards the role of women that made violence against women and children, especially in rural areas and in informal settlements, a way of life and an accepted social phenomenon.[58] At the core of this violence was the unequal power, gender relations, patriarchy, homophobia, sexism and other harmful discriminatory beliefs and practices.[59] Therefore, it has been argued, that the high rates of GBVF in the country can be attributed to the violence inherited from the apartheid-era and which continues to resonate profoundly today.[60]

---

[53] General Recommendation 19, para 9: "States may also be responsible for private acts if they fail to act with due diligence to prevent violations of rights or to investigate and punish acts of violence, and for providing compensation."

[54] Bott et al. (2005).

[55] Office of the United Nations High Commissioner for Human Rights (1993), Article 2.

[56] Coalition of Feminists for Social Change (2017).

[57] Mosavel et al. (2011).

[58] Boonzaier and van Schalkwyk (2011).

[59] Presidency of South Africa (2018).

[60] Human Rights Council (2016).

When looking at the definition in *DEVAW*, this inequality and patriarchal narrative contributes to the stereotypes against women and men that rely on the gender binary and depends on the division of sexes into two distinct, hierarchically ranked categories. In consideration thereof, it becomes clear that GBV specifically delineates the problem of violence against women and girls. In addition, violence against women has been documented as taking many forms, including but not limited to, spousal/intimate partner violence (physical, sexual and/or psychological); sexual violence by persons other than a spouse/partner, including other family members, friends, acquaintances, or strangers (i.e., non-partner sexual violence); femicide, including murders in the name of "honor" and, trafficking of women. Violence by a husband or male intimate partner (or other male family member) is the most pervasive form of violence against women globally.[61] Therefore, in addition to emphasizing that GBV takes many forms, *DEVAW* makes the link between patriarchy and GBV clear by emphasizing that violence against women is "a manifestation of historically unequal power relations between men and women, which have led to the domination over and discrimination against women by men and to the prevention of the full advancement of women."[62]

The *1995 Beijing Platform for Action* later expanded on this definition, specifying that GBV includes violations of the rights of women in situations of armed conflict, such as systematic rape, sexual slavery, forced pregnancy, forced sterilization, forced abortion, coerced or forced use of contraceptives, prenatal sex selection and female infanticide.[63] It further recognizes the particular vulnerabilities of women belonging to minorities, the elderly and the displaced, indigenous, refugee and migrant communities, women living in impoverished rural or remote areas and women in detention. GBV is consequently domestic, physical, sexual, psychological, emotional, socioeconomic and any other harmful practice that can result in serious long-term effects for victims/survivors ranging from "permanent disability or death to a variety of physical, psychosocial and health-related problems that often destroy the survivor's self-worth and quality of life and expose her or him to further abuse."[64] The term "gender-based violence" also strengthens the understanding of this violence as a social, rather than merely an individual problem. Such an understanding would translate to requiring a comprehensive and systemic response to GBV beyond addressing simply individual cases.[65]

A significant regional instrument that speaks to curbing GBV is the 2003 *Protocol to the African Charter on Human and Peoples' Rights, on the Rights of Women in Africa*,[66] also known as the *Maputo Protocol*. The *Maputo Protocol* prohibits GBV as part of women's rights to life, integrity and security of person,

---

[61] World Health Organization (2021a).

[62] The *CRC, 1989*; World Health Organization (2021a).

[63] United Nations (1995).

[64] United Nations High Commissioner for Refugees (2010).

[65] United Nations (2017).

[66] Adopted in Maputo on 11 July 2003 and entered into force on 25 November 2005.

and dignity. Article 1 defines violence against women as "all acts perpetrated against women" including acts or threats of violence in both the private and public spheres, in peacetime as well as during armed conflict. It includes physical, sexual, or psychological violence, economic abuse and exploitation, deprivation, or neglect. Explicit mention of violence against women is made in Article 4, which deals with the rights to life, integrity, and security of the person. The *Maputo Protocol* notes several violations related to the aforementioned rights including protection of women from trafficking. It stresses that women should be protected from scientific experiments without their informed consent and calls upon state parties to enact and enforce laws to prohibit all forms of violence against women. The states are also required to allocate adequate budgetary resources for the implementation and monitoring interventions geared towards eradicating violence against women.

It needs to be mentioned herein that an important regional instrument in the *African Charter on Human and People's Rights* (*African Charter*),[67] does not explicitly address violence against women or violent cultural practices. However, this is remedied by Article 5 of the *Maputo Protocol* which deals exclusively with women's protection from harmful practices. The section outlaws all forms of Female Genital Mutilation (FGM), scarification and medicalization of FGM. The *Maputo Protocol* also specifically prohibits early or forced marriage and sets the minimum age of marriage at 18. State parties are required to eradicate elements in traditional and cultural beliefs, stereotypes, practice which exacerbate violence against women and to end all forms of harmful practices which negatively affect the human rights of women.[68] The *Maputo Protocol* encompasses the provisions of *CEDAW* and further expands on women's human rights concerning GBV, calling on all Member States to give greater attention to the realization of women's human rights to eliminate all forms of discrimination and GBV against women and girls.

Regarding the LGBTQ+ community specifically, while research on sexual and intimate partner violence against LGBTQ+[69] people is still in its relative infancy,[70] the evidence suggests that members of these communities encounter such violence at rates similar to, if not higher than, cisgender heterosexual women.[71] LGBTQ+ communities are themselves far from homogeneous, and rates of violence differ

[67] Organization of African Unity (OAU), *African Charter on Human and Peoples' Rights*, 27 June 1981, CAB/LEG/67/3 rev. 5, 21 I.L.M. 58 (1982).

[68] In Africa, the most prevalent forms of GBV reported and documented, include, among others, intimate partner violence, which manifests in physical, sexual or psychological violence by an intimate partner; female genital mutilation (FGM), which is a common cultural practice in some parts of Africa; early child and forced marriage where girls below 18 years are forced into marriage; as well as sexual violence in conflict which includes rape, sexual assault with violent physical assault, kidnapping, sexual slavery and forced prostitution in conflict situations. See African Union (2021).

[69] The abbreviation "LGBTQ+" is used to collectively refer to the lesbian, gay, bisexual, transgender, queer, and intersex sector.

[70] Rollè et al. (2018).

[71] Cense et al. (2017).

within and across these groups.[72] Transgender women and specifically transgender women of color, experience particularly high rates of GBV.[73] Although men are victims of GBV, including physical and sexual abuse, there are specific gendered factors and contributors that render violence against women different to that of men and which require a specific gendered analysis.[74] In particular, men's violence against women is located within specific cultural, social and economic contexts which are rooted in unequal structural power relations and gendered norms within a patriarchal framework.[75] The use of the term GBV highlights these gendered contexts of violence against women which are rooted in inequalities between women and men.

Similarly, some authors[76] have emphasized the importance of an intersectional analysis[77] since the incidences of GBV makes it clear that one can no longer approach the gendered aspects of GBV as if there is "a stable, coherent or shared category of 'woman' or 'man'."[78] Rather, gender is itself co-constituted by factors such as race, class and sexuality.[79] An intersectional approach to GBV recognizes that all oppressions exist simultaneously, and that categories of oppression mutually construct each other to create unique experiences of violence for women and girls. For instance, violence that is "gender-based" is likewise inflected and entangled with racist, homophobic, transphobic, heterosexist and other forms of violence. Indeed, this type of approach is necessary in all areas of work relating to ending violence against women and girls. It was noted by the UN that "lack of attention to intersectionality not only inhibits policymakers from assessing inequalities between women and men, but also inhibits their ability to assess how differently positioned women experience discrimination and violence. The Special Rapporteur considered how violence is contingent on women's material conditions, individual attributes,

---

[72] Callander et al. (2019).

[73] LGBTIQ Domestic and Family Violence Interagency and The Centre for Social Research in Health (2014).

[74] Bows and Fileborn (2020), p. 305.

[75] African Union (2003).

[76] Crenshaw (1991).

[77] Intersectionality has been described as referring to overlapping social identities and the related systems of oppression and domination that use these to marginalize and exclude. Although all women face discrimination some women face multiple forms of oppression because of their race, ethnicity, religion, socioeconomic background, abilities, and sexual orientation, which in turn shapes their experiences of violence. Intersectionality looks at the relationships between these different forms of oppression and allows for analysis of social problems more fully, shapes more effective interventions, and promotes more inclusive responses. See Government of South Africa (2020), p. 13.

[78] Bows and Fileborn (2020), p. 302.

[79] Bozzoli (1983); Judge and Smythe (2020), p. 60.

and social locations, and recommended a holistic approach that addresses systematic discrimination and marginalization."[80]

What is clear from these definitions and recognitions of the types of violence that women experience is that the act of "violence against women encompasses but is not limited to the physical, sexual and psychological violence occurring in the family, including battering, sexual abuse of female children in the household, dowry-related violence, marital rape, female genital mutilation and other traditional practices harmful to women, non-spousal violence and violence related to exploitation."[81] The scope of the definition of "gender-based violence" together with its various interpretations reveals the complexity of the issue itself.

The term "gender-based violence" is clearly used to encompass a very broad range of specific offenses against a person and against several types of people, including women, children, men, straight, gay, lesbian, bi-sexual, and transgender. Men are particularly vulnerable where they are perceived to have transgressed the predominant concepts of masculinity. GBV includes domestic violence; sometimes referred to as intimate partner violence; and violence subjected by a stranger. However, the most common form of GBV is inflicted by men on women and girls because of the unequal distribution of power in society between women and men. Therefore, there are specific consequences of this violence for women and girls. It has been acknowledged that:

> The primary targets of GBV are women and adolescent girls, but not only are they at high risk of GBV, but they also suffer exacerbated consequences as compared with what men endure. As a result of gender discrimination and their lower socio-economic status, women have fewer options and less resources at their disposal to avoid or escape abusive situations and to seek justice. They also suffer (...) consequences [on their sexual and reproductive health], including forced and unwanted pregnancies, unsafe abortions and resulting deaths, traumatic fistula, and higher risks of sexually transmitted infections (STIs) and HIV.[82]

This acknowledgment highlights that gender is hierarchical and contributes to increasing disparities that intersect with other social and economic inequalities. Gender-based discrimination intersects with other factors of discrimination, such as ethnicity, socioeconomic status, disability, age, geographic location, gender identity and sexual orientation, among others.[83] This "intersectionality"[84] is an

---

[80] As reported by Rashida Manjoo, special rapporteur on violence against women in United Nations Human Rights Council (2015), p. 1.

[81] Enaifoghe (2019).

[82] United Nations Population Fund (2009), p. 7.

[83] World Health Organization (2023).

[84] The concept of intersectionality was first coined in 1989 by Black feminist activist and academic Professor Kimberlé Crenshaw. Crenshaw offered intersectionality as a tool to contextualize the specific ways African American women were being subjected to both sex and race discrimination, and the barriers they faced when trying to seek redress around this. She argued that the existing frameworks did not recognize that Black women's experiences of inequality occurred at the intersection of racism and sexism; that the systems which had been developed to challenge sexism were constructed around white women, and that those which had been developed to challenge

important consideration for policy development and initiatives aimed at eliminating GBV. The concept of "intersectionality" in GBV expands ones understanding of how gender power dynamics interact with other power hierarchies of privilege or disadvantage, resulting in inequality/oppressions (race, sexuality, gender identity, ethnicity, indigeneity, immigration status, disability, etc.) to produce unique experiences of violence for women and girls.[85]

2.2.1.1 Sex vs Gender

It also becomes important to note here that whilst the term "gender" interacts with "sex," it is different from "sex." The WHO states that "sex" refers to "the biological and physiological characteristics that define men and women" such as chromosomes, hormones and reproductive organs and "gender" refers to "the socially constructed roles, behaviours, activities, and attributes that a given society considers appropriate for men and women."[86] This includes norms, behaviors, and roles associated with being a woman, man, girl, or boy, as well as relationships with each other. As a social construct, gender varies widely within and across cultures and changes over time.[87] Diverse societies value the capacities, abilities and traits attributed to men and women differently. Those defined as feminine are often treated as inferior to those defined as masculine.[88] These so-called cultural norms then become instrumental in establishing and maintaining unequal relations between men and women on a range of dimensions, as well as sustaining societies characterized by masculinist domination.

Dominant conceptions of gender assume that first, people are only attracted to those whose sex is different to their own, constructing heterosexuality as the only "normal," acceptable form of sexual practice and second, that there are only two sexes, entailing that people's gender identities[89] will always correspond with their bodily features.[90] When these assumptions are prevalent societies police men and women's behavior to prevent deviation from these gendered heterosexual norms. It leads to, for example, women being perceived as signaling their sexual availability

racism had been designed around Black men. Since then, the term "intersectionality" has been used to understand women's experiences at the intersection of several simultaneous oppressions including [but not limited to] race, class, caste, gender, ethnicity, sexuality, disability, nationality, immigration status, geographical location, religion, and so on. See Crenshaw (1989), p. 139.

[85] Crenshaw (1991), p. 1241.

[86] Council of Europe (2023).

[87] UNICEF (2017).

[88] UNICEF (2017).

[89] Gender identity refers to a person's deeply felt, internal and individual experience of gender, which may or may not correspond to the person's physiology or designated sex at birth. See Lindqvist et al. (2021).

[90] UNGA, "Protection Against Violence and Discrimination Based on Sexual Orientation and Gender Identity" (2018) A/73/152 [2].

through their conduct or dressing, while men may be excused for their violence on the grounds of them being a male and their innate overwhelming sexual urges. Where persons are perceived as not complying with social expectations, discrimination, abuse, and violence are considered acceptable methods to punish and force conformity or to assert dominance and so enforce gendered social relations and hierarchies. In some contexts, especially when this violence is targeted at someone based on their sexual orientation or gender identity, it may also be defined in law as a hate crime.[91]

The term GBV has thus been coined in recognition of the ways in which gender shapes particular manifestations of violence. For this study, the concept of "gender" is used in reference to violence that is directed against a person because of that person's gender or violence that affects persons of a particular gender disproportionately. In addition, whilst there are various forms of violence experienced by women and girls including physical, sexual, emotional, psychological, and economical, this book focuses on only some forms of violence against women: physical and/or sexual intimate partner violence, femicide and non-partner sexual violence. These types of violence are some of the most prevalent forms in South Africa. However other forms of violence may also be referred to from time to time and where appropriate.

2.2.2 *Femicide*

GBV lies at the heart of femicide. Femicide was a concept devised in the 1970s by Diana Russell, a leading feminist activist and scholar.[92] In its early iteration by Russell, femicide was defined as "the murder of women by men motivated by hatred, contempt, pleasure, or a sense of ownership of women" and "the misogynistic killings of women by men."[93] Most recently, this definition evolved to its most commonly-used form as gender-related killings or "the killing of one or more females by one or more males because they are female."[94] Whilst "femicide" is a relatively new concept, it remains the dominant term in official documents, as well as scientific and grey literature, albeit "feminicide" is also employed elsewhere.[95] As mentioned it indicates the specific crime of intentionally murdering a female person, either woman or girl, because of her gender. Since the early 1990s, this concept has been used by women's movements and, from the turn of the millennium, it was also adopted in the social sciences to grasp those characteristics which distinguish between the killings of women and men, which were hitherto obscured by the

[91] Erickson-Schroth et al. (2020), p. 113.
[92] Russell (2012).
[93] Radford and Russell (1992).
[94] Russell (2012), p. 2.
[95] Corradi (2021), p. 6.

neutral term "homicide."[96] In its broadest sense, the term "femicide," has been defined as the intentional killing, with a gender-related motivation connected to its root causes, which may range from stereotyped gender roles, discrimination towards women and girls, to unequal power relations between women and men in society.[97] It represents the tragic end to a perpetual cycle of multiple and interconnected forms of GBV.[98]

Femicide's classification differs according to different contexts of victim-perpetrator relationships and takes place in different situations within both private and public spheres. Some significant examples include the stoning to death of females, murders of females for so-called "honor," rape murders/rape femicide,[99] murders of women and girls by their husbands, boyfriends, and dates for various reasons, wife-killing by immolation because of too little dowry, deaths as a result of genital mutilations, female sex slaves, trafficked females, and prostituted females, murdered by their "owners," traffickers, "johns," and pimps, and females killed by misogynist strangers, acquaintances, and serial killers,[100] killing by an intimate partner or family member, witch-hunting deaths, pre- and post-natal excess female mortality, infanticide and deliberate neglect, rooted in a preference for sons over daughters.[101] The act of femicide is often the last in an abusive relationship. There is a continuum of femicides ranging from one-on-one sexist murders, for example, a man strangling his wife because she plans to leave him; to one or more males killing a group of women for, for example, refusing to wear the correct attire in public; to the other end of the continuum, for example, mass femicides such as when preference for male children results in the killing, or death from neglect, of millions of female babies and girls.

Depending on whose perspective is being examined or where it is being examined the term as well as its accepted meaning often varies[102] between disciplines and scientific traditions.[103] Furthermore, the disciplines and scientific traditions themselves place different emphases on what constitutes femicide. For example, some criminologists refer to intimate partner homicide or intimate partner femicide as femicide. This interpretation effectively reduces femicide to one specific, albeit most

---

[96] Femicide, as coined by feminist activists in 1976, places the male-female opposition at its root, in a time when "man" and "woman" were taken for granted. More recently, studies have criticized binary conceptions of sexual orientation and gender identity and they have argued for a more fluid understanding. Scholars studying victimisation of the LGBTQ+ communities prefer concepts such as "hate crime," or "anti-LGBT homicide." See Gruenewald and Kelley (2014).

[97] United Nations Office on Drugs and Crime (2022b).

[98] United Nations Office on Drugs and Crime (2022a).

[99] A prevalent form of femicide includes rape femicides. Rape femicides are those femicides where a female is raped and killed in the same crime. It is very prevalent in countries like South Africa. See Gqola (2015), p. 7.

[100] Radford and Russell (1992), p. 14.

[101] Corradi (2021), p. 6.

[102] Harmes and Russell (2005), p. 5.

[103] Dawson and Carrigan (2020), p. 2.

common type of femicide. On the other hand, the gender-sensitive literature on the concept uses the terminology of femicide or feminicide.[104] In some world regions, such as Latin America, the term *feminicidio* (or feminicide in English) was introduced into the debate on the killings of women in the Latin American context to stress the complicity of Latin American states in the killing of women through their roles in neglecting such killings and failing to take them seriously.[105] This term is consequently intended to highlight the role of institutional or state violence and focuses on the complicity of the state (institutional violence, misogynistic and discriminatory practices) in the deaths of women.[106] Thus, suggesting that the State both implicitly and explicitly support such gender-related killings.[107]

Furthermore, supporters of the seminal work of Kelly, argue for the broader adoption of the phenomenon of femicide by placing it on the continuum of violence that remains persistent in women's lives. Consequently, the phenomenon of femicide, its scope, content, and implications continue to be the subject of much discourse in academia, policy and grassroot activists' levels.[108] Internationally, and the one adopted in South Africa, a broader definition of femicide is often used that includes any killings of women and girls. This is not to say that in some cases or types of femicide, female family members or females in other contexts may not sometimes be involved. It is still however internationally recognized that men remain the primary perpetrators of femicide and that most femicides are committed by current or former male partners; a pattern that exists worldwide although proportions vary across world regions.

It has recently been argued by Hefti[109] that the concept of femicide should extend beyond the killings of women and girls alone and that it should not only be equated with a female homicide which is considered an intrinsically individualistic crime. She argues that femicide is more like a female genocide (with the social subordination of the group being its aim), embedded in structural inequality. By focusing on killings, she argues that it tends to reinforce the male experience of human rights violations exclusively and that killings are only one means of achieving the subordination of the social group in question.[110] Hefti's conceptualization of femicide is in line with the architecture of the genocide framework,[111] which may include the murder of a woman—among many other acts—as the method by which the female social group is subordinated in society.[112]

---

[104] Corradi and Stöckl (2014), p. 603.

[105] Castañeda-Salgado (2016), p. 4.

[106] Menjívar and Walsh (2017).

[107] Dawson and Carrigan (2020), pp. 1–2.

[108] Lagarde De Los Ríos (2010), pp. xi–xxvi.

[109] Hefti (2022), p. 2.

[110] Hefti (2022), p. 21.

[111] Dworkin (1974), p. 93; Warren (1985); Hagay-Frey (2011), p. 131.

[112] Hefti (2022), p. 3.

Whilst Hefti's arguments remain food for thought, using the genocide framework in cases of femicide has its own issues. Firstly, femicide does not fit the legal requirements of genocide[113] given that the female social group cannot constitute a group targeted for destruction, and that women in femicide are attacked rather than destroyed by virtue of their gender.[114] Secondly, femicide is not defined in international criminal law (ICL),[115] let alone recognized as a sub-form or method of genocide.[116] Femicide, as conceptualized in this book, is considered to be the most extreme form of violence directed against a woman because she is a woman, or which affects women disproportionately. Femicide here is accepted to mean "the culmination of many forms of gender violence against women that represent an attack on their human rights and that lead them to various forms of violent death."[117] Since this perspective sees femicide as representing the lethal end point of a continuum of multiple, overlapping, and interconnected forms of GBV, not all acts of GBV can be qualified as femicide.

This book accordingly relies on a broad definition of femicide as "structural violence," while acknowledging that femicide is an individual act with a specific motivation.[118] It acknowledges that femicide is also based in an unequal gender structure and is thus a form of "structural violence," "based on gender discrimination, sexism and misogyny, taking advantage of any of the relationships of trust, kinship, authority or other unequal power relationships with the victim."[119] Contextual factors such as "patriarchy, sexism, and gender roles" are also included in analyses of femicide.[120] This definition is in line with the recognition and acknowledgement that femicide remains an impediment towards the SDGs,[121] and that this type of violence is perpetuated and maintained through a broader patriarchal systems of oppression and ongoing gender inequality.[122]

It is important to note that irrespective of the perspective that is chosen, femicide has found its way into the public discourse and is officially recognized as a form of discrimination and a human rights violation.[123] To this end, the most important development for women in international law, was the adoption of *CEDAW* and the creation of the *CEDAW* Committee to oversee its enforcement. *CEDAW* provides a comprehensive framework for challenging the various forces that have created and sustained discrimination based upon sex. *CEDAW* was followed by a range of global

[113] Cassese et al. (2015), p. 124.
[114] Randall (2022), p. 3.
[115] United Nations (1951).
[116] Grover (2014), p. 274.
[117] López et al. (2010), pp. 160–163.
[118] United Nations Office on Drugs and Crime (2022a), pp. 11–12.
[119] European Institute for Gender Equality (2021), p. 10.
[120] Cunha and Goncalves (2019), p. 2574.
[121] United Nations (2015).
[122] National Inquiry into Missing and Murdered Indigenous Women and Girls (2017).
[123] Harmes and Russell (2005), p. 4.

and regional declarations, recommendations and comments addressing various rights of women, resulting in a body of international law that deals exclusively with the needs and well-being of women.[124]

It should be noted however that even though *CEDAW* marked the first international step toward recognizing women's rights to equal protection before the law *CEDAW* protects individuals from discrimination and only considers violence indirectly. It was not until the 1990s that violence against women was recognized as a violation of human rights.[125] In 1992 the *CEDAW* committee incorporated violence against women into its jurisprudence with the adoption of *General Recommendation 19* interpreting CEDAW's scope to include GBV.[126] *General Recommendation 19* is supplemented by *General Recommendation No. 35* of 2017 (*General Recommendation 35*).[127] *General Recommendation 19* prohibits a wide range of violence and established a firm correlation between discrimination and GBV. In general violence against women is said to include "acts that inflict physical, mental or sexual harm or suffering, threats of such acts, coercion and other deprivations of liberty."[128] It

[124]Some of these include, inter alia, the *Convention on the Nationality of Women, O.A.S. Treaty Series* No. 4, 38, entered into force Aug. 29, 1934; *Convention on the Political Rights of Women*, 193 U.N.T.S. 135, entered into force July 7, 195; *Optional Protocol to the Convention on the Elimination of Discrimination against Women*, G.A. res. 54/4, annex, 54 U.N. GAOR Supp. (No. 49) at 5, U.N. Doc. A/54/49 (Vol. I) (2000), entered into force Dec. 22, 2000; *Declaration on the Protection of Women and Children in Emergency and Armed Conflict*, G.A. res. 3318 (XXIX), 29 U.N. GAOR Supp. (No. 31) at 146, U.N. Doc. A/9631 (1974); *DEVAW*, *Beijing Declaration and Platform for Action*, U.N. Fourth World Conference on Women, U.N. Doc. A/CONF.177/20 (1995) &. A/CONF.177/20/Add.1 (1995) (*Beijing Declaration); Protocol to Prevent, Suppress and Punish Trafficking in Persons, Especially Women and Children, Supplementing the United Nations Convention Against Transnational Organized Crime*, G.A. Res. 25, annex II, U.N. GAOR, 55th Sess., Supp. No. 49, at 60, U.N. Doc. A/45/49 (Vol. I) (2001), entered into force Sept. 9, 2003; *United Nations High Commissioner for Human Rights Principles and Guidelines on Human Rights and Trafficking*, E/2002/68/Add.1 (2002); Office of United Nations High Commissioner for Refugees, *Guidelines on International Protection: Gender-Related Persecution within the Context of Article 1a (2) of the 1951 Convention and Its 1967 Protocol Relating to the Status of Refugees*, U.N. Doc. HCR/GIP/02/01 (2002); the creation of the United Nations Report of the Special Rapporteur on Violence Against Women, its Causes and Consequences, U.N. ESCOR, 52d Sess., U.N. Doc. E/CN.4/1996/53 (1996); *Inter-American Convention on the Granting of Civil Rights to Women*, 1438 U.N.T.S. 51, entered into force March 17, 1949; *Inter-American Convention on the Granting of Political Rights to Women*, 1438 U.N.T.S. 63, entered into force March 17, 1949; *Convention of Belem Do Para* and the African Union's *Protocol to the African Charter on Human and Peoples' Rights on the Rights of Women in Africa of 2003.*

[125]Simmons (2009), p. 207.

[126]UN General Recommendation No 19: Violence Against Women, CEDAW/A/47/38 (1993).

[127]UN General Recommendation No 35: General Recommendation No 35 on Gender-based Violence Against Women, updating General Recommendation No 19, CEDAW/C/GC/35 (2017). In its general recommendation No. 35, the Committee noted that GBV was one of the fundamental social, political and economic means by which the subordinate position of women with respect to men and their stereotyped roles were perpetuated.

[128]General Recommendation 19, para 6.

confirmed expressly that domestic violence impedes gender equality and that the "full implementation of the Convention required states to take positive measures to eliminate all forms of violence against women." *General Recommendation 19* also makes a bold statement about cultural autonomy. It rejects traditional practices and prejudices that may "justify gender-based violence as a form of protection or control of women."[129] The major concern with *General Recommendation 19* is that it is of interpretive value only and not legally binding. The provisions of *General Recommendation 19* did however form the basis for *DEVAW*.

Furthermore, whilst *General Recommendation 35* does not add anything new to the conceptualization of violence against women, it does, through the lens of discrimination, see violence as "a critical obstacle to achieving substantive equality between women and men."[130] It clearly frames violence against women as a form and manifestation of gender-based discrimination, used to subordinate and oppress women.[131] It explicitly highlights the structural extent to which women are subjected to. It does so by specifically identifying "gender-based violence against women" instead of the general "violence against women" used in *General Recommendation 19*.[132] Consequently, *General Recommendation 35* considers GBV as a "social, rather than an individual problem" entrenched in societal norms which "assert male control or power, enforce gender roles, or prevent, discourage or punish what is considered to be unacceptable female behaviour."[133] It also specifically states that "harmful practices ....are also forms of gender-based violence against women affected by such cultural, ideological and political factors."[134] *General Recommendation 35* unequivocally brings violence outside of the private sphere and into the realm of human rights.

General Recommendation 35 does recognize the interplay between many human rights violations in femicide. However, it only mentions femicide in the context of data collection, limiting the complex phenomenon to "gender-based killings of women."[135] Despite these concerns, it is important to note though that on an international level, *CEDAW's* General Recommendations can be considered positively as it could provide some responses to femicide.

DEVAW recognizes a plethora of acts which can constitute femicide, such as "battering, sexual abuse of female children in the household, dowry-related violence, marital rape, female genital mutilation and other traditional practices harmful to women, non-spousal violence and violence related to exploitation."[136] *DEVAW* consequently summarizes three forms of violence as violations of international

[129] General Recommendation 19, para 11.
[130] General Recommendation 35, para 10.
[131] OHCHR (2017), p. 1.
[132] General Recommendation 35, para 9.
[133] General Recommendation 35, para 19.
[134] General Recommendation 35, para 14.
[135] General Recommendation 35, para 34(b).
[136] Preamble and Article 2 of *DEVAW*.

law, namely, violence in the family, public violence, and violence that is condoned by the state, irrespective of where it occurs. It also stipulates that states should exercise "due diligence to prevent, investigate and, in accordance with national legislation, punish acts of violence against women, whether those acts are perpetrated by the State or by private persons."[137] Finally, *DEVAW* directs states to develop sanctions to punish perpetrators of violence against women and to make the system of justice accessible for injured women.[138]

Of significance, in 1994, the General Assembly of the Organization of American States (OAS) adopted the *Inter-American Convention on the Prevention, Punishment and Eradication of Violence against Women*, commonly referred to as the *Convention of Belem Do Para.*[139] This regional convention developed an even more expansive definition of violence against women and identified violence as one of the historic impediments to women achieving equality and a violation of their right to dignity.[140] In many respects, the *Convention of Belem Do Para* is considered a stronger legal instrument than its international equivalent, *DEVAW*. In addition, the *Convention of Belem Do Para* is a binding treaty, whereas *DEVAW* is a declaration, constituting an interpretation of a treaty (CEDAW).[141] Since the *Convention of Belem Do Para* is an American regional instrument, it does not constitute a principle of international law as a whole. It is however mentioned here as it does add value to the discourse that there is a growing norm against systemic intimate violence.

In addition, this treaty was the first instrument in the world that focused on the problem of violence against women,[142] and is a key instrument used by the Inter-American Commission on Human Rights and the Inter-American Court of Human Rights (IACtHR) in both GBV[143] and femicide cases.[144] The IACtHR is the only

---

[137] Article 4(c) of *DEVAW*.

[138] Article 4(d) of *DEVAW*.

[139] Inter-American Convention on the Granting of Political Rights to Women, 1438 U.N.T.S. 63, entered into force March 17, 1949.

[140] See the Preamble to the *Convention of Belem Do Para.*

[141] Meyersfeld (2006), p. 90.

[142] Mechanism to the Belém do Pará Convention (MESECVI) (n.d.), p. 3.

[143] Its first judgment in the matter was in 2006 in the *Miguel Castro Castro Prison v. Peru*, Inter-Am. Ct.H.R. (ser. C) No. 160 (Nov. 25, 2006) and the most recent case is *Case Guzmán Albarracín y otras v. Ecuador*, Inter-Am. Ct.H.R. (ser. C) No. 405 (Jun. 24, 2020).

[144] Some cases include the emblematic case *of González et al. ("Cotton Field") v. Mexico*, Inter-Am. Ct.H.R. (ser. C) No. 205 (Nov. 16, 2009); *Véliz Franco et al. v. Guatemala*, Inter-Am. Ct.H.R. (ser. C) No. 277 (May 19, 2014) and *Velásquez Paiz et al. v. Guatemala*, Inter-Am. Ct.H.R. (ser. C) No. 307 (Nov. 19, 2015). In their femicide judgments, the Court has widely adopted the concept of femicide and promoted the use of the term in the region. Moreover, through femicide cases, the Court has obliged States to acknowledge the problem of feminicide and to create legislation frameworks to prevent, to investigate, and to sanction it. When analyzing the various femicide cases the IACtHR has focused on three important aspects: (a) the duty of prevention and due diligence during investigations; (b) the eradication of gender stereotypes as barriers to femicide investigations, and (c) comprehensive reparations for victims.

regional court that acknowledges gender-based murders of women as femicides.[145] The adoption of this term by a regional court entails a clear understanding of the fact that not all murders of women can qualify as gender-based killings, and that the root of femicide has different variations. In its most extreme form, it is the manifestation of hate and intolerance against women and their rights and freedoms.

Looking at the African continent, Africa has several regional platforms for ensuring human rights, such as the Economic Community of West African Court of Justice (ECOWAS Court), which is the judicial institution of the Economic Community of West African States and the African regional systems of human rights (RSHR). In addressing the issue of femicide specifically, Africa has a few powerful instruments in the form of the *Maputo Protocol* and *African Charter*. However, despite this the RSHR have been silent on femicide in the decisions and jurisprudence. This however does not seem to apply to the ECOWAS Court. The ECOWAS Court was empowered to address cases of human rights violations since 2005 and despite some doubts about its mandate and suitability,[146] the ECOWAS Court has taken some advantage of the African RSHR in gender topics during the last few years.[147] The problem is that the ECOWAS Court, does not use the term "femicide" for gender-based killings, thereby creating challenges in defining the concept and in prevention strategies. Indeed, the adoption of a concept of femicide to name and define a problem is important especially when gender-based killings of women is a problem of such global proportions. By comparison, the fact that the IACtHR has adopted and used the concept of femicide has contributed to consolidate the term in the American region, and to compel the States of the region to consider this topic in their agendas.[148]

However, although the adoption of the term by a Court is important, this is just one of several actions through which the regional Courts can contribute to the elimination of femicides. An example of a case dealt with by the ECOWAS Court, is the 2018 domestic violence case of *Mary Sunday v. Federal Republic of Nigeria* in Nigeria.[149] Here the ECOWAS Court delivered its judgment on the case for women's human rights violations in Africa. This decision has been described as a "historic milestone" for the promotion of the protection of women's rights, as well as an important step towards the recognition of the violence against women as a violation of human rights.[150] The jurisprudence on GBVF is still developing in the

[145] *González et al. ("Cotton Field") v. Mexico*, Inter-Am. Ct.H.R. (ser. C) No. 205 (Nov. 16, 2009).

[146] Ebobrah (2010).

[147] In 2017, the ECOWAS Court delivered a judgment about vagrancy laws that targeted female sex workers. *Dorothy Chioma Njemanze & 3 Ors v. Federal Republic of Nigeria*, ECOWAS Court, ECW/CCJ/JUD/08/17 (2017).

[148] Inzunza (2020), p. 80.

[149] *Mary Sunday v. Federal Republic of Nigeria*, ECOWAS Court, ECW/CCJ/JUD/11/18 (2018).

[150] In a decision that can be interpreted a historic milestone and a "triple high-five" for the promotion of accountability for women's human rights in Africa; for the recognition of violence against women as a violation of human rights, and for the emerging role of African regional courts in addressing human rights issues, on the 24th of January, 2017, the ECOWAS Court (the ECCJ or

region but of importance is that the RSHR offers its platforms to victims of gender-based killings to raise their cases and to obtain justice and reparations from States.

Furthermore, the UN Special Rapporteur on Violence against Women, its Causes and Consequences was appointed in 1994. Their primary objective was to submit annual reports on measures taken to eliminate violence against women.[151] The 1995 *Beijing Declaration* furthermore recognizes violence against women as a human rights violation and sets the agenda for States to identify and eradicate GBV. However, there are two issues here as these approaches are not legally binding but importantly, they fail to address the issue of femicide directly.

It should be further noted that there are several UN Security Council (UNSC) resolutions on women's rights that concern women, peace and security, as well as sexual violence in armed conflict.[152] The UNSC also adopted Resolution 2467 in April 2019 that deals with sexual violence in armed conflict.[153] The United Nations General Assembly (UNGA) also issued a resolution on gender-related killings of women and girls, expressing concern about femicide.[154] In addition the International Labor Organization's (ILO) *Violence and Harassment Convention, 2019* on sexual harassment in the workplace is the first binding treaty explicitly addressing violence against women. It states that harassment includes "a range of unacceptable behaviours and practices or threats whether a single occurrence or repeated, that aim at, result in, or are likely to result in physical, psychological, sexual or economic harm, and includes gender-based violence and harassment."[155] The problem is that this 2019 Convention is limited to the "workplace" sphere, limiting its application for femicide.

Despite *CEDAW* providing the most specific and, arguably, the most progressive analysis concerning women's rights,[156] there is no universal treaty that exists which

---

the Court) ruled that it has the competence to hear a case of domestic violence instituted against the Federal Government of Nigeria by two NGOs. See Ruling ECW/CCJ/APP/26/15, 24th January 2017, INTLAWGRRLS (2017).

[151] OHCHR, Resolution XI.-E/CN.4/1994/132 (4 March 1994), paras 6–7.

[152] UNSC Resolution 1325 (2000). Clause 10 recognizes the proliferation of gender-based atrocities in situations of conflict; UNSC Resolution 1820 (2010). This 1820 resolution focuses principally on sexual violence in armed conflict. In its preamble, it reaffirms the importance of ending impunity for all forms of violence against women and girl civilians both during and after armed conflicts, especially sexual violence, and in so doing aims to bridge the gap between international humanitarian law and international human rights law. This link is reinforced by recognition that the use of rape as a weapon of war and other sexual violence may continue beyond the cessation of armed conflict. See in this regard Barrow (2010), p. 232; UNSC Resolution 1960 (2010). The 1960 resolution stresses the importance of ending impunity for sexual violence and requests that sanctions be considered as a possible response to rampant sexual violence.

[153] UNSC Resolution 1467 (23 April 2019) UN Doc S/RES/1467.

[154] UNGA Res 68/119 (18 December 2013) UN Doc A/68/457 68/191.

[155] Article 1(b) of the ILO *Convention concerning the Elimination of Violence and Harassment in the World of Work*, 2019 (No. 190). The Convention was adopted in June 2019, by the International Labour Conference of the ILO, and came into force on 25 June 2021.

[156] Hefti (2022), p. 111.

exclusively deals with violence against women and girls, let alone femicide. However, *CEDAW's* definition of GBV can serve as a catch-all provision for currently undefined acts of femicide.

On the regional front, the *Maputo Protocol* was a historical milestone in the realization of the rights of women in Africa. The *Maputo Protocol* contains a broad definition of "violence against women," covering all acts perpetrated against women which cause or could cause them physical, sexual, psychological, and economic harm, including the threat to commit such acts.[157] Several articles in the *Maputo Protocol* are relevant to GBV in Africa. For example, Article 4 provides that every woman is entitled to respect for her life and the integrity and security of her person.[158] State parties are obliged to enact and enforce laws to prohibit all forms of violence against women, including unwanted or forced sex, whether the violence takes place in private or public.[159] In addition, Article 5 deals exclusively with women's protection from harmful practices. State parties are obliged to create public awareness in all sectors of society regarding harmful practices.[160] Of specific significance is the obligation on state parties to prohibit, through legislative measures backed by sanctions, all forms of female genital mutilation.[161] Finally, Article 11 provides for the protection of women in armed conflicts and emphasizes the obligations incumbent upon state parties in terms of international humanitarian law.[162]

2.3 Selected Forms of GBV in South Africa

Every day, millions of women and girls worldwide experience violence in many forms, including, inter alia, intimate physical and sexual partner violence, female genital mutilation, child and forced marriage, sex trafficking, and rape.[163] Since 1998, numerous prevalence studies from different settings and populations confirm that GBV is highly prevalent and endemic in South Africa with physical violence being the most common form of GBV.[164] In addition, data on the prevalence and reported manifestations of GBV reveal high levels and persistence of different forms of "other" violence.[165] Such "other" forms include any acts or omissions that is intended or likely to cause or result in death or physical, sexual, psychological or

[157] Article 1(j) of the *Maputo Protocol.*

[158] Article 4(1) of the *Maputo Protocol.*

[159] Article 4(2) of the *Maputo Protocol.*

[160] Article 5(a) of the *Maputo Protocol.*

[161] Article 5(b) of the *Maputo Protocol.*

[162] Articles 11 (1) & (2) of the *Maputo Protocol.*

[163] The Lancet Series (2014).

[164] Demographic and Health Survey (2019); Jewkes et al. (1999), p. 2.

[165] United Nations High Commissioner for Refugees (2016).

economic harm or suffering for women and girls, threats of such acts, harassment, coercion and arbitrary deprivation of liberty.[166] While GBV is a global problem it has a local character in South Africa that is shaped by the country's history and closely connected to the many social, economic and political challenges facing it today.[167] Indeed, violence against women in South Africa is embedded in a history of brutality characterized by race, class and a gender divide[168] that has been fundamental to the building of the country.[169] The following provides explanations of some of the most prevalent forms of GBV in the country.

2.3.1 *Femicide*

One of the most excessive and extreme forms of GBV experienced in South Africa is femicide.[170] In South Africa, femicide is specifically defined as the killing of a female person, or someone who is perceived as a female person on the basis of gender identity, whether committed within the domestic relationship, interpersonal relationship or by any other person, or whether perpetrated or tolerated by the State or its agents[171] and private intimate femicide is defined as the murder of women by intimate partners, i.e., "a current or former husband or boyfriend, same-sex partner, or a rejected would-be lover."[172] The killing of a woman by their partner is the most extreme consequence of intimate partner violence and South Africa has some of the highest rates of intimate femicide in the world.[173] Recent reports indicate that femicide is five times higher in South Africa than the global average.[174]

Scholars have argued that femicide in South Africa is rampant because of the prevalence of impunity[175] and that killings of women exemplified the role of the State where individuals act with impunity.[176] South African women are consequently victims of this systemic disorder. This impacts prevention and responses to femicide and violence against women, which effects the prevalence rates.

[166] United Nations (2017).
[167] Goldblatt (2016), p. 3.
[168] Salo (2004).
[169] Bozzoli (1983).
[170] Stop Gender Violence Campaign (2019).
[171] Stats SA (2020), p. 10.
[172] Abrahams et al. (2013).
[173] Norman et al. (2010).
[174] Stats SA (2020), p. 5.
[175] Fagbadebo (2021), p. 113.
[176] Menjívar and Walsh (2017), p. 222.

2.3.2 Domestic Violence and Intimate Partner Violence

Domestic violence is one of the most common forms of GBV. South Africa is ranked as one of the countries with the highest rates of domestic violence in the world.[177] Many incidences of domestic violence can escalate over time, leading to the women's death.[178] According to South African law, domestic violence includes physical abuse; sexual abuse; emotional, verbal and psychological abuse; economic abuse; intimidation; harassment; stalking; entry into the complainants' residence without her consent or any other controlling or abusive behavior taking place in domestic relationships.[179] Whilst some reports[180] indicate that over a quarter of women in South Africa experience domestic violence from their intimate partners other reports suggests that the rate of domestic violence in South Africa may be higher than the recorded figures, given that many cases go unreported.[181] Research shows that many survivors tend not to report abuse from their partners[182] due to factors like, fear that the abuser will retaliate, desire to protect the family, financial dependence on the perpetrator, and fear of ending the marriage.[183] What is interesting to note is that domestic violence is not recorded by the South African Police Service (SAPS) as a specific crime category and therefore there are no national statistics available. When cases of domestic violence are reported to the police, they are recorded under a range of different categories such as assault, malicious damage to property, pointing a firearm, murder, etc.

Intimate partner violence in South Africa is currently higher than it is has ever been,[184] where approximately 58% of female homicide deaths are by an intimate partner[185] and as many as 51% of South African women have experienced violence at the hands of an intimate partner in their lifetimes.[186] Domestic violence is "any incident of threatening behaviour, violence (psychological, physical, sexual, financial, emotional), or abuse between adults who are or have been an intimate partner or family member, regardless of gender or sexuality."[187] Intimate partner violence is "abuse or aggression that occurs in a romantic relationship."[188]

[177] Jewkes et al. (2013).
[178] Swemmer (2021).
[179] Section 1 of the *Domestic Violence Act 116 of 1998.*
[180] Demographic and Health Survey (2019).
[181] Mshweshwe (2023).
[182] Jewkes and Abrahams (2002).
[183] Mshweshwe (2023).
[184] Stats SA (2020) and Stop Gender Violence Campaign (2019).
[185] Abrahams et al. (2012).
[186] Stats SA (2020).
[187] Karystianis et al. (2019).
[188] National Center for Injury Prevention and Control, Division of Violence Prevention (2022).

Intimate partner violence is one type of violence dealt with by South Africa's *Domestic Violence Act* (*DVA*).[189] It is regarded as domestic violence by a current or former spouse or partner in an intimate relationship against the other spouse or partner.[190] Intimate partner violence can take various forms, including physical, verbal, emotional, economical, and sexual abuse, as well as stalking and intimidation, or any other form of controlling behavior. It includes by law "engagement, dating or customary relationship, including an actual or perceived romantic, intimate or sexual relationship of any duration" irrespective of whether these relationships are heterosexual or same sex. In the most extreme cases, it results in women's deaths.[191] Furthermore, according to the *DVA*, domestic relationships can exist between people who share a residence but have no sexual or romantic relationship. This brings both housemates and students in residences within the ambit of the *DVA's* protection.

While domestic violence and intimate partner violence may appear to be the same thing, and certainly have much overlap, they differ a little in terms of meaning. Domestic violence is violence that takes place within a household and can be between any two people within that household.[192] Domestic violence can occur between a parent and child, siblings, or even roommates. Intimate partner violence can only occur between romantic partners who may or may not be living together in the same household.[193] Intimate partner violence may also be referred to as intimate partner domestic violence. Intimate partner violence includes any behavior that one intimate partner (current or former) uses to establish power and control over another intimate partner. This may include physical or sexual violence and/or financial, emotional/psychological, cultural, spiritual, and reproductive abuse, as well as other forms of controlling behavior. In relationships affected by intimate partner violence, the survivor of intimate partner violence is regarded as the partner who the controlling behavior is aimed at.[194]

In the same context, the perpetrator of intimate partner violence is regarded as the partner leveraging power and control over the other partner. Intimate partner violence can occur regardless of whether the individuals involved are/were living together or not. This distinction is what separates it from the term domestic violence, which generally refers to violence occurring between residences within one single location. The term "intimate partner domestic violence" more specifically refers to the abusive behavior of residences of one single location who are in an intimate relationship with each other, in turn excluding family members or other residents living within the household who would fall under the broader term of domestic

[189] 116 of 1998.

[190] Hamel and Russell (2022), pp. 3–4.

[191] Spencer and Stith (2020).

[192] Meyersfeld (2010).

[193] Ellsberg et al. (2015).

[194] World Health Organization (2013).

Violence. Often, it is difficult to identify various forms of abuse, particularly when they are indirect or not as obvious as physical and/or sexual violence.

2.3.3 *Non-Partner Sexual Violence*

Rates of non-partner sexual violence in South Africa is extremely high. Non-partner sexual violence is particularly common, but reporting to police is very low. One study found that a mere one in 13 women in Gauteng had reported non-partner rape, and only one in 25 rapes had been reported to the police.[195] In addition, some lifetime estimates suggest the prevalence of non-partner rape ranges from 5% to 12%.[196] Other population-based studies indicate lifetime non-partner rape perpetration by men to be as high as 21%.[197] It should be noted that there has been steady growth in the number of countries with surveys documenting women's experiences of sexual violence perpetrated by non-partners such as other family members, friends, acquaintances or strangers.[198] However, there are still significantly fewer studies on this compared with those on intimate partner violence.

2.3.4 *Sexual Violence*

The most common form of GBV in South Africa is sexual violence. Sexual violence is "any sexual act, attempt to obtain a sexual act, unwanted sexual comments or advances, or acts to traffic, or otherwise directed, against a person's sexuality using coercion, by any person regardless of their relationship to the victim, in any setting, including but not limited to home and work."[199] The forms that sexual violence takes are generally grouped into intimate partner violence and non-partner violence, which may include gang rape, rape homicide, school- and workplace-related violence, etc. These forms of violence occur in the spaces and environments within which women's general life experiences occur, including their homes, schools, workplaces, neighborhoods and communities.[200] Sexual violence within the South African context is occurring on such a large scale[201] that it appears to be socially normalized and legitimized through a culture of acceptance.[202] Its enormous scale is indicative that

---

[195] Machisa (2011).

[196] Gibbs et al. (2020).

[197] Jewkes et al. (2011).

[198] World Health Organization (2021a).

[199] Jewkes et al. (2002).

[200] Kabeer (2014).

[201] Stats SA (2019).

[202] Deane (2018).

society's beliefs of what does and does not constitute rape may be legitimizing acts of sexual violence or providing a space for these crimes to occur.[203]

2.3.5 *Harmful Practices*

Although femicide and sexual violence are two of the most horrendous forms of the GBV problem, South Africa faces the additional burden of local problems wherein practices are upheld that continue to place men in a powerful position and intended to keep women in a subordinate position. Some of these harmful customary or traditional practices include harmful honor killings,[204] *lobola* (bride-price) violence,[205] forced marriage,[206] female genital mutilation,[207] and marriage by abduction (*ukuthwala*).[208] These practices often become accepted and normalized, where both males and females become "socialized" into conforming to these cultural and religious practices. The sad reality is that some of these practices implicitly or explicitly condone and tolerate GBV.[209]

2.3.5.1 Ukuthwala

The practice of *ukuthwala*, is of particular concern as it often involves the culturally acceptable practice of the kidnapping and rape of a girl by a man and his friends or peers with the intention of compelling the girl or young woman's family to agree to marriage.[210] Traditionally, *ukuthwala* was an accepted path to marriage. In the past *ukuthwala* was intended to start and build families. It did not involve rape or consensual sex until the marriage negotiations were concluded. Today, *ukuthwala* is being practiced in different ways from the original tradition, as it is marked by

---

[203] Jewkes et al. (2005).

[204] Women or girls are killed because of the perceptions related to their "unacceptable" behavior or contact with men who are not relatives, choice of partner, education, or their dressing. The behavior of the woman is viewed as bringing shame upon her family or concerned person and it is believed that only her death will restore the so-called lost honor. See Gill et al. (2014), pp. 99–100.

Additionally, a report has indicated that in South Africa, honor femicide cases have been detected mostly from incestuous relationships and in "sordid" sexual relationships which resulted in unwanted pregnancies or exposures. These cases often go unreported because of secrecy, concealment and mystery attached to the killing. See Department of Justice and Constitutional Development (n.d.), para 6.

[205] Eniola et al. (2020), p. 31.

[206] Rembe et al. (2011).

[207] Muteshi et al. (2016).

[208] South African Law Reform Commission (2014) and UNICEF (2015).

[209] Centre for the Study of Violence and Reconciliation (2016), p. 8.

[210] Department of Justice and Constitutional Development (2021), para 3.

violence and rape where girls as young as 12 are abducted and raped,[211] often by significantly older men, and routinely exposed to HIV/AIDS transmission.[212] One study of young girls aged 12–19 reported that 56% were forcibly married through *ukuthwala*[213] and a further survey revealed that an estimated 10,600 women are victims of forced marriage.[214]

2.3.5.2 Child Marriage

Whilst not specifically dealt with in this book child marriages are a growing cause for concern[215] and is therefore included herein for completeness. It is also linked with the practice of *ukuthwala* where minor girls are being forced to wed.[216] Indeed, in South Africa much of the attention on child marriage has been focused on the customary practice of *ukuthwala*.[217] Child marriage[218] or early marriage deserves attention as it is a detrimental practice. Not only does this practice rob girls of their childhood, but it is also a violation of their human rights and creates obstacles to achieving development goals related to gender, health, and education.

In addition to the harms to a child brides' health, several reports draw attention to other harms associated with early marriages like physical violence and marital rape.[219] Reports indicate that the practice continues to be commonly practiced in the rural parts of the Eastern Cape and KwaZulu-Natal.[220] Despite the devasting consequences attached to child marriage, South Africa's *Recognition of Customary Marriage Act*,[221] a law that governs customary marriages, read with the *Marriages*

---

[211] Department of Justice and Constitutional Development (2021), para 4.

[212] South African Law Reform Commission (2014).

[213] Jewkes et al. (2007).

[214] Walk Free Foundation (2015).

[215] Deane (2017).

[216] Mwambene (2018).

[217] *Jezile v S and Others* (A 127/2014) [2015] ZAWCHC 31; 2015 (2) SACR 452 (WCC); 2016 (2) SA 62 (WCC); [2015] 3 All SA 201 (WCC) (23 March 2015).

[218] This term is used in its widest sense to cover a betrothal or union between two people, recognized under civil law, religious law and/or customary rites, and understood to be binding by the spouses concerned, their families and the wider community, whether it has been formally registered in law. See Deane (2021).

[219] Deane (2021); World Vision (2008), pp. 18–24.

[220] Department of Justice and Constitutional Development (2021), para 5; Mwambene (2018).

[221] *Recognition of Customary Marriages Act 108 of 1998*, which entered into force on 15 November 2000.

Act[222] allows minors to get married provided they have the necessary consent.[223] These laws are arguably contributing to the rates of child marriages and to the challenge of ending child marriages, and consequently violence against women and girls in South Africa.[224]

2.4 Concluding Remarks

The definition of gender and GBVF varies in different contexts and epistemological approaches, and different understandings may raise conflicts. This chapter provides a foundation for an understanding and conceptualization of what is meant by GBVF by defining various terminologies associated with this phenomenon. How these concepts relate to each other are also given some consideration. It also highlights some of the most prevalent forms of GBVF, specific to the South African context. This framework is developed to contribute to the understanding of GBVF as well as to the data collection and analysis of GBV in academic environments and research workplaces. The next chapter will analyze why it is important for a country like South Africa to focus on the elimination of GBVF.

References

Abrahams N et al (2012) Every eight hours: intimate femicide in South Africa 10 years later! Medical Research Council, Cape Town

Abrahams N et al (2013) Intimate partner femicide in South Africa in 1999 and 2009. PLoS Med 10(4):e1001412. https://doi.org/10.1371/journal.pmed.1001412

[222] *Marriage Act 25 of 1961.*

[223] Sections 3(a) and (b) of the *Recognition of Customary Marriages Act*, read with section 25 of the *Marriage Act* allows both boys and girls of under 18 to get married provided they have the consent of a parent, guardian, or Commissioner of Welfare/Minister of Home Affairs. In particular, section 3 (a) of the *Recognition of Customary Marriages Act* provides that [i]f either of the prospective spouses is a minor, both his or her parents, or if he or she has no parents, his or her legal guardian must consent to the marriage. Section 3(b) provides: If the consent of the parent or legal guardians cannot be obtained, section 25 of the *Marriage Act, 1961* applies.

[224] At the time of the drafting of this chapter, Cabinet has approved the publication of the Draft *Marriage Bill of 2022* for public comment. Currently, marriages in South Africa are recognized under three separate acts—the *Marriage Act*, the *Civil Union Act 17 of 2006* and the *Recognition of Customary Marriages Act*. The Bill gives effect to the *White Paper on Marriages in South Africa* (Department of Home Affairs 2022) which was approved by Cabinet in March 2022 and empowers the Department of Home Affairs to develop a single Marriage Act for the country. A key feature of the Bill is that it will outlaw child marriages, meaning it will no longer be permissible for parents to consent to marriages of individuals under the age of 18. Anybody who allows somebody under the age of 18 to be married whether the marriage officer or the parent, will be guilty of an offense.

Africa Health Organisation (2021, January 14) Gender based violence fact sheet: South Africa. https://aho.org/news/gender-based-violence-fact-sheet-south-africa/. Accessed 18 Nov 2022

African Development Fund (2009) The National Gender Machinery, gender mainstreaming and the fight against gender-based violence. https://www.afdb.org/fileadmin/uploads/afdb/Documents/Project-and-Operations/South%20Africa%20-%20The%20National%20Gender%20Machinery%20Gender%20Mainstreaming.pdf. Accessed 8 Aug 2023

African Union (2003) Protocol to the African Charter on Human and Peoples' Rights on the Rights of Women in Africa. African Union, Maputo

African Union (2021) Press releases: African Union legal frameworks aim to break the cycle of violence against women and girls. https://au.int/en/pressreleases/20211125/african-union-legal-frameworks-aim-break-cycle-violence-against-women-and. Accessed 20 Dec 2023

Barrow A (2010) UN Security Council Resolutions 1325 and 1820: constructing gender in armed conflict and international humanitarian law. Int Rev Red Cross 92(877):221–234

Boonzaier FA, van Schalkwyk S (2011) Narrative possibilities: poor women of color and the complexities of intimate partner violence. Violence Against Women 17(2):267–286. https://doi.org/10.1177/1077801210397796

Bott S et al. (2005) Preventing and responding to gender-based violence in middle and low-income countries: a global review and analysis. In: The World Bank (ed) Policy research working papers. https://doi.org/10.1596/1813-9450-3618

Bows H, Fileborn B (2020) Space, place and GBV. J Gender-Based Violence 4(3):299–307. https://doi.org/10.1332/239868020x15983760944114

Bozzoli B (1983) Marxism, feminism and South African studies. J South Afr Stud 9(2):139–171. https://doi.org/10.1080/03057078308708055

Callander D et al (2019) The 2018 Australian Trans and Gender Diverse Sexual Health Survey: report of findings. The Kirby Institute, UNSW Sydney, Sydney

Carpenter RC (2006) Recognizing gender-based violence against civilian men and boys in conflict situations. Secur Dialogue 37(1):83–103. https://doi.org/10.1177/0967010606064139

Cassese A et al (eds) (2015) International criminal law, critical concepts in law. Routledge

Castañeda-Salgado MP (2016) Feminicide in Mexico: an approach through academic, activist and artistic work. Curr Sociol 64(7):1054–1070. https://doi.org/10.1177/0011392116637894

Cense M et al (2017) Sexual victimisation of transgender people in the Netherlands: prevalence, risk factors and health consequences. J Gender-Based Violence 1(2):235–252. https://doi.org/10.1332/239868017x15009036473945

Centre for the Study of Violence and Reconciliation (2016) Gender-based violence (GBV) in South Africa: a brief review. https://www.csvr.org.za/pdf/Gender%20Based%20Violence%20in%20South%20Africa%20-%20A%20Brief%20Review.pdf. Accessed 26 Jan 2023

Coalition of Feminists for Social Change (2017) Reframing the language of "GBV" away from feminist underpinnings. https://Cofemsocialchange.org/Learning-Advocacy-Tools/Cofem-Svri-Paper-Video-Series/Paper-2/. Accessed 16 Jan 2023

Corradi C (2021) Femicide, its causes and recent trends: what do we know? European Union, Brussels

Corradi C, Stöckl H (2014) Intimate partner homicide in 10 European countries: statistical data and policy developments in cross-national perspective. Eur J Criminol 11(5):601–618

Council of Europe (2011) Council of Europe Convention on preventing and combating violence against women and domestic violence. Council of Europe Treaty Series - no. 210. https://www.coe.int/en/web/gender-matters/council-of-europe-convention-on-preventing-and-combating-violence-against-women-and-domestic-violence. Accessed 29 Apr 2023

Council of Europe (2023) Gender matters. https://www.coe.int/en/web/gender-matters/sex-and-gender#18. Accessed 12 Dec 2023

Crenshaw K (1989) Demarginalizing the intersection of race and sex: a black feminist critique of antidiscrimination doctrine, feminist theory and antiracist politics. Univ Chic Leg Forum 1:139–167. (Article 8)

Crenshaw K (1991) Mapping the margins: intersectionality, identity politics, and violence against women of color. Stanf Law Rev 43(6):1241–1299
Cunha SO, Goncalves AR (2019) Predictors of intimate partner homicide in a sample of Portuguese male domestic offenders. J Interpersonal Violence 34(2):2573–2598
Daily Maverick (2022, June 14). South Africa's staggering intimate partner violence stats aren't shifting – here's what we can do about it. https://www.dailymaverick.co.za/article/2022-06-14-intimate-partner-violence-in-s-africa-the-staggering-stats-and-the-solutions/#:~:text=in%20South%20Africa%3F. Accessed 11 Nov 2022
Dawson M, Carrigan M (2020) Identifying femicide locally and globally: understanding the utility and accessibility of sex/gender-related motives and indicators. Curr Sociol 69(5):1–23
Deane T (2017) Searching for best practice: a study on trafficking in persons in West Africa and South Africa. Afr Insight 47(1):42–63
Deane T (2018) Sexual violence and the limits of laws' powers to alter behaviour: the case of South Africa. J Int Women's Stud 19(2):84–103
Deane T (2021) Marrying young: limiting the impact of a crisis on the high prevalence of child marriages in Niger. Laws 10(3):61. https://doi.org/10.3390/laws10030061
Demographic and Health Survey (2019, January) South Africa Demographic and Health Survey 2016. SA, DHS
Department of Home Affairs (2022) White paper on marriages in South Africa. http://www.dha.gov.za/images/PDFs/White-Paper-on-Marriage-in-SA-5-May2022.pdf. Accessed 9 Aug 2023
Department of Justice and Constitutional Development (2021) Justice/resources/publications/ukuthwala. https://www.justice.gov.za/brochure/ukuthwala/ukuthwala.html. Accessed 22 Dec 2022
Department of Justice and Constitutional Development (n.d.) Forms of femicide. https://www.justice.gov.za/vg/femicide/forms.html#:~:text=In%20South%20Africa%2C%20honour%20femicide,mystery%20attached%20to%20the%20killing. Accessed 7 Aug 2023
Dworkin A (1974) Woman hating. Penguin Books
Ebobrah ST (2010) Critical issues in the human rights mandate of the ECOWAS Court. J Afr Law 1(54):1–25
Ellsberg M et al (2008) Intimate partner violence and women's physical and mental health in the WHO multi-country study on women's health and domestic violence: an observational study. Lancet 371(9619):1165–1172. https://doi.org/10.1016/s0140-6736(08)60522-x
Ellsberg M et al (2015) Prevention of violence against women and girls: what does the evidence say? Lancet 385(9977):1555–1566. https://doi.org/10.1016/s0140-6736(14)61703-7
Enaifoghe AO (2019) South Africa gender based violence and the global gendered viewpoint approach mechanisms in building a peaceful world. J Soc Dev Sci 10(2(S)):15–25. https://doi.org/10.22610/jsds.v10i2(s).2905
Eniola O et al (2020) Bride price and sexual and reproductive rights of women: a case study of South Africa and Nigeria. J Law Policy Glob 96:26–33
Erickson-Schroth L et al (2020) Sexual and gender-based violence in lesbian, gay, bisexual, transgender, and queer communities. In: Ades V (ed) Sexual and gender-based violence. Springer, Cham, pp 113–116. https://doi.org/10.1007/978-3-030-38345-9_6
European Institute for Gender Equality (2021) Gender-based violence: defining and identifying femicide: a literature review. Publications Office of the European Union, Luxembourg
Fagbadebo O (2021) A discourse on the plight of South African women in the face of abuse and neglect. Law Democr Dev 25(spe):95–117. https://doi.org/10.17159/2077-4907/2020/ldd.v25.spe5
Garcia-Vergara E et al (2022) A comprehensive analysis of factors associated with intimate partner femicide: a systematic review. Int J Environ Res Public Health 19(12):7336. https://doi.org/10.3390/ijerph19127336
Gibbs A et al (2020) Non-partner sexual violence experience and toilet type amongst young (18–24) women in South Africa: a population-based cross-sectional analysis. Glob Public Health 16(4):1–7. https://doi.org/10.1080/17441692.2020.1813787

Gill K et al (eds) (2014) Honour' killing and violence theory, policy and practice. Palgrave Macmillan. https://doi.org/10.1057/9781137289568

Goldblatt B (2016, November 18) Violence against women in South Africa – constitutional responses and opportunities. https://papers.ssrn.com/sol3/papers.cfm?abstract_id=2872478. Accessed 4 Sept 2022

Government of South Africa (2020) National strategic plan on gender-based violence & femicide: 2020-2030. https://www.gov.za/sites/default/files/gcis_document/202006/stratplan-gbvs.pdf. Accessed 4 Aug 2023

Gqola PD (2015) Rape a South African nightmare. Mfbooks, Auckland Park

Grover L (2014) Interpreting crimes in the Rome Statute of the International Criminal Court. Cambridge University Press

Gruenewald J, Kelley K (2014) Exploring anti-LGBT homicide by mode of victim selection. Crim Justice Behav 41(9):1130–1152. https://doi.org/10.1177/0093854814541259

Hagay-Frey A (2011) Sex and gender crimes in the new international law: past, present, and future. Brill Nijhoff

Hamel J, Russell B (eds) (2022) Gender and domestic violence: contemporary legal practice and intervention reforms. Oxford University Press

Harmes RA, Russell DEH (2005) Femicide in global perspective. Teachers College, New York

Hefti A (2022) Conceptualizing femicide as a human rights violation. Edward Elgar Publishing Limited, Massachusetts

Human Rights Council (2016) Human Rights Council thirty-second session: agenda item 3 - promotion and protection of all human rights, civil, political, economic, social and cultural rights, including the right to development Report of the Special Rapporteur on violence against women, its causes and consequences on her mission to South Africa. https://evaw-global-database.unwomen.org/-/media/files/un%20women/vaw/country%20report/africa/south%20africa/sr%20south%20africa.pdf?vs=1106. Accessed 11 Nov 2022

Inzunza IAO (2020) Femicides: different approaches from the regional protection of human rights. Mexican Law Review New Series XIV(1):53–87

Jewkes R, Abrahams N (2002) The epidemiology of rape and sexual coercion in South Africa: an overview. Soc Sci Med 55(7):1231–1244. https://doi.org/10.1016/s0277-9536(01)00242-8

Jewkes R et al. (1999) "He must give me money, he mustn't beat me": violence against women in three South African provinces. CERSA (Women's Health) Technical Report. Pretoria, Medical Research Council

Jewkes R et al. (2002) Sexual violence. https://www.ojp.gov/ncjrs/virtual-library/abstracts/sexual-violence-world-report-violence-and-health-p-147-181-2002. Accessed 10 Oct 2022

Jewkes R et al (2005) "If they rape me, I can't blame them": reflections on gender in the social context of child rape in South Africa and Namibia. Soc Sci Med 61(8):1809–1820. https://doi.org/10.1016/j.socscimed.2005.03.022

Jewkes R et al. (2007, March) Evaluation of stepping stones: a gender transformative HIV prevention intervention. https://www.endvawnow.org/uploads/browser/files/Evaluation%20of%20Stepping%20Stones.pdf. Accessed 4 Nov 2023

Jewkes R et al (2011) Gender inequitable masculinity and sexual entitlement in rape perpetration South Africa: findings of a cross-sectional study. PLoS ONE 6(12):e29590. https://doi.org/10.1371/journal.pone.0029590

Jewkes R et al (2013) Prevalence of and factors associated with non-partner rape perpetration: findings from the UN multi-country cross-sectional study on men and violence in Asia and the Pacific. Lancet Glob Health 1(4):e208–e218. https://doi.org/10.1016/s2214-109x(13)70069-x

Judge M, Smythe D (2020) Striking women: the politics of gender, sexuality and the law in South Africa. In: Ashford C (ed) Research handbook on gender, sexuality and the law. Alexander Maine, pp 60–75

Kabeer N (2014, January 1) Violence against women as "relational" vulnerability: engendering the Sustainable Human Development Agenda. https://hdr.undp.org/content/violence-against-women-relational-vulnerability-engendering-sustainable-human-development. Accessed 4 Feb 2023

Karystianis G et al (2019) Automated analysis of domestic violence police reports to explore abuse types and victim injuries: text mining study. J Med Internet Res 21(3):e13067. https://doi.org/10.2196/13067

Lagarde De Los Ríos M (2010) Preface: feminist keys for understanding feminicide: theoretical, political and legal construction. In: Fregoso RL, Bejarano C (eds) Terrorizing women. Feminicide in the Americas. Duke University Press, Durham, pp xi–xxvi

LGBTIQ Domestic and Family Violence Interagency & The Centre for Social Research in Health (2014) Calling it what it really is: a report into lesbian, gay, bisexual, transgender, gender diverse, intersex and queer experiences of domestic and family violence. CSRH, UNSW, Sydney

Lindqvist A et al (2021) What is gender, anyway: a review of the options for operationalising gender. Psychol Sex 12(4):332–344. https://doi.org/10.1080/19419899.2020.1729844

López AC et al (2010) Feminicide in Latin America and the movement for women's rights. In: Fregoso RL, Bejarano C (eds) Terrorizing women, feminicide in the Americas. Duke University Press

Machisa MT (2011) The war at home: the Gauteng GBV indicators research study: gender links and the South African Medical Research Council. https://www.researchgate.net/publication/299627061_The_War_at_Home_The_Gauteng_GBV_Indicators_Research_Study_Gender_Links_and_the_South_African_Medical_Research_Council. Accessed 16 Nov 2022

Mail & Guardian (2022, June 17) South Africa ranks 118 out of 163 in the 2022 Global Peace Index. https://mg.co.za/opinion/2022-06-17-south-africa-ranks-118-out-of-163-in-the-2022-global-peace-index/. Accessed 9 Nov 2022

Mechanism to the Belém do Pará Convention (MESECVI) (n.d.) Inter-American Convention on the Prevention, Punishment, and Eradication of Violence against Women (Belem do Pará), OAS, 3. https://www.oas.org/en/mesecvi/docs/Folleto-BelemdoPara-EN-WEB.pdf. Accessed 2 Nov 2023

Menjívar C, Walsh SD (2017) The architecture of feminicide: the state, inequalities, and everyday gender violence in Honduras. Latin Am Res Rev 52(2):221. https://doi.org/10.25222/larr.73

Meyersfeld A (2006) Theory of domestic violence in international law. https://openyls.law.yale.edu/handle/20.500.13051/17631. Accessed 5 Dec 2023

Meyersfeld B (2010) Domestic violence and international law. Hart Publishers, Oxford

Mosavel M et al (2011) Perceptions of gender-based violence among South African youth: implications for health promotion interventions. Health Promot Int 27(3):323–330. https://doi.org/10.1093/heapro/dar041

Mpani P, Nsibande N (2015) Understanding gender policy and gender-based violence in South Africa: a literature review. Legal Advocacy Centre, Tshwaranang

Mshweshwe L (2023) Support for abused rural women in the Eastern Cape: views of survivors and service providers. https://ujcontent.uj.ac.za/esploro/outputs/doctoral/Support-for-abused-rural-women-in/9912832807691. Accessed 9 Apr 2023

Muteshi JK et al (2016) The ongoing violence against women: female genital mutilation/cutting. Reprod Health 13:44. https://doi.org/10.1186/s12978-016-0159-3

Mwambene L (2018) Recent legal responses to child marriage in Southern Africa: the case of Zimbabwe, South Africa and Malawi. Afr Hum Rights Law J 18(2):527–550. https://doi.org/10.17159/1996-2096/2018/v18n2a5

National Center for Injury Prevention and Control, Division of Violence Prevention (2022) Preventing intimate partner violence. https://www.cdc.gov/violenceprevention/intimatepartnerviolence/fastfact.html. Accessed 14 Nov 2022

National Inquiry into Missing and Murdered Indigenous Women and Girls (2017) The interim report: our women and girls are sacred. https://www.femicideincanada.ca/sites/default/files/2017-12/MMIWG%20INTERIM%20REPORT%20%282017%29%20%281%29.pdf. Accessed 8 Apr 2023

News24 (2020) South Africa ranks 123 out of 163 on the 2020 Global Peace Index. https://www.news24.com/news24/southafrica/news/south-africa-ranks-123-out-of-163-on-the-2020-global-peace-index-20200615. Accessed 3 Aug 2023

Norman R et al (2010) Interpersonal violence: an important risk factor for disease and injury in South Africa. Popul Health Metr 8(1). https://doi.org/10.1186/1478-7954-8-32

Office of the United Nations High Commissioner for Human Rights (1993, December 20) Gender-based violence against women and girls. https://www.ohchr.org/en/women/gender-based-violence-against-women-and-girls. Accessed 14 Mar 2023

OHCHR (2017) CEDAW general recommendation no. 35 on gender-based violence against women, updating general recommendation no. 19 - launch event – concept note. https://www.ohchr.org/sites/default/files/Documents/HRBodies/CEDAW/GR35/ConceptNoteLaunchGR35.pdf. Accessed 6 Dec 2023

Oram S et al (2022) The Lancet Psychiatry Commission on intimate partner violence and mental health: advancing mental health services, research, and policy. Lancet Psychiatry 9(6):487–524. https://doi.org/10.1016/S2215-0366(22)00008-6

Pandea AR et al (eds) (2019) Gender matters: a manual on addressing gender-based violence affecting young people. Council of Europe, Hungary

Presidency of South Africa (2018, November 2) Declaration of the Presidential summit against gender-based violence and femicide. https://www.thepresidency.gov.za/content/declaration-presidential-summit-against-gender-based-violence-and-femicide. Accessed 16 Sept 2022

Radford J, Russell DEH (1992) Femicide: the politics of woman killing. Open University Press

Randall AE (ed) (2022) Genocide and gender in the twentieth century: a comparative survey, 2nd edn. Bloomsbury Academic Publishers

Rembe S et al. (2011) Child and forced marriage as violation of women's rights, and responses by member states in Southern African Development Community. Agenda: Empowering Women Gender Equity 25(1 (87)): 65–74

Rollè L et al (2018) When intimate partner violence meets same sex couples: a review of same sex intimate partner violence. Front Psychol 9(1506). https://doi.org/10.3389/fpsyg.2018.01506

Russell DEH (2012, November) Defining femicide. https://www.dianarussell.com/defining-femicide-.html. Accessed 8 Apr 2023

Salo ER (2004) Respectable mothers, tough men and good daughters. Langaa Publishers

Simmons B (2009) Mobilizing for human rights: international law in domestic politics. Cambridge University Press

South African Government (2022a, August 19) Minister Bheki Cele: quarter one crime statistics 2022/2023. https://www.gov.za/speeches/minister-bheki-cele-quarter-one-crime-statistics-20222023-19-aug-2022-0000. Accessed 6 Nov 2022

South African Government (2022b, November 1) President Cyril Ramaphosa: second Presidential summit on gender-based violence and femicide. https://www.gov.za/speeches/president-cyril-ramaphosa-second-presidential-summit-gender-based-violence-and-femicide-1. Accessed 4 Nov 2022

South African Human Rights Commission (2021, August 10) Action on gender equality: the past, present and future are weighted against women. https://www.sahrc.org.za/index.php/sahrc-media/opinion-pieces/item/2769-action-on-gender-equality-the-past-present-and-future-are-weighted-against-women. Accessed 1 Mar 2023

South African Law Reform Commission (2014) The practice of *Ukuthwala*. https://www.justice.gov.za/salrc/dpapers/dp132-ukutwala.pdf. Accessed 16 Oct 2022

Spencer CM, Stith SM (2020) Risk factors for male perpetration and female victimization of intimate partner homicide: a meta-analysis. Trauma Violence Abuse 21:527–540. https://doi.org/10.1177/1524838018781101

Stats SA (2019, August 14) Governance, public safety and justice survey 2018/19. http://www.statssa.gov.za/publications/P0340/P03402019.pdf. Accessed 26 Dec 2022

Stats SA (2020) Crimes against women in South Africa: an analysis of the phenomenon of GBV and femicide. https://www.parliament.gov.za/storage/app/media/1_Stock/Events_

Institutional/2020/womens_charter_2020/docs/30-07-2020/A_Statistical_Overview_R_Maluleke.pdf. Accessed 23 Dec 2022
Stop Gender Violence Campaign (2019) National strategic plan on gender-based violence shadow framework. https://genderjustice.org.za/publication/national-strategic-plan-on-gender-based-violence-shadow-framework/. Accessed 18 Dec 2022
Swemmer S (2021) Femicide and the continuum of gender-based violence. In: Leal Filho W et al (eds) Gender equality: encyclopedia of the UN sustainable development goals. Springer, Cham. https://doi.org/10.1007/978-3-319-95687-9_44
Temmerman M (2015) Research priorities to address violence against women and girls. Lancet 385(9978):e38–e40. https://doi.org/10.1016/s0140-6736(14)61840-7
The Lancet Series (2014) Violence against women and girls. https://www.thelancet.com/series/violence-against-women-and-girls. Accessed 10 Nov 2022
UNICEF (2015, November 23) A profile of child marriage in Africa. https://data.unicef.org/resources/a-profile-of-child-marriage-in-africa/. Accessed 19 Dec 2022
UNICEF (2017) Glossary of terms and concepts. https://www.unicef.org/rosa/media/1761/file/Genderglossarytermsandconcepts.pdf. Accessed 12 Dec 2023
United Nations (1951) *Convention on the prevention and punishment of the crime of genocide* adopted 9 December 1948, entered into force 12 January 1951) 78 UNTS 277
United Nations (1993) Declaration on the elimination of violence against women. https://www.ohchr.org/en/instruments-mechanisms/instruments/declaration-elimination-violence-against-women. Accessed 2 Aug 2023
United Nations (1995) Fourth world conference on women: Beijing Declaration. http://www.un.org/womenwatch/daw/beijing/platform/declar.htm. Accessed 15 Nov 2022
United Nations (2013) Agreed conclusions on the elimination and prevention of all forms of violence against women and girls. https://www.un.org/womenwatch/daw/csw/csw57/CSW57_Agreed_Conclusions_(CSW_report_excerpt).pdf. Accessed 20 Apr 2023
United Nations (2015) Transforming our world: the 2030 agenda for sustainable development. https://sdgs.un.org/2030agenda. Accessed 2 Apr 2023
United Nations (2017) OHCHR general recommendation no. 35 (2017) on gender-based violence against women, updating general recommendation no. 19 (1992). https://www.ohchr.org/en/documents/general-comments-and-recommendations/general-recommendation-no-35-2017-gender-based#:~:text=Twenty%2Dfive%20years%20later%2C%20despite,violence%20against%20women%20and%20girls. Accessed 7 Aug 2023
United Nations Committee on the Elimination of Discrimination Against Women (CEDAW) (1992) CEDAW general recommendation no. 19: violence against women. https://www.un.org/womenwatch/daw/cedaw/cedaw25years/content/english/General_Recommendations_1-25-English.pdf. Accessed 7 Apr 2023
United Nations High Commissioner for Refugees (2010) Handbook for the protection of internally displaced persons. https://www.unhcr.org/protection/idps/4c2355229/handbook-protection-internally-displaced-persons.html. Accessed 19 Dec 2022
United Nations High Commissioner for Refugees (2016, June 14) Report of the Special Rapporteur on violence against women, its causes and consequences on her mission to South Africa. https://www.refworld.org/docid/57d90a4b4.html. Accessed 14 Sept 2022
United Nations Human Rights Council (2015) Report of the Special Rapporteur on violence against women, its causes and consequences. Special rapporteur on violence against women: A/HRC/26/38/Add.1. https://www.ohchr.org/sites/default/files/HRBodies/HRC/RegularSessions/Session29/Documents/A_HRC_29_27_AEV.doc. Accessed 24 Dec 2023
United Nations Office on Drugs and Crime (2019) Global study on homicide. https://www.unodc.org/documents/data-and-analysis/gsh/Booklet1.pdf. Accessed 30 Nov 2022
United Nations Office on Drugs and Crime (2021) Killings of women and girls by their intimate partner or other family members. https://www.unodc.org/documents/data-and-analysis/statistics/crime/UN_BriefFem_251121.pdf. Accessed 25 Nov 2022

United Nations Office on Drugs and Crime (2022a) Gender-related killings of women and girls (femicide/feminicide). https://www.unodc.org/documents/data-and-analysis/briefs/Femicide_brief_Nov2022.pdf. Accessed 3 Dec 2023

United Nations Office on Drugs and Crime (2022b) Statistical framework for measuring the gender-related killing of women and girls. https://www.unodc.org/documents/data-and-analysis/statistics/Statistical_framework_femicide_2022.pdf. Accessed 6 Aug 2023

United Nations Population Fund (2009) UNFPA strategy and framework for action to addressing gender-based violence 2008-2011. https://www.unfpa.org/sites/default/files/pub-pdf/2009_add_gen_vio.pdf. Accessed 20 Apr 2023

Walk Free Foundation (2015) South Africa - Global Slavery Index 2016. https://legacy.globalslaveryindex.org/country/south-africa/#. Accessed 3 Apr 2023

Warren MA (1985) Gendercide, the implications of sex selection. Rowman & Allanheld Publishers

Wirtz AL et al (2018) Lifetime prevalence, correlates and health consequences of gender-based violence victimisation and perpetration among men and women in Somalia. BMJ Global Health 3(4):e000773. https://doi.org/10.1136/bmjgh-2018-000773

World Bank (2019) Gender-based violence: violence against women and girls. World Bank, Washington DC

World Bank (2023) International Women's Day 2023: three important facts (and charts) from the World Bank's Gender Data Portal. https://blogs.worldbank.org/opendata/international-womens-day-2023-three-important-facts-and-charts-world-banks-gender-data#:~:text=Almost%20one%20in%20three%E2%80%94or,explore%20in%20the%20graph%20below. Accessed 8 Aug 2023

World Bank Group (2014) Voice and agency: empowering women and girls for shared prosperity. https://www.worldbank.org/en/topic/gender/publication/voice-and-agency-empowering-women-and-girls-for-shared-prosperity. Accessed 3 Nov 2022

World Health Organization (2013) Global and regional estimates of violence against women. https://www.who.int/publications/i/item/9789241564625. Accessed 4 Dec 2023

World Health Organization (2021a) Violence against women prevalence estimates, 2018: global, regional and national prevalence estimates for intimate partner violence against women and global and regional prevalence estimates for non-partner sexual violence against women. https://www.who.int/publications/i/item/9789240022256. Accessed 18 Mar 2023

World Health Organization (2021b, March 9) Violence against women. https://www.who.int/news-room/fact-sheets/detail/violence-against-women. Accessed 11 Nov 2022

World Health Organization (2023) Gender and health. https://www.who.int/health-topics/gender#tab=tab_1. Accessed 19 Dec 2023

World Vision (2008) Before she's ready: 15 places girls marry by 15. https://resourcecentre.savethechildren.net/document/shes-ready-15-places-girls-marry-15/. Accessed 6 Nov 2022

Chapter 3
Why Focus on Gender-Based Violence and Femicide

3.1 An Overview: The Sustainable Development Goals and Gender-Based Violence and Femicide

GBVF undermines global efforts to achieve human rights, gender equality and sustainable development. It is one of the most fundamental social, political and economic means by which the subordinate position of women with respect to men and their stereotyped roles are perpetuated.[1] Not only does its continued prevalence remain a critical obstacle to achieving substantive equality between women and men, but it acts as a barrier to women's enjoyment of their human rights and fundamental freedoms.[2] In recognition that women and girls must have equal rights and opportunity, and must be able to live free of violence and discrimination the UN Sustainable Development Goals (SDGs)[3] specifically calls for the elimination of violence against women. Adopted by United Nations Member States in 2015,[4] the SDG Agenda with its 17 Goals and 169 targets acknowledges the relationship between peace and security, poverty and inequality, economic growth, and environmental protection and mitigation.[5] Specifically, SDG 3 encompasses a set of hugely ambitious health targets that build on the progress of the Millennium Development Goals, which concluded in 2015.[6]

The SDG Agenda goes further by including broad and diverse global health challenges. It encompasses the main drivers of inequality, mortality and morbidity and calls for countries to build sustainable health systems for the future. SDG 5, which addresses gender equality and the empowerment of women and girls, is

[1] United Nations (2017).

[2] United Nations Office on Drugs and Crime (2022).

[3] United Nations (2015b).

[4] United Nations Development Group (2015).

[5] United Nations (2015a).

[6] Sachs et al. (2019). See, also, World Health Organization (2018).

T. Deane, *Gender-Based Violence and Femicide in South Africa*, Gender, Justice and Legal Feminism 5, https://doi.org/10.1007/978-3-031-61053-0_3

equally comprehensive and ambitious. Embedded in SDG 5 is the need to break down barriers to gender equality, including by transforming the underlying norms, structures and practices that prevent women and girls from enjoying their rights. Recognized as a core tenet of the 2030 Agenda, gender equality is both a stand-alone goal of sustainable development and a cross-cutting priority for achieving all the SDGs.

The inclusion of a specific target to "eliminate all forms of violence against all women and girls in private and public spheres, including trafficking and sexual and other types of exploitation" under SDG5,[7] as well as other related targets,[8] reflects the recognition by the global community that eliminating GBV is central to the empowerment of women and necessary for achieving sustainable development.[9] This includes ensuring the paramountcy of safety and dignity for victims while holding the perpetrators accountable for acts of violence.[10] Despite growing global awareness and evidence on effective prevention strategies, progress on reducing violence against women and girls over the past two decades has been inadequate. There is the concerning acknowledgement that a failure to act to achieve these SDGs will translate to the 2030 Agenda becoming "an epitaph for a world that might have been."[11]

The elimination of violence against women is therefore a key commitment of the 2030 Agenda for Sustainable Development. Member States must make the world a place "in which every woman and girl enjoys full gender equality and all legal, social and economic barriers to their empowerment have been removed."[12] The 2030 Agenda notes that "the achievement of full human potential and of sustainable development is not possible if one half of humanity continues to be denied its full human rights and opportunities."[13] The achievement of gender equality is seen as integral to all dimensions of inclusive and sustainable development. In short, all the SDGs depend on the achievement of Goal 5. Gender inequality has a strong relationship with a range of types of violence, especially sexual violence, and domestic and family violence. These forms of violence are generally considered inherently gendered due to the overwhelming perpetration of the violence by men towards women and children throughout the world. The SDGs are as much about development and transformation as they are about the restoration of the dignity of people around the world, more so in South Africa with its history of deprivation and exclusion of the majority of its people.

The achievement of gender equality by 2030 requires urgent action to eliminate the many root causes of discrimination that still curtail women's rights in private and

---

[7] Specifically, SDG target 5.2 of the UN SDG's.

[8] See, for example, SDG targets 11.7, 16.1, and 16.2 United Nations (2015b).

[9] Kendall (2020).

[10] United Nations Women (2019).

[11] António Guterres, Secretary-General of the United Nations, in United Nations (2023), p. 2.

[12] United Nations (2015b), p. 8.

[13] United Nations (2015b), para 20.

public spheres. Eliminating GBV is clearly a priority, given that this is one of the most pervasive human rights violations in the world today. Based on data from 87 countries, 1 in 5 women and girls under the age of 50 will have experienced physical and/or sexual violence by an intimate partner within the last 12 months.[14] The SDGs have highlighted interpersonal violence and violence against women and girls as impediments to development globally.[15] South Africa is adversely affected by GBV. Achieving gender equality and the empowerment of women and girls will require more vigorous efforts, to counter deeply rooted gender-based discrimination that often results from patriarchal attitudes and related social norms. This chapter therefore calls for an ambitious national benchmark to, for the purpose of this book, eradicate poverty and reduce inequality by focusing on key areas like expanding social protection and addressing gender inequality through the elimination of GBVF. The reality is that despite various normative standards having been set, violence against women[16] remains a global epidemic, which is further complicated when considering the multiple and intersecting forms that discrimination can take. Accordingly, an intersectional approach is needed and will require an analysis on how violence is responded to in policy and legislation across the country.

The 2030 SDG Agenda presents a potentially transformative framework for urgent change, not only in South Africa, but throughout the world. A failure to make substantive progress means inequalities will continue to deepen, increasing the risk of a fragmented, two-speed world.[17]

[14] United Nations Economic and Social Council (2018).

[15] SDG 5 aims to achieve gender equality and to empower all women and girls. The targets in SDG 5 encompass a wide range of issues, such as eliminating discrimination and gender-based violence, recognising unpaid domestic and care work, increasing access to reproductive healthcare, land, and various economic resources, and implementing legislation and policies that serve to provide an enabling environment for women's empowerment.

[16] Any act of GBV that results in, or is likely to result in, physical, sexual, or mental harm or suffering to women, including threats of such acts, coercion, or arbitrary deprivation of liberty, whether occurring in public or in private life. United Nations General Assembly (1994) *Declaration on the Elimination of Violence Against Women: Resolution (48th session: 1993-1994) (A/RES/48/104)*. This Resolution refers to violence directed at a woman because she is a woman and that affects her disproportionately. It takes a range of forms including but not limited to: intimate partner violence; non-partner sexual assault; trafficking; so-called honour crimes; sexual harassment and exploitation; stalking; witch craft related violence; gender related killings. See, also, United Nations (2017) *OHCHR General Recommendation No. 35*.

[17] United Nations (2023), p. 2.

3.2 The SDGs and the National Development Plan

Specifically in South Africa, the SDGs are closely aligned to the country's National Development Plan (NDP): Vision 2030[18] which prioritizes the elimination of poverty, reduction of inequality and growing an inclusive economy by 2030. The NDP therefore potentially holds the key to accelerate the realization of the NDP's vision, notably by fostering greater policy coherence and reducing duplication and inefficiencies.

South Africa has also established a national coordinating mechanism to strengthen implementation of development policies.[19] The coordination arrangement further facilitates national engagements and reporting in a coordinated and integrated manner on the developmental agendas of the UN 2030 Agenda, the African Union (AU) Agenda 2063,[20] the Southern African Development Community (SADC) Regional Indicative Strategic Development Plan (RISDP)[21] as well as its Vision 2030, as encapsulated in the NDP. The NDP goals are consequently aligned to the SDGs and to the AU Agenda 2063 and are integrated into the government's planning systems and processes at national, provincial, and local level.[22] The NDP has indeed contributed to improved living conditions for millions of South Africans in a context where, for historical reasons, South Africa is amongst the most unequal of societies. The country is therefore seemingly well placed towards meeting the SDGs. However, the SDGs require the vigorous pursuit of gender equality by eliminating all forms of discrimination against women and to eliminate all forms of violence against all women and girls by 2030. South Africa's current persistent levels of inequalities, discrimination, and high rates of GBVF[23] is worrying.

As previously mentioned, the attainment of gender equality is not only a fundamental human right, but a necessary foundation for a peaceful, prosperous, and sustainable country and world. The alarmingly high rates of GBV makes being a woman in South Africa more dangerous than being in some of the world's war-torn areas.[24] This situation does not bode well for the achievement of equality and non-discrimination and the rest of the SDGs. South Africa's achievement of the

[18] The National Development Plan (NDP): Vision 2030—"Our future – make it work" was adopted in 2012, as South Africa's development lodestar and roadmap. It predated the post-2015 development agenda of the United Nations 2030 Agenda for Sustainable Development as well as the African Union Agenda 2063. The NDP has a 74% convergence with the Sustainable Development Goals (SDGs), and prioritises job creation, the elimination of poverty, the reduction of inequality and growing an inclusive economy by 2030. See Stats SA (2019).

[19] Stats SA (2019).

[20] African Union (2013).

[21] South African Development Community (2020).

[22] Stats SA (2019).

[23] United Nations (2019).

[24] SAHRC (2021).

SDGs will require some significant interventions to eliminate GBV and inequality. As the country looks to ensure a more equal society for all going forward, focus must be on ensuring that today's girl child develops to her full potential, thereby promoting intergenerational gender justice.[25] The SDGs recognize the importance of ensuring that the girl child's survival, development, and protection needs are met, to build a stronger and more resilient future for all.

The government therefore has the task of eradicating GBV in the country, restructuring a historically unequal economy that marginalizes women and youth, while preparing for a future that may bring further inequalities. The government, to achieve the SDGs, must therefore adopt appropriate responses and include various role players to not only address a system that is fundamentally discriminatory and violent towards women, but also to ensure that such measures will be sustainable and effectively responds to the needs of women and girls.

3.3 Too Costly to Ignore

GBVF is a fundamental human rights violation and deserves condemnation and attention at all levels. This alone is sufficient justification for urgent action against GBV. However, violence against women and girls goes further as it also hampers development. New evidence indicates that ending violence against women is not only a moral imperative, but it also benefits the economy.[26] It has enormous social, economic and productivity costs for individuals, families, communities, and societies. In 2013, the 57th session of the Commission on the Status of Women specially noted the economic and social harm caused by such violence.[27] Compounding this situation is the fact that funding allocations to specifically address violence against women are often lacking or inadequate.[28]

3.3.1 Why Highlight the Costs of Violence

It is important to highlight the costs of violence for the following reasons. First, measuring the costs of violence demonstrates how violence drains resources from many sectors, not just the perpetrators and victims, but also presents significant costs to the businesses and the private sector, all levels of government and civil society.[29] This is particularly important for South Africa where it is crucial not to remove scare

[25] SAHRC (2021).

[26] KPMG (2017), p. 3.

[27] United Nations Women (2013a).

[28] Commonwealth Secretariat (2019).

[29] KPMG (2017), p. 12.

resources from the promotion of healthy and viable communities. Essentially, the cost of violence demonstrates the waste of resources that can be more effectively used. Thus, if society could eliminate violence against women, the equivalent costs associated with GBVF could be avoided. Such resources can then be dedicated to development purposes which would contribute towards closing the resource gap and enhancing efforts to achieve gender equality, the empowerment of all women and girls, and the sustainable development goals at large.[30] The costs associated with GBV therefore provides strong arguments for why preventing and responding to such violence should be a priority for governments, donors, and the private sector.[31]

Second, highlighting the scale of the costs will aid in the prioritization of relevant policies. The WHO amongst others have indicated that cost calculation and economic analysis of violence, particularly in low income and developing countries, should be a prioritized task in the policy making process.[32] It is also important to highlight that the analysis of the cost of violence indicates that most responses to GBVF focuses primarily on intervening with affected women after the violence has occurred.[33] Whilst such strategies are key to mitigating the devastating effects of violence for survivors thereof, focus should also be on implementing programs to prevent the violence from occurring in the first place. Such an approach will ensure the prevention of significant human rights violations and reduce the social and economic costs of violence.

In addition, to make informed decisions about how public and private resources should be allocated, and to ensure that enough financial resources are directed toward understanding the issue of violence, policy makers need to have scientific information about the initial size of the problem. By measuring economic costs and consequences of violence, policymakers can be better informed about the prioritization of resource allocation across various social and economic priorities, including within efforts to address GBV.[34] An understanding of the costs of providing services is therefore necessary to ensure sufficient budgets are allocated and that inadequate funding will not compromise essential services to victims and survivors.

Third, the progress on reducing violence against women globally has been slow. International commitments to attain gender equality and end violence against women and girls remain at the heart of priorities for sustainable development and economic growth.[35] Of concern, the latest progress reports on sustainable development and economic growth shows that the world is not on track to achieve gender equality by

[30] Puri (2016).

[31] In addition to investing in prevention it is critical that government and donors continue to support high quality response and support services to prevent re-occurrence of violence against women.

[32] World Health Organization (2021).

[33] Puri (2016).

[34] KPMG (2017), p. 13.

[35] Commonwealth Secretariat (2019).

2030.[36] It has been reported that without dedicated investment in scaling up prevention programs, implementing effective policies and providing support services to address violence, countries will not achieve the target of eliminating violence against women and girls by 2030.[37] Gender equality, women's empowerment and the prevention of violence against women in private and public spaces is a precondition for and objective of sustainable development. Much more will need to be done to achieve the SDGs on gender, particularly goal 5.2 on the elimination of violence against women and girls.[38]

3.3.2 *Costing GBV*

Whilst costing GBV is still an emerging area of research that requires collection of sensitive information from women who have been victims of violence, global studies on the economic impact of GBV has increased over the past few decades. Various papers have successfully attempted to measure comprehensive national costs, while others research forms partial exercises measuring only a particular subcategory of costs.[39] However, all the research has contributed to an understanding that violence against women and girls bring huge economic costs to any society. It exacts an economic cost to countries in terms of prevention, response and opportunity costs.[40] The nature of these costs varies and may be direct or indirect,[41] monetarily tangible or intangible.[42] Importantly, these costs are not just immediate, as they have

[36] See United Nations (2023) and the United Nations (2022). The 2022 SDG Gender Index indicates that between 2015 and 2020 little progress in gender equality has been made around the world. The score of the Global Gender Equality Index for 2020 reached 67.8—a small improvement of less than two points since 2015. Even more concerningly, the combined effects of COVID-19 have resulted in several reversals of the gains achieved. The report indicates that this is especially the case for girls' education, gender-based violence, women's employment and sexual and reproductive health and rights. Lost learning and the surge in school dropouts potentially leads to a loss in earnings for an entire generation, estimated at US$10 trillion.

[37] United Nations (2023), p. 23.

[38] SDG Target 5.2 is to "eliminate all forms of violence against women and girls in public and private spheres, including trafficking and sexual and other types of exploitation."

[39] Some examples of studies would include Walby (2004); Morrison and Orlando (2005); European Institute for Gender Equality (2014); CARE (2018); Spence (2020) and Commonwealth Secretariat (2022).

[40] Opportunity costs, sometimes also regarded as indirect costs, are the costs foregone when a victim's options are limited by the circumstances of violence, such as being in or leaving a violent relationship. They represent the loss of potential which have a monetary value that can be estimated.

[41] Direct costs are in relation to goods and services for which there is a monetary exchange. Indirect costs are those costs for which a monetary value can be calculated even though there is no monetary exchange, such as foregone benefits or opportunity costs.

[42] The costs of violence against women and the impact on their children are typically described as direct (or tangible), indirect (or intangible) and opportunity costs. The literature varies in how costs are classified according to these types, and some studies treat direct and tangible as different things,

multiplier[43] effects for society and the economy.[44] Examples of such costs include health, justice and other service costs, lost earnings, where GBV negatively impacts women's participation in education, it results in lost employment and productivity and undermines poverty reduction.[45] Importantly it has second-generation costs or dimensions, which are the cost of children witnessing and living with violence.[46] GBV therefore effectively drains resources from social services, the justice system, health-care agencies and employers. Consequently, violence against women has been acknowledged as a clear barrier to sustainable development. Indeed, for the first time, violence against women and girls is included as a target area under Goal 5 on gender equality, reaffirming that such violence is a barrier to gender equality, women's empowerment, and overall sustainable development, as well as a barrier to the achievement of the other SDGs.

3.3.3 Specific Costs from Studies

According to the UN, the cost of violence against women (public, private, and social) amounts to US$1.5 trillion at the global level.[47] It is noted that while such

---

but essentially the point is to identify all the different costs associated with violence in order to quantify the full impact.

Direct, or tangible, costs are those representing actual paid expenses, or real money spent, on the provision of services, facilities, or expenses incurred by the victim or the household.

Indirect, or intangible, costs are those which do not have a monetary value, such as pain, fear and suffering or social and psychological costs of violence. These costs may be approximated by a quality or value of life measure or use of a reasonable proxy measure, such as those used credibly in the justice system for establishing compensation. See Duvvury et al. (2012).

[43] The multiplier effect relates to the reduction in output which translates to even larger reductions because of the economic multiplier effect, which means that a dollar lost represents more than just that dollar. Rather it represents the lost savings and spending that is passed on to others to save and spend many times over as money circulates through the economy. When violence is reduced, not only can resources be reallocated to more productive uses that result in economic growth, but the multiplier effect also serves to augment that growth. See KPMG (2017).

[44] United Nations (2020).

[45] Morrison and Orlando (2005).

[46] GBV has a significant effect on children, whether those children are also direct victims of abuse or witnesses to the abuse. Witnessing family violence in childhood is associated with a greater likelihood that sons and daughters will be either perpetrators or victims of violence. For example, a woman who has experienced violence in childhood is 3.11 times more likely to have experienced violence in last 12 months and 2.78 times more likely to experience violence in her lifetime, whilst a woman who has witnessed violence in childhood is 1.89 times more likely to experience violence in her lifetime. In this regard, see Duvvury et al. (2012). Men's risk of perpetration of domestic violence starts in childhood and is more common if they have witnessed violence between parents or if they themselves have been exposed to physical or sexual abuse in childhood. In this regard, see Abrahams et al. (2013).

[47] Puri (2016).

costs are profound, they are not well calculated due to an absence of data globally. However, discussed below are some estimates of a range of costs, obtained from national studies and other research, that are associated with violence against women and girls. While the economic costs of different countries highlighted below are not directly comparable[48] to each other due to differences in the types of violence studied, different costs considered, and differences in population and Gross Domestic Product (GDP) sizes, what it is evidence of is that the cost (however studied) of violence against women is universal and significant.[49] The scale of the problem worldwide and the costs to each country fall within broader estimates of the cost to the global economy as a whole. This global cost has been estimated at approximately 2% of global GDP, or US$1.5 trillion. This is comparable to approximately the size of the Canadian economy.[50] Another study indicates that based on costing done for various countries globally, GBV costs economies an estimated 1.2–3.7% of GDP. [51]

In addition, more than 30 studies have been conducted, mostly from developed countries, that attempt to quantify the costs of various forms of violence against women.[52] Some of the most comprehensive of these studies, in both developed and developing countries, estimate the cost of violence to be between 1–2% of GDP. These reports are however widely accepted to be underestimates, given the conservatism of the methodology and the gross underreporting of GBV in many countries.[53] The Walby study in the UK,[54] considered the most comprehensive of the studies,[55] estimated that the aggregate costs of intimate partner violence, including service-related costs, the value of economic output lost, and human and emotional costs,[56] is close to 1.91% of the GDP or £23 billion (US$34.5 billion) annually. In England and Wales specifically, domestic violence alone costed approximately US$32.9 billion. A similar cost estimation in Australia put the costs at an estimated US$11.38 billion per year. In the United States, intimate partner violence is estimated to cost approximately US$5.8 billion a year and 1.78% of GDP[57] whilst in Canada it is estimated at US$1.16 billion.

[48] Cross country comparisons are challenging and should be approached with caution. This is because country specific considerations vary, including the scope and definition of violence, populations measured, reporting rates, the units of measurement and the comparisons in terms of the year of study and total costs may vary according to inflation and exchange rate fluctuations.

[49] CARE (2018).

[50] Puri (2016).

[51] World Bank (2018).

[52] These studies focus largely on the costs of services, and the economic losses due to lost output, decreased productivity and lower earnings resulting from violence.

[53] KPMG (2017).

[54] Walby (2004).

[55] Duvvury et al. (2012).

[56] Some researchers argue for and against the inclusion of pain and suffering in the costing measures mainly because it is considered immoral or demeaning to put a price on a victim's suffering. However, these costs are significant and cannot be ignored. See Vyas et al. (2021).

[57] United Nations Women (2013b).

As part of studies completed in Africa, the results highlight how GBV remains a major threat to economic development specifically within the sub-Saharan African region.[58] This region has been identified as having the highest level of domestic violence against women. However empirical studies about its potential economic impact are scarce, mainly due to data limitations. Therefore, once again, researchers caution that in the estimates given, it should be taken as partial or minimum estimates of the true costs, due to challenges of data availability and capturing all costs. What the estimates do however provide is indicative economic costs in the countries. The results of studies suggest that an increase in violence against women by 1 percentage point is associated with a 9% lower level of economic activity.[59]

Within the sub-Saharan region, GBV within South Africa has been costed at up to 1.3% of GDP.[60] Specifically, the economic impact of that violence is between at least ZAR4 billion and ZAR4 billion for the year 2012/2013, representing 0.9% and 1.3% of GDP, respectively. While national prevalence rates of all types of GBV, not just those that result in death, are not available for South Africa, it is clear that it is a problem of great magnitude. However, apart from one study by KPMG in 2017,[61] very little attempt has been made to comprehensively estimate the full economic impact that this has had on the South African economy. This is especially concerning as South Africa's NDP and Vision 2030 has set forth the country's plan for economic transformation, poverty eradication, and full employment.[62] The continued prevalence of GBV is resulting in wasted resources that could be used towards the NDP and productive economic growth. In addition, and as will be discussed in detail later,[63] the country has made some significant investments towards the elimination of GBVF in the country. However, these investments made by government and the private sector to grow the South African economy will be eroded if the prevalence of violence against women prevails. In short, the continued prevalence of GBV erodes both the inputs and outputs of growth. In addition, despite the obvious limitations in making comparisons the international studies together provide an important reference point for South African policymakers on the scale and magnitude of GBV across other jurisdictions and raises pertinent questions on the scale and cost of GBV locally.

Looking at a study conducted in Nigeria, and taking into account that estimates of costs to the economy of 1.3% GDP were done for South Africa at prevalence rates of 20–30%, and Nigeria had rates of 38% during the pre-COVID period,[64] the cost to Nigeria, due to the substantive increase in GBV during lockdown, has increased the

---

[58] Ouedraogo and Stenzel (2021).

[59] Ouedraogo and Stenzel (2021).

[60] KPMG (2017).

[61] KPMG (2017).

[62] National Planning Commission (2011), Chapter 12.

[63] See Chap. 7.

[64] This will also be discussed in detail under "*GBV During Times of Crisis*" below.

costs to the economy significantly.[65] In Zambia, GBV has been costed at 2.27%[66] and a study conducted in Lesotho has estimated the total economic cost of GBV to be around 462.9 million maloti,[67] implying an approximate 1.333% of GDP.[68]

This comprised an estimated direct cost of M428.2 million (1.234% of GDP) plus an economy-wide indirect cost of M34.7 million (0.100% GDP). In Ghana, GBV has been costed around 0.9% of GDP.[69] In Uganda, approximately 9% of violent incidents forced women to lose time from paid work, amounting to nearly 11 days a year, which is equivalent to half a month's salary. This affected not only the incumbent person but the family unit and dependents.[70] A study conducted in India, showed that women can lose an average of at least five paid workdays for each incident of intimate partner violence. This fact would mean the affected woman would get 25% less of her salary each time an incident of violence happens.[71] Whilst not many studies have been conducted that explored the impact of domestic violence in the global South, one important study did find that Colombian women who suffered physical violence have 14% lower earnings than women who did not suffer violence and in Brazil, productivity loss due to violence-related injuries accounted for approximately 12% of the total health budget or 1.2% of GDP.[72]

It has been reported that women and girls who survive the violence bear the brunt of costs, estimated to be as much as six times the cost to the state.[73] These overall costs of violence against women are comparable to state budgets for essential services.[74] For example, in Zambia, the cost of GBV at 2.27% of GDP or US$473 million was comparable to the entire health budget for the country in 2016.[75] In Bangladesh, the cost of domestic violence at US$2.3 billion (equivalent to 2.1% of GDP in 2010) was equal to the health and nutrition budget for the whole country in that year.[76] In Uganda, the US$22.2 million costs borne by providers of public services for domestic violence was 0.75% of the country's national budget in 2010/2011.[77]

The nature of the current crisis of GBV and attendant challenges in prevention and response efforts indicate that while incidents of GBV increase, the magnitude of the economic costs will continue to be significant and be borne in the medium to

[65] International Growth Centre (2020).

[66] CARE (2018).

[67] Lesotho's currency, M. See Commonwealth (2020).

[68] Commonwealth Secretariat (2019).

[69] Raghavendra et al. (2019), p. 939.

[70] CARE (2018).

[71] Puri (2016).

[72] Butchard and Khanh-Huynh (2008).

[73] Walby (2004), pp. 97–98.

[74] CARE (2018).

[75] Zulu et al. (2017), p. 7.

[76] Siddique (2011), p. 51.

[77] Kasirye (2013), p. 4.

longer term with multiplier effects. Studies show that investing in the prevention of violence is a cost-effective approach for states.[78] One study argued that international studies demonstrate that each $1 invested in GBV prevention saves the economy $5–20 in future service cost.[79] Another study highlighted that an estimated total of US$12 trillion could be added to global GDP by 2025 by closing the gender gap and advancing women's equality in the public, private and social sectors, which in turn will have a positive impact on stopping violence against women.[80] US$12 trillion is equal to the combined GDPs of Japan, Germany, and the United Kingdom in 2015.[81]

While the estimates per country vary depending on the scope and focus of the study, the magnitude is clear. By investing in the effective implementation of behavioral, legal, and regulatory solutions, states will save on the cost of responding to violence. A gender-responsive design and provision of essential services and physical and social infrastructure is essential. It also provides strong arguments to governments that investing in prevention programs that treat the causes of GBV are far more economical and cost-effective than treating the symptoms.

3.4 Concluding Remarks

This chapter has highlighted that GBV has a fundamental impact on economic growth which can span several generations. It drains resources from many sectors, not just the perpetrators and victims. Measuring the costs of GBV demonstrates that GBV is a social and economic issue that wastes scarce resources, and that inaction translates to an immense global cost. Highlighting costs and the potential benefits shows the critical importance of accelerating efforts to prevent and respond to violence against women across the world. Given the scale and prevalence of the problem globally, and the related social and economic costs, it is critical that governments, donors, and the private sector work actively and collaboratively to end GBVF.

Finally, creating an enabling environment for realizing the three main attributes of women's human rights embodied in SDG 5—namely, physical security, safety and integrity and control over their bodies, participation and leadership in decision, equal access to opportunities, productive resources, capabilities, and choices with regards to their economic, social, and personal life, remains essential to combatting GBV.

The next chapter will focus on developing a theoretical framework for understanding GBVF to offer a deeper understanding of the continued violence that is targeted towards women and girls.

---

[78] Laxminarayan et al. (2006), Chapter 2.

[79] United Nations Population Fund: Ukraine (2018).

[80] Woetzel et al. (2015), p. iv.

[81] CARE (2018).

References

Abrahams N et al (2013) Intimate partner femicide in South Africa in 1999 and 2009. PLoS Med 10(4):e1001412. https://doi.org/10.1371/journal.pmed.1001412

African Union (2013) Agenda 2063: the Africa we want. https://au.int/en/agenda2063/overview. Accessed 14 Mar 2023

Butchard A, Khanh-Huynh A (2008) Manual for estimating the economic costs of injuries due to interpersonal and self-directed violence. US, World Health Organization & Centers for Disease Control and Prevention

CARE (2018) Counting the cost: the price society pays for violence against women. https://www.care-international.org/files/files/Counting_the_costofViolence.pdf. Accessed 23 Apr 2023

Commonwealth (2020) The economic cost of violence against women and girls a study of Lesotho. Marlborough House Maseru, Kingdom of Lesotho, London

Commonwealth Secretariat (2019) The economic cost of violence against women and girls. Commonwealth Secretariat, London

Commonwealth Secretariat (2022) Measuring the economic costs of violence against women and girls: facilitators guide. Commonwealth Secretariat, London

Duvvury N et al. (2012) Estimating the costs of domestic violence against women in Vietnam. https://asiapacific.unwomen.org/sites/default/files/Field%20Office%20ESEAsia/Docs/Publications/2013/estimating%20the%20cost%20of%20domestic%20violence%20against%20women%20in%20viet%20nam.pdf. Accessed 25 Apr 2023

European Institute for Gender Equality (2014) Costs of gender-based violence in the European Union. https://eige.europa.eu/gender-based-violence/costs-of-gender-based-violence?language_content_entity=en. Accessed 8 Aug 2023

International Growth Centre (2020, May 19) The shadow pandemic: gender-based violence and COVID-19. https://www.theigc.org/blogs/covid-19/shadow-pandemic-gender-based-violence-and-covid-19. Accessed 22 Apr 2023

Kasirye I (2013) Economic costs of domestic violence in Uganda. Kampala, Centre for Domestic Violence Prevention

Kendall T (2020) A synthesis of evidence on the collection and use of administrative data on violence against women: background paper for the development of global guidance. https://giwps.georgetown.edu/resource/a-synthesis-of-evidence-on-the-collection-and-use-of-administrative-data-on-violence-against-women-background-paper-for-the-development-of-global-guidance/. Accessed 4 Oct 2022

KPMG (2017) Too costly to ignore – the economic impact of gender-based violence in South Africa. https://assets.kpmg.com/content/dam/kpmg/za/pdf/2017/01/za-Too-costly-to-ignore.pdf. Accessed 14 Apr 2023

Laxminarayan R et al (2006) Intervention cost-effectiveness: overview of main messages (Chapter 2). In: Jamison DT et al (eds) Disease control priorities in developing countries. The International Bank for Reconstruction and Development/The World Bank Oxford University Press, New York

Morrison AR, Orlando MB (2005) The costs and impacts of gender-based violence in developing countries: methodological considerations and new evidence. http://gender.careinternationalwikis.org/_media/morrisonorlandogenderbasedviolence.pdf. Accessed 10 Aug 2023

National Planning Commission (2011) Chapter 12: building safer communities. https://www.nationalplanningcommission.org.za/assets/Documents/NDP_Chapters/devplan_ch12_0.pdf. Accessed 10 Nov 2022

Ouedraogo R, Stenzel D (2021) The heavy economic toll of gender-based violence: evidence from sub-Saharan Africa. International Monetary Fund

Puri L (2016, September 21) The economic costs of violence against women. https://www.unwomen.org/en/news/stories/2016/9/speech-by-lakshmi-puri-on-economic-costs-of-violence-against-women. Accessed 19 Apr 2023

Raghavendra S et al. (2019) The macroeconomic loss due to violence against women and girls: the case of Ghana. Economics working paper archive
Sachs JD et al (2019) Six transformations to achieve the sustainable development goals. Nat Sustain 2:805–814. https://doi.org/10.1038/s41893-019-0352-9
Siddique K (2011) Domestic violence against women: cost to the nation. CARE
South African Development Community (2020) Regional Indicative Strategic Development Plan 2020-2030. https://www.sadc.int/pillars/regional-indicative-strategic-development-plan-2020-2030. Accessed 14 Mar 2023
South African Human Rights Commission (2021, August 10) Action on gender equality: the past, present and future are weighted against women. https://www.sahrc.org.za/index.php/sahrc-media/opinion-pieces/item/2769-action-on-gender-equality-the-past-present-and-future-are-weighted-against-women. Accessed 1 Mar 2023
Spence I (2020) The cost of violence: assessing the economic cost of gender-based violence in Rwanda. Eur J Public Health 30(5):ckaa166.169. https://doi.org/10.1093/eurpub/ckaa166.169
Stats SA (2019) Sustainable Development Goals (SDGs): country report 2019 - South Africa. https://www.statssa.gov.za/MDG/SDGs_Country_Report_2019_South_Africa.pdf. Accessed 25 Apr 2023
United Nations (2015a) The 17 goals. https://sdgs.un.org/goals. Accessed 9 Aug 2023
United Nations (2015b) Transforming our world: the 2030 agenda for sustainable development. https://sdgs.un.org/2030agenda. Accessed 2 Apr 2023
United Nations (2017) OHCHR general recommendation no. 35 (2017) on gender-based violence against women, updating general recommendation No. 19 (1992)
United Nations (2019) South Africa: sustainable development knowledge platform. https://sustainabledevelopment.un.org/memberstates/southafrica. Accessed 26 Mar 2023
United Nations (2020, May 4) Gender-based violence in Nigeria during the Covid-19 crisis: the shadow pandemic. https://nigeria.un.org/sites/default/files/2020-05/Gender%20Based%20Violence%20in%20Nigeria%20During%20COVID%2019%20Crisis_The%20Shadow%20Pandemic.pdf. Accessed 24 Apr 2023
United Nations (2022) The progress on the sustainable development goals: the gender snapshot 2022. https://unstats.un.org/sdgs/report/2022/. Accessed 20 Apr 2023
United Nations (2023) The sustainable development goals report: a special edition. https://unstats.un.org/sdgs/report/2023/. Accessed 9 Aug 2023
United Nations Development Group (2015) Socio-economic impact of the Ebola virus disease in West Africa. https://www.undp.org/africa/publications/socio-economic-impact-ebola-virus-disease-west-africa. Accessed 19 Dec 2022
United Nations Economic and Social Council (2018) Progress towards the sustainable development goals. https://digitallibrary.un.org/record/1627573?ln=en. Accessed 14 Sept 2022
United Nations General Assembly (1994) Declaration on the elimination of violence against women: resolution (48th session: 1993-1994) (A/RES/48/104). https://digitallibrary.un.org/record/179739?ln=en#:~:text=TitleDeclaration%20on%20the%20Elimination,adopted%20by%20the%20General%20Assembly.&text=Solemly%20proclaims%20the%20Declaration%20on,becomes%20generally%20known%20and%20respected.&text=Date%5BNew%20York%5D%20%3A%20UN,1994. Accessed 12 Sept 2022
United Nations Office on Drugs and Crime (2022) Statistical framework for measuring the gender-related killing of women and girls (also referred to as "femicide/feminicide"). https://oig.cepal.org/sites/default/files/statistical_framework_femicide_2022.pdf. Accessed 26 Nov 2022
United Nations Population Fund: Ukraine (2018, June 28) Economic costs of violence against women in Ukraine. https://ukraine.unfpa.org/en/publications/economic-costs-violence-against-women-ukraine-0. Accessed 25 Apr 2023
United Nations Women (2013a) Agreed conclusions on the elimination and prevention of all forms of violence against women and girls (E/2013/27 E/CN.6/2013/11). https://www.un.org/womenwatch/daw/csw/csw57/CSW57_Agreed_Conclusions_(CSW_report_excerpt).pdf. Accessed 19 Apr 2023

United Nations Women (2013b) Commission on the status of women 2013. https://www.unwomen.org/en/news/in-focus/csw57-stop-violence-against-women. Accessed 24 Apr 2023

United Nations Women (2019) Turning promises into action: gender equality in the 2030 agenda for sustainable development. https://www.unwomen.org/en/digital-library/publications/2018/2/gender-equality-in-the-2030-agenda-for-sustainable-development-2018. Accessed 15 Nov 2022

Vyas S et al (2021) The economic cost of violence against women and girls in low- and middle-income countries: a systematic review of the evidence. Trauma Violence Abuse 24(1): 152483802110160. https://doi.org/10.1177/15248380211016018

Walby S (2004) The cost of domestic violence. Women and Equality Unit (DTI), London

Woetzel J et al (2015) The power of parity: how advancing women's equality can add US$12 trillion to global growth. McKinsey Global Institute, New York

World Bank (2018) Fact sheet: update on addressing gender-based violence in development projects. https://www.worldbank.org/en/news/factsheet/2018/08/30/fact-sheet-update-on-addressing-gender-based-violence-in-development-projects. Accessed 20 Apr 2023

World Health Organization (2018, February 19) Millennium development goals (MDGs). https://www.who.int/news-room/fact-sheets/detail/millennium-development-goals-(mdgs)#:~:text=The%20United%20Nations%20Millennium%20Declaration. Accessed 19 Jan 2023

World Health Organization (2021, March 9) Violence against women. https://www.who.int/news-room/fact-sheets/detail/violence-against-women. Accessed 11 Nov 2022

Zulu MJ et al. (2017) The cost of gender based violence in Zambia. http://gender.careinternationalwikis.org/_media/zambia_covaw_ii_-_summary_rpt_june_2017.pdf. Accessed 25 Apr 2023

Chapter 4
Towards an Understanding of Gender-Based Violence and Femicide

4.1 An Overview: The Theory of Gender and Violence

In comparison to the rest of the world, South Africa's prevalence rates of GBVF stands at approximately five times higher.[1] This unacceptable situation presents a critical context for the theorization of violence against women and girls in general. Theories becomes critical as it provides key insights into the study of human behavior, i.e., it can provide explanations for specific behaviors as well as provide foundations for predicting certain behaviors.[2] It can therefore be used to inform policy, guide practice and direct research.[3] Currently, there is no single perspective or theory that offers a definitive explanation regarding the causes of violence against women. Despite this, a combination of factors has emerged from various perspectives that provide some understanding of those factors that substantially increases a women's risk of being killed, especially by intimate partners, and those associated with an increased risk that men will perpetrate GBVF.[4] This understanding can go a long way towards finding solutions to address GBVF. The aim of this chapter is to therefore develop a broad understanding of the root causes of GBVF and to highlight how these causes act as barriers to combating GBVF.

One method of understanding the high rates of GBV is to look at the theory of gender and violence. In this regard the feminist theory has, since the early 1970s, been one of the predominant theoretical models used to explain GBV, specifically domestic and intimate partner violence. This theory has been used to strengthen interventions, advocacy initiatives and legislative agendas regarding GBVF. The feminist theory relates to "theories of empowerment," which is concerned with the

---

[1] Govender (2004).

[2] Robbins et al. (2012).

[3] Hanson and Patel (2014).

[4] Russell and Hamel (2022), pp. 3–4.

T. Deane, *Gender-Based Violence and Femicide in South Africa*, Gender, Justice and Legal Feminism 5, https://doi.org/10.1007/978-3-031-61053-0_4

dynamics of prejudice and oppression, or culture, power, and gender.[5] It is founded on the belief that patriarchy and, consequentially, oppression are common threads in the structures of society. GBV is seen as a product of a system of unequal power relations, it is both reproduced and in turn reproduces in society. Its historical origins and forms can be meaningfully understood in the context of patriarchy, dominance and unequal power relations embedded in different economic, political, cultural, and social structures of any given society. Violence is consequently used a means to reproduce and reinforce these unequal social relations.[6] In a classic work from this position, Bograd's posits that:[7]

> As feminists, we believe that the social institutions of marriage and family are special contexts that may promote, maintain, and even support men's use of physical force against women.

In particular, the violence used by men against their partners is exerted to maintain power and coercive control over their partner. It has been argued that this not only explains the rates of perpetration, in that it is a result of a structurally granted right to maintain control over women, but it also explains the expectation of women to be submissive in a violent relation and how this submissiveness, may be the only means to survival.[8] However, the feminist model has been subject to criticism by various scholars since its inception.[9] The main criticisms of this theory relates to its narrow focus on gender and violence,[10] in that feminist theories that examine gender-specific violence focus on violence within the confines of the male/female binary.[11] In addition, this model tends to omit conversations with key stakeholders including those working on the front lines of the violence against women movement, that is, shelter workers, domestic violence service providers, and counsellors in GBV intervention programs.[12]

However, the feminist perspective remains extremely important and relevant as it provides a deeper understanding of violence by analyzing how it is connected to, and embedded in, patriarchal structures of power. It is undisputed that "gender power

---

[5] Yllö and Bograd (1988).

[6] Department of Higher Education and Training (2020).

[7] Yllö and Bograd (1988), p. 12.

[8] Walker (1979).

[9] Hooks (1984); Felson (2006).

[10] A limitation of the feminist theory was found in the explanation of violence in same-sex relationships, where the concept of gendered power is not enough. It is apparent that intimate partner violence in the context of same-sex relationships calls for a more comprehensive analysis and conceptual reasoning. Another challenge of this feminist theorization of violence is observed in understanding violence perpetrated by women outside the context of intimate relationships, for instance at work, with peers or with children. See Sibanda-Moyo et al. (2017, April 28); see, also, Shaw (2013).

[11] Lawson (2003); Renzetti (1992).

[12] Schechter (1982).

shapes the dynamic of every interaction."[13] In addition despite gender specific violence having been recognized since the 18th century[14] with the first official reference to femicide appearing in British legal discourse in 1848,[15] femicide was not developed as a feminist theory until it re-emerged in conjunction with the second wave feminism in the 1970s.[16] The femicide framework is consequently valuable and necessary firstly because it communicates something language such as murder and homicide cannot.[17] Secondly, it is a useful tool in response to the alarming escalation of violent murders and murders of women and girls. As has been correctly pointed out, "you cannot mobilise against something with no name."[18] Within this context, the theory of femicide highlights the patriarchal power structures that impose masculine dominance over the female.[19] The act of femicide intersects with complex economic, cultural and geographical factors, revealing that violence is embedded in patriarchal structures of power.[20] In sum, femicide is a crucially important feminist theory to highlight violence against women and acts as a useful starting point to reveal how masculine dominance asserts itself within power structures.[21]

It must be noted that the aim of this chapter is not to position feminist theories against each other or to construct a gendered hierarchy of suffering or to completely ignore the fact that men also suffer from several forms of violence. It is hoped that by examining the various theories of gender and violence it can offer a deeper understanding of the violence that is targeted towards women and girls. Consequently, the intention of this discussion is to provide an understanding of how theories can be applied to the analysis of gender specific violence with the aim of the elimination thereof.

4.2 Patriarchy

The ideology of patriarchy is a central feminist explanation for the rates of GBV in South Africa. The feminist theory further points out that discriminatory patriarchal practices against women are likely to be the root causes of GBVF.[22] The ideology

[13] Cockburn (2004), p. 28.

[14] Grech (2015).

[15] Wharton (1848).

[16] When Diana Russell (1977) used the term at the International Tribunal on Crimes against Women. See Russell (2012, November).

[17] Corradi et al. (2016), p. 977.

[18] Radford and Russell (1992), p. 7.

[19] Corradi et al. (2016), p. 981.

[20] Cockburn (2004), p. 30.

[21] Corradi et al. (2016), pp. 976–977.

[22] Centre for the Study of Violence and Reconciliation (2016).

suggests that the male-dominated power structure throughout institutionalized South Africa and in individual relationships forms the underlying bias that enables violence against women and girls. At the level of community life, celebration of aggressive or toxic masculinity[23] and, reciprocally, the devaluation of women's roles are the most important risk factors. According to proponents, "oppressive views of women are not only culturally sanctioned but also embedded in and expressed through all social institutions."[24] The fundamental tenet of patriarchy is power, where power is distributed unequally between men and women and violence is the tool men use to keep women under their control.

It is argued that when there is violence against women and girls there is a legitimization of this by some elements within the "dominant culture." This is mainly because the dominant culture in virtually all societies is patriarchal.[25] Patriarchal culture seems to inevitably validate violence as an acceptable, sometimes even desirable, attribute of masculinity.[26] However it is not just masculinity but a "crisis of masculinity" that is the issue. According to the "crisis of masculinity" thesis, men are increasingly confused and insecure because of women's so-called assault on "male bastions of power" and the growing "social and cultural disapproval of traditional displays of masculinity."[27]

Since the balance of social power is tilted to the advantage of men, their perspectives and their rights in this dominant culture consequently enables the formation and entrenchment of norms and attitudes that disadvantage women and girls.[28] Women living in traditional communities are especially vulnerable.[29] When these women are seen to transgress patriarchal norms that define what is acceptable gender behavior and sexual life, the likelihood of femicide increases. When looking at the broader societal level, low access to justice and little to no public measures to close the gender inequality gap increases women's vulnerabilities whilst perceived impunity increases the likelihood of becoming a perpetrator without fear of consequences.[30]

---

[23] Toxic masculinity refers to "harmful behaviour and attitudes commonly associated with some men, such as the need to repress emotions during stressful situations and to act in an aggressively dominant way."

[24] Taylor and Jasinski (2011), p. 342.

[25] Sagot and Carcedo (2010), pp. 138–156.

[26] As in other patriarchal cultures, traditional and outdated ideals or notions of masculinity and femininity are still prevalent in the country. Historically, men were taught that being masculine meant they had to revere violence and stoicism and to hyper-sexualize women. As a result, boys are often pressured to distance themselves from associations of weakness and homosexuality. Thus, it is argued that to fight gender-based violence, one must demonstrate care and understanding to boys and assist them in dealing with the internal and external pressures that can make them abusive.

[27] Hamber (2010), p. 81.

[28] Namy et al. (2017).

[29] World Health Organization (2012).

[30] Corradi (2021).

Using patriarchy alone to explain violence against women advances the pre-eminence of gender in understanding GBV. This should however not limit explanations of women's experiences of violence. Beyond the category of gender, women in South Africa have had (differential) historical and continuing experiences of other forms of oppression and inequality, including racism, heterosexism, and colonialism, which must be accounted for in the understanding of violence. This view is also consistent with the domestic violence literature that has "challenged the primacy of gender as an explanatory mode and. . .emphasized the need to examine how other forms of inequality and oppression, such as racism, ethnocentrism, class privilege, and heterosexism, intersect with gender oppression in women's experiences of violence."[31]

Various research indicates clear links between an imbalance in power between males and females and gender inequality.[32] By giving violence legitimacy it increases the acceptability of specific acts of violence against individuals who are socially devalued and discriminated against by the dominant culture. Transformed into "the norm," acts of violence remain unquestioned, acquiring impunity. Ultimately, violence against women can only be overcome when the "culture of violence" is replaced by a culture of equality and respect.

Developed from structural violence the notion that a culture can sanction violent acts become known as the culture of violence theory. Established by Franco Ferracuti and Marvin Wolfgang[33] in 1967 the cultural acceptance of violence is a theory that emphasizes that cultural norms and religious beliefs may lead to distinctive aspects in the experience and excusing of gendered violence.[34] This theory addresses the pervasiveness of specific violent patterns within a societal dimension, where sub-groups in a society will establish values and norms that justify and encourage the use of physical force. Examples of culture legitimizing violence can be seen in rape myths and victim blaming.[35]

In addition, men usually rely on assumptions of gendered roles and expectations of appropriate or "unacceptable" female behavior in the performance of domestic or sexual duties. The supposition is that there are times when women "deserve" to be chastised, even if beatings and other forms of abuse might be considered excessive or "uncivilized." Furthermore, the culture of violence theory potentially accounts for

---

[31] Sokoloff and Dupont (2005), p. 39.

[32] Patil (2013); Sokoloff and Dupont (2005), p. 39.

[33] Ferracuti and Wolfgang (2013).

[34] Wolfgang and Ferracuti developed the Subculture of Violence Theory in 1967 to explain homicides, or murders. They developed this theory after extensive work in subculture theory criminology where they analyzed patterns in data on homicides. They found that those in certain subcultures were more likely to commit these crimes. They believed that the members of these subcultures that were committing violent acts were perpetuating a learned behavior of violence.

[35] Rape myths lead to misconstrued notions of blame. It is common for the responsibility associated with the rape to be placed on the victim rather than the offender. Finchilescu and Dugard (2018); Meger (2016).

inter-generational theories of violence and domestic violence.[36] One's childhood exposure to violence in the household may lead to similar patterns in marital relations. Similarly, early experiences of domestic violence will likely increase an individual's potential for the development of clinical symptoms.[37] Additionally, presence of a pre-existing mental disorder may heighten the chances of becoming involved in an abusive relationship. In South Africa, most reported rapes involve female victims. However, there is a growing body of evidence to support the notion that women can perpetuate relational cycles of violence.[38] A detailed discussion will not be entered into here as this ideology falls outside the scope of this chapter.

There are consequently many factors which contribute to the persistence of violence among individuals and on a societal level, gender remains one relevant factor to understanding the culture of violence theory. This theory therefore shows the incessant cultural attitudes based on gender inequality and male entitlement in domestic and social arrangements. This culture of violence theory has also created the models that examples of pornography and violent images on TV contribute to a "culture of violence" toward women.[39]

4.3 Apartheid

Of the explanations for the continued and escalating violence against women, the most distinctive for the purposes of South Africa, has been the concept of the apartheid legacy of violence and brutality. With the first democratic elections in 1994, the decades-long struggle against the apartheid regime ended. This end brought with it not only the hope of democracy but equality. However, even after the end of the apartheid system, South Africa remains characterized by divisions based on race, class, and gender, inherited from its violent apartheid past.[40] Apartheid was rooted in the hegemonic European colonization of South Africa.[41] During apartheid violence against the disempowered by the dominant group was legitimized by harmful cultural and discriminatory legal practices.[42] Violence is the single most determining factor in South African political history. For many years the apartheid state, being categorized by a highly militarized state and civil society, sanctioned

[36] Where toxic ideals are passed down through generations, so each generation carries on the violent behavior. This approach is criticized for allowing abusers to avoid responsibility, or even to "justify" it on religious or cultural grounds.

[37] Sabri and Granger (2018).

[38] Both et al. (2019).

[39] To see the various expressions of such violence, go to CRAM (n.d.).

[40] United Nations High Commissioner for Refugees (2016, June 14). See, also, South African Human Rights Commission (2017).

[41] Chandhoke (1986).

[42] Moffett (2006).

violence as a means of maintaining political power. Further injustices manifested in racist policies depriving Black people of rights[43] and status[44] reserved for white South Africans.[45] Violence here is therefore not only a reference to physical or overt violence, but also to the violence of the law or what is often referred to as institutional or structural violence.[46]

Regarding the status of women, during apartheid, very few legal and social structures existed to protect women against GBV. The judicial system of the time was generally detrimental to the protection of victims of color but especially women. Research found that since rape was recognized during that time only if the perpetrator used his penis to penetrate the victim, a high prevalence of rapes against women were perpetrated using bottles and tin cans as penetrative weapons. The most severe charge that perpetrators who utilized objects in such cases could receive was that of assault.[47]

After the end of apartheid, the South African Department of Justice did not establish sentencing guidelines for rape and other kinds of sexual assault, leaving judges to use their own biases to inform cases. For many years, the "cautionary rule" was in effect, which required the courts to use extreme scrutiny when evaluating the validity of women's rape testimonies that were uncorroborated by physical evidence or eyewitnesses. As a result, many women were discredited, and in 1992 rape cases had a conviction rate of only 53%, while perpetrators of non-sexual assault were

---

[43] Numerous laws were passed in the creation of the apartheid state. Listed below are just a few of the pillars on which it rested; The *Population Registration Act, 1950* demanded that people be registered according to their racial group. This meant that the Department of Home affairs would have a record of people according to whether they were white, colored, Black, Indian, or Asian. People would then be treated differently according to their population group, and so this law formed the basis of apartheid. The *Group Areas Act, 1950* started physical separation between races, especially in urban areas. The *Group Areas Act* also called for the removal of some groups of people into areas set aside for their racial group. The *Promotion of Bantu Self-Government Act, 1959* provided for different racial groups to live in different areas. Only a small percentage of South Africa was left for Black people (who comprised the vast majority) to form their "homelands." This *Promotion of Bantu Self-Government Act* also got rid of "black spots" inside white areas, by moving all Black people out of the city. Well known removals were those in District 6, Sophia Town, and Lady Selborne. They were then placed in townships outside of the town and were made to rent as they could not own property there. This *Promotion of Bantu Self-Government Act* caused much hardship and resentment. People lost their homes, were moved off land they had owned for many years and were moved to undeveloped areas far away from their place of work. Other important laws were the *Prohibition of Mixed Marriages Act, 1949*; *Immorality Amendment Act, 1950* and the *Separate Representation of Voters Act, 1951.*

[44] The apartheid state was typified by rigid racial segregation and stratification in which whites occupied the most favored positions in the racial hierarchy, followed by Indians, coloreds, and Africans.

[45] Apartheid law was considered a crime that was institutionalized by the state. The purpose of law was to legitimize the system, and hence to provide a means of self-justification for those whose task it was to pass, enforce, and defend the law. Indeed, law became the major instrument of oppression. See *The African Charter on Human and Peoples' Rights*, Chap. 2.

[46] Truth Commission (1998), subsection 8.

[47] Armstrong (1994).

convicted at a rate of 86%.[48] This translated to a subjective judicial landscape wherein sexual assault charges varied wildly and women were not taken seriously when they reported incidents of assault.[49] Additionally, the state condoned the corporal punishment of wives by their husbands. At the time, wife-beating was both normalized and legal, creating an environment in which domestic abuse was rampant and virtually unpunishable.[50] The distortions of apartheid rendered domestic violence either a private issue or in the case of rape, one confined to black residential areas and therefore of no concern to the police.[51]

The disordering of gender relations and colonialism made women's relatively disadvantaged position in South African society worse.[52] Apartheid policies that sanctioned geographical and economic segregation, either along racial or gendered lines, socio-culturally reinforced the unequal status of women in both the private and public spheres of life.[53] Under apartheid, citizenship was granted only to men, and women were classified exclusively as dependents. Remnants of this standard persisted in post-apartheid laws that restricted protections for women for example, under African customary law, women were always under the perpetual tutelage of a male, whether their father, husband or even a son.[54] Customary marriages were not previously recognized as legal unions because they were potentially polygamous.[55] This legal non-recognition meant that the wives in these unions did not have or acquire rights.[56] For African women, these laws operated to deprive them of rights to rent or buy their own homes, custody of their children, an education or a having wage. These laws were argued to be enforced by products of the system, i.e., white bureaucrats or their African surrogates,[57] whose position was within the apartheid system that codified and sustained patriarchy.[58]

---

[48] Nowrojee and Manby (1995).

[49] Nowrojee and Manby (1995).

[50] Stauffer (2015).

[51] Andrews (1999).

[52] Baden et al. (1998).

[53] The laws and policies which regulated the movement of black labor and access to housing, with their deleterious impact on family life, cemented the economic inferiority of black South Africans.

[54] This position was codified in KwaZulu, in KwaZulu Government Notice 47 (1982); *KwaZulu Act on the Code of Zulu Law, 1981*. These rules have now been eradicated with the passage of the *Recognition of Customary Marriages Act No 120 of 1998*.

[55] This situation applied to African and Muslim marriages. See Andrews (2009). See, also, Moosa (1997), p. 197.

[56] These patriarchal legal structures were given legitimacy because it was enforced by a culture that did not question the fundamental logic of such gender inequality. Albie Sachs, a then judge of the Constitutional Court, described patriarchy as the only truly non-racial institution in South Africa. Sachs (1990), p. 1.

[57] Andrews (1999).

[58] Chanock (1991).

The migrant labor or influx control system[59] was particularly pernicious as it ensured that African women[60] remained dependent on men as men could more easily obtain permission to work in the cities. Women's livelihoods depended on absent husbands or sons sending them allowances.[61] The homelands or rural areas were the women stayed behind did not provide the women with many employment or economic opportunities for self-sufficiency.[62] Under apartheid women were rendered subordinate to men and Black women have been left overwhelmingly bereft of rights and resources.[63] The racially discriminatory and violent nature of the apartheid state, together with the ensuing conflicts and the eventual transition to democratic governance in South Africa produced an entrenched culture of violence that sustains and different forms of violence, including GBV. The reasons for the continued violence against women are historical and deeply rooted in class, gender, and racial discriminations. Whilst systemic discrimination has been addressed by many government and social ventures, cultural gender inequality persists. This is evidenced by the rates of GBVF throughout South Africa.

4.4 Culture and Tradition

The influences of culture and tradition on GBV is a critical area of discussion. Some norms supporting harmful cultural practices include female genital mutilation (FGM), sex selection,[64] child marriage,[65] dowry-deaths, *ukuthwala* and "honor"

---

[59]This system was authorized by the *Black (Urban Areas) Consolidation Act of 1945* and its subsidiary regulations. Section 10 (1) of the *Act* stated that it was illegal for a Black person to remain in a prescribed (white) area for longer than 72 hours and provided four exceptions:

(a) a person who had been born there and resided there continuously since birth;
(b) a man who had worked continuously for one employer for ten years, or who had resided lawfully in the area for 15 years;
(c) the wife or dependent child of someone who qualified under Sec 10 (1) (a) or (b);
(d) a person who had been given permission to remain.

See *East Rand Administration Board and Another v Rikhoto*, 1983 (3) SA 595 and Cock (1989).

[60]White women also suffered legal discrimination and were subjected to paternalistic and sexist attitudes, were victims of domestic violence and other forms of abuse. However, their subordination as women was compensated for by the "privilege" of being members of the highest-ranked group in the racial hierarchy. They could, therefore, offset their gender subordination with their racial elevation. See Andrews (2007).

[61]Kemp et al. (1995), p. 131.

[62]Small and Kompe (1992).

[63]Gouws (2016).

[64]Sex selection, sometimes known as gender selection or family balancing, is the process of determining the genetic sex, male or female, of each embryo created through in vitro fertilization. The rise in sex selection is alarming as it reflects the persistent low status of women and girls.

[65]Deane (2021).

killings[66] are harmful cultural practices supported by various social norms and beliefs.[67] Often the perpetrators resort to femicide "to protect" toxic traditions, a family's "reputation," or to adhere to misconceived interpretations of religious demands. These norms reinforce existing power inequalities in society. Looking at the chapter on "Perceptions of Crime and the Fear of Crime" it highlights that the continuation of these practices is oftentimes supported by both women and men. The power imbalance can become internalized and violence even acceptable for the victim, who may be afraid of challenging shared norms out of fear of backlash (or may not even be aware of alternatives to the norm). Explicit and implicit cultural legitimation for violence against women accordingly becomes legitimized in South African society.

4.5 Individual Factors

At the individual level, the drivers of GBVF include inter alia growing up in a home characterized by violence, mental health problems (frequently observed in femicide-suicide), violations of protection orders and having an absent father or a father who is not a positive role model.[68] Another explanation offered is linked to the social problems of South Africa which includes high levels of poverty[69] and unemployment or general socioeconomic insecurity.[70] Of importance and as previously

[66] "Honor"-related murders involve a girl or woman being killed by a male or female family member for an actual or assumed sexual or behavioral transgression, including adultery, sexual intercourse, or pregnancy outside marriage—or for even being raped.

[67] Some of these toxic beliefs and norms include inter alia:

- Female genital mutilation or FGM which is traditionally believed to preserve virginity until marriage. Non-conformity to the practice may lead to social exclusion, stigma, and the inability to find a husband.
- Sex selective abortions, infanticide, neglect of female children, mistreatment and severe health consequences for women who did not bear male children are manifestations of pervasive son preference typically grounded in rigid patriarchal family systems and the special role of sons in religious rituals.
- The dowry system is a practice that strengthens son preference as it leads parents to consider daughters as liabilities and has often been linked to brutal violent acts against women to extract more resources from the wife's family, including harassment, domestic violence, murders, and suicides, leading to the infamous dowry-deaths.
- Widows are sometimes victims of violence from in-laws and humiliating rites and isolation as part of the mourning process to demonstrate grief and innocence for their husband's death.

See Milazzo (2016, May 25).

[68] Centre for the Study of Violence and Reconciliation (2016).

[69] The Stats SA report on Poverty Trends in South Africa reveals that the female headed households remain significantly poorer than male headed households. Stats SA (2022).

[70] Stats SA (2022). In the third quarter of 2022, the unemployment rate in South Africa reached 27.9% among workers aged 35 to 44 years. The figure dropped from 29.1% in the same quarter in

discussed, the GBV pandemic in South Africa is rooted in unequal power in gender relations,[71] differing economic statuses among men and women where for example, the economic power balance between men and women is skewed, and many women believing that they are obliged to stay in abusive relationships.[72]

In addition, patriarchy, homophobia, sexism, harmful discriminatory beliefs, and practices add to the risk factors for GBV. Such violence is reinforced by the widespread use of drugs and alcohol.[73] Also mentioned are the persistent stereotypical portrayal of women in the media,[74] as well as the high incidence of and challenges related to HIV and AIDS.[75] These problems have been shown to either exacerbate or act as triggers of GBV in South Africa and are closely associated with re/assertions of masculinities where men often validate their masculinity through violent behavior towards women and girls. Some of the well documented risk factors of being GBVF include inter alia; attempted strangulation (the victim's highest risk factor of all); pregnancy during a violent relationship; being a victim of rape (and thus being targeted as "dishonored") and having low educational levels. In addition, witnessing domestic abuse in the family of origin is a risk factor for both perpetrator and victim.[76]

These explanations do not operate independent of each other. They interact in a complex manner to support and sustain an environment of GBV. Therefore, any explanation of violence against women and girls needs to consider the interrelationship between these explanations as all these explanations impact women's access to justice and consequently act as barriers to justice.

4.6 Equality and Structural Violence

It has been said that any approach to a theory of violence needs to be with a look at the structural violence[77] in South Africa. This is especially so since as a starting point, feminists claim that the main cause of femicide is the structural inequality of

---

the previous year. The age group corresponded to the largest share of labor force participation in the country. Among young South Africans (15 to 24 years), the unemployment rate was at its highest at 59.6%.

[71] At the economic level, factors include poverty, unemployment and differing economic statuses among men and women. In many cases the economic power balance between men and women is skewed, and many women believe that they have no choice but to stay in abusive relationships.

[72] Sibanda-Moyo et al. (2017, April 28).

[73] Stats SA (2022).

[74] Koziol-Mclain et al. (2006).

[75] United Nations High Commissioner for Refugees (2016, June 14).

[76] Corradi (2021).

[77] The concept of "structural violence" was introduced by Johan Galtung in 1969. It refers to a form of violence wherein some social institution may harm people by preventing them from meeting their basic needs. See Galtung (1969).

gender[78] and the real or perceived impunity of the justice system.[79] GBV does not take place simply at individual level. It is anchored in the cultural and institutional structures of societies. The interplay between discriminating behaviors at all three levels is referred to as "structural" violence. Institutional and structural violence is any form of structural inequality or institutional discrimination that maintains a woman in a subordinate position, whether physical or ideological, to other people within her family, household, or community.[80] Examples include discriminatory rules, laws, traditions and customs, as well as misogynistic language.[81] These structures have both a conscious and subconscious influence on the way people think and behave. In turn, people who are socialized within these structures continue to preserve them, leading to a cycle which ensures that sexism and its expressions continue to exist, in turn perpetuating the violence against women that results from this sexism. Women can be affected by many other forms of discrimination at the same time, including sexism, racism, and ableism. These reinforce each other, increasing the risks of women experiencing violence.

Structural violence differs from behavioral violence in many respects. Structural violence is marked by unequal access to the determinants of health (e.g., housing, good quality health care, unemployment, education), which then creates conditions where interpersonal violence can occur, and shape gendered forms of violence that place women in vulnerable positions.[82] Johan Galtung in 1969 originally framed the term structural violence to refer to any constraint on human potential due to economic and political structures and correctly stated that "when one husband beats his wife, there is a clear case of personal violence, but when one million husbands keep one million wives in ignorance, there is structural violence."[83]

Winter and Leighton define structural violence as the violence of injustice and inequity which is embedded in "ubiquitous social structures [and] normalized by stable institutions and regular experience."[84] Structural violence poses unique challenges because, in comparison to direct violence whose brutality grabs attention, is immediately visible and can be responded to, structural violence is almost always invisible. It is intertwined within the fabric of society and is normalized as the "status quo." It consequently is more difficult to recognize and even harder to meaningfully address. Further, to recognize the existence of structural violence would also require

[78] Católicas por el Derecho a Decidir (2012).

[79] While an effective and well-functioning criminal justice system provides disincentives to potential lawbreakers and inhibits crime, an ineffective and corrupt system provides no deterrence. See Agrast et al. (2012).

[80] Paul (1997), pp. 261–283.

[81] Misogyny refers to the dislike of, contempt for, or ingrained prejudice against, women.

[82] Montesanti (2015).

[83] Galtung (1969), p. 171.

[84] Winter and Leighton (2001), p. 1.

asking questions about how and why it is tolerated, who is harmed, and importantly, who it benefits.[85]

Structural violence apart from being virtually invisible functions almost independently of individual behaviors. Furthermore, its problematic effects operate continuously not just sporadically.[86] The values, morals and cultural traditions of society is framed or "structured" in such a way as to keep women in an inferior position to men, which is the root cause of GBV in society.[87] Feminist scholars and gender activists agree that an equal society will remain elusive until there are concrete attempts to shift the gender power relations in politics, the economy and society.[88] The feminist theoretical framework can be summarized as one that sees the prevalence of GBV as a process and a conflict that oppresses women, as well as expresses the ills of society. Considering that multiple kind of violence stem from the interaction of patriarchy with structural factors such as culture and economic opportunity, to stem the rising tides of GBVF, there must be cross-national studies on violence against women. Such a study would help to identify the structural factors impacting GBVF across the world, regardless of content. The question that this raises is how then does one assess the degree of structural violence.

Various methods of assessment have been put forth by theorists. For example, Koenig's work has stressed the interrelated effects of contextual and community level factors, individual and household level characteristics, and women's autonomy.[89] On the other hand Farmer emphasizes the impact of poverty on women, forcing them to accept jobs that place them in a position of vulnerability.[90] According to Anderson,[91] a multiple level of gendered violence should be examined, She stresses that "to date, studies have generally conceptualized and examined gender at only one level. We need to identify the ways structural gender inequalities, gender performances and accountability, and gender identities interact to facilitate or challenge coercive control." Heise argues for an integrated ecological framework which can account for the interplay among personal, situational, and sociocultural

[85] Winter and Leighton (2001).

[86] Gilligan (2006).

[87] Jewkes and Morrell (2015). Gender stereotypes are often used to attempt to justify GBV. For example, cultural norms often dictate that men are aggressive, controlling, and dominant, while women are meant to be docile, subservient, and rely on men as providers. These norms have been shown foster a culture of abuse, such as early and forced marriage or female genital mutilation (FGM). When challenged these norms can proliferate the culture of violence.

[88] The structural causes of violence against women include socialized gender roles with patriarchal roots, clichés about gender, and the resulting power relations. Whereas dominance, power and strength are seen to be masculine, qualities such as submissive, passive, or indulgent are assigned to women. Even today these attributions lead to women being excluded from important political decision-making processes and offices. This lack of representation in relevant areas of society then leads to the needs of women being neglected and violence becoming established. See Verena (2021).

[89] Koenig et al. (2003).

[90] Paul (1997).

[91] Anderson (2009).

factors, and which view will be explored further below.[92] Research and statistics on GBV have historically focused more on individual-level actions rather than the larger structural systems that maintain an environment where violence is prevalent.[93] Understanding this broader context is essential in developing successful GBV policy interventions.[94]

4.7 Intersectionality

It is clear that GBVF does not exist in isolation. When looking holistically at the factors discussed above, GBVF as an issue of importance needs to be discussed and addressed through an intersectional lens. The intersectionality theory, coined by the legal theorist Kimberlé Crenshaw, asserts that different social identities, especially those of gender, race, and class, intersect to impact on one's level of subordination and oppression within a society.[95] According to this feminist theory all social identities must be broken down and analyzed in order to gain a full understanding about the level and types of oppression that a person faces through a complete social justice lens. This means that a single social identity should not be the basis of how one experiences oppression, where oppression refers to "the absence of choices,"[96] but rather every category that one identifies with. Through this intersectional and multidimensional approach to oppression, those who face subordination on multiple social levels can acknowledge how their personal and specific identity experiences oppression.

As an example, Crenshaw explained that:[97]

> Black women are sometimes excluded from feminist theory and antiracist policy discourse because both are predicated on a discrete set of experiences that often does not accurately reflect the interaction of race and gender. These problems of exclusion cannot be solved simply by including Black women within an already established analytical structure. Because the intersectional experience is greater than the sum of racism and sexism, any analysis that does not take intersectionality into account cannot sufficiently address the particular manner in which Black women are subordinated. Thus, for feminist theory and antiracist policy discourse to embrace the experiences and concerns of Black women, the entire framework that has been used as a basis for translating "women's experience" or "the Black experience" into concrete policy demands must be rethought and recast.

---

[92] Heise (1998).

[93] Montesanti and Thurston (2015).

[94] Structural violence is represented by inequities in determinants of health such as access to affordable housing, quality health care, or living wages. Determinants of health create conditions where different forms of gender-based violence take shape and thereby exploit those who are vulnerable. See Farmer (2009).

[95] Crenshaw (1989), pp. 139.

[96] Hooks (2014), p. 5.

[97] Crenshaw (1989), p. 141.

It develops the argument that the challenges faced by a Black woman in a racist and misogynistic society like South Africa cannot simply be equated to the challenges faced by a Black man or combined with those faced by a white woman. This is based on the argument that a Black woman is subject to oppression not only because she is Black and because she is a woman, but because she is specifically a Black woman. Additionally, being poor, disabled, part of the LGBTQ+ community, or an immigrant comes with its own social, economic, and political challenges. Any combination of those identities results in an oppression that is more than the sum of each individual identity.

The importance of an intersectional lens therefore cannot be overestimated when analyzing the varied levels of oppression that a society may face which contributes to a culture wherein which GBVF is prevalent. Women of sexualities other than heterosexual, of color and of low economic class may face multiple layers of intersectional oppression in addition to their experience of gender oppression.[98] Every level is consequently key to discussing the roots of GBVF and each one cannot be analyzed independently from one another. As Hooks articulates in *Feminist Theory: From Margin to Center*:[99]

> . . . male violence in the family is an expression of male domination. . . violence is inextricably linked to all acts of violence in this society that occur between the powerful and the powerless, the dominant and the dominated. While male supremacy encourages the use of abusive force to maintain male domination of women, it is the Western philosophical notion of hierarchical rule and coercive authority that is the root cause of violence against women, of adult violence against children, of all violence between those who dominate and those who are dominated. It is this belief system that is the foundation on which sexist ideology and other ideologies of group oppression are based; they can be eliminated only when this foundation is eliminated. . . . . . .

The idea of male dominance, especially when built upon this Western foundation, paves the way for justifying the use of violence as a form of subjugation against women. This is also seen in cases of sexual oppression, one form of GBV. A society that allows GBV to continue with impunity creates an environment for the escalation of occurrences of rape and perpetuates a rape culture[100] together with other forms of violence against women.[101] It also helps to sustain various rape myths including those that blame women for their rapes or those that provide a rationale for the perpetrators of rape that they have ravenous sexual appetites which must be satisfied. These myths are based upon the idea that rape and GBV is a form of legitimate coercion and control of women by men.[102] Furthermore, within the context of the sexual oppression of women, there is a focus on conforming to norms and to

---

[98] Crenshaw (1991), p. 1241.

[99] Hooks (2014), p. 199.

[100] Rape culture refers to the trend in which violence against women is normalized and prevalent due to patriarchal domination of women and conceptions about the role and status of women within a society. Deane (2018).

[101] Burt (1980), p. 217; Marin and Russo (1999), p. 18.

[102] Russo and Pirlott (2006), p. 178.

heterosexuality. This focus on heterosexuality "promotes objectification [of, and] ... makes everyone, especially women, into sex objects.[103] Women are consequently denied the same level of choice in their sexuality as men, which creates a pattern of sexual oppression that has created and perpetuates rape culture and consequently GBVF.[104]

Since many people who are affected by GBVF in South Africa are subject to intersecting forms of oppression, an intersectional framework becomes extremely important in considering the experiences of GBV in the country. More crucially, the implementation of any truly meaningful initiative will likely fail without recognizing the intersectionality of many GBV survivors and the vulnerability of people with intersecting identities to GBV.

4.8 Alternative to the Feminist Framework

The above discussion has highlighted some of the key explanations for why violence against women persists in the country despite significant efforts to combat it. These include, inter alia, the complexities around the distribution and complex interconnectedness of different forms of power relations that disadvantage women, the problems in sociocultural learnings of what is acceptable in society, gaps in the implementation of GBVF laws and policies and psychosocial explanations. Femicide results from the complex interaction of the risk factors, characterizing the condition and behavior of persons involved, how they relate to each other, the presence or lack of dedicated services (such as risk assessment centers, safe houses, trained police officials, etc.), as well as the dominant representation of male and female roles in society and the downgrading of status of women in society, all of which is an obstacle to their empowerment.[105] Therefore whilst different theories have clear benefits what is needed is an integrated approach towards GBVF. In this regard researchers in the field suggest a multi-level "ecological approach" to GBVF where aspects belonging to diverse levels of social life come together in different ways, depending on norms and socially accepted behaviors in local contexts.[106]

[103]Hooks (2014), p. 157.

[104]Hooks (2014), pp. 157–158.

[105]Bandelli and Corradi (2021).

[106]Brankovic (2019, April 30).

4.8.1 Ecological Model

The ecological model is most widely used for understanding any form of violence, not only domestic violence or intimate partner violence.[107] The ecological framework identifies many causes of violence against women and is believed to be more integrative.[108] The framework proposes that violence is influenced by risk factors operating at four levels: individual, family/relationship, community, and societal or structural (which relates to laws, policies and wider societal influences).[109] Addressing and prevention of GBV is the addressing and prevention of entrenched oppression of women and girls. When one looks at the interrelation between GBV and how it is inherently linked to current systems of power, privilege, societal and structural inequalities, it becomes clear that the unacceptable persistence of the various manifestations of violence, is complex and has many causes. It further reveals how difficult it is to break down structural inequalities, specifically in relation to patriarchal, discriminatory, and violent cultural patterns. It becomes critical to acknowledge the historical, structural, societal, community, relationship, and individual impacts of such violence; none of which operate in a vacuum.

An advantage of the ecological model therefore is that it allows for the development of strategies that reduce or eliminate the risk factors leading to GBVF though a broad-based prevention strategy. This can be done through, for example, interventions that target childhood abuse (individual level), exposure to parental conflict as a child (relationship level), weak community sanctions against GBV (community level), and poverty (society level). Such a strategy will allow for the development of a broader understanding of the complex interplay of biological, psychological, social, cultural, economic, and political factors that increase women's and girl's likelihood for experiencing violence as well as men's likelihood for perpetrating violence.[110] It is also critical to understand and support protective factors. For example, some protective factors that can inform prevention efforts for intimate partner violence that has been identified through multi-country research on health and domestic violence include ensuring that both girls and boys complete secondary education,[111] the delaying of age of marriage to 18,[112] ensuring women's economic autonomy and access to skills training, employment and social norms that promote gender equality.[113] The ecological approach will allow for the reduction and elimination of risk factors at all levels.

Feminists have played a significant role in the fight against GBVF. It has successfully advocated for reforms to strengthen state power and punish gender-

107 Heise et al. (1999).

108 Heise (1998).

109 World Health Organization (2012).

110 Buvinic et al. (1999), pp. 3–34.

111 Deane (2018).

112 Deane (2018).

113 World Health Organization (2005).

based crimes. Feminism has increasingly been associated with crime control and the proper conviction and imprisonment of men.[114] Of concern though is that the movement has also shown that a "punitive, retribution-driven agenda" now constitutes "the most publicly accessible face of the women's movement."[115] The widespread implementation of rape and domestic violence reforms and the shift in mindsets on gendered crimes during the late 20th century has allowed for a shift in conversation. There is an opportunity based on the literature and theories discussed to reframe GBV and move the conversation beyond individual acts to the root causes of violence, including structural violence such as inequality, poverty, and racism.

There is now a clearer understanding that the responsibility to end GBV shifts from survivors to those who have caused harm, and importantly to the community and society as a whole.[116] Attitudes, beliefs and behaviors that allow GBV to persist do not just exist within individuals. They are supported by broader social environments, social structures, history and its current-day influences and peer networks. Deconstruction of patriarchy and gendered norms for example, should therefore not only be a victim-centered societal project but it should also break down structures that enhance patriarchal practices that in turn give rise to GBV.[117] This would also allow for a more targeted initiative aimed at preventing and addressing the propensity of men to be violent towards women in general. By adopting a more integrative model like the ecological model, it will allow for the strengthening of efforts to address and prevent GBV. This can be done by investigating, if and how, efforts and initiatives intersect with each level of the model. For example, one can explore how efforts are addressing learning and community needs from the individual, relationship, community, societal, structural, and historical levels.

Resolutions and interventions aimed at the elimination of GBVF, must take the complexity of these factors into account. Accordingly, one must move away from policy and interventions that have a narrow focus. Policymakers may be tempted to view GBV as the collective experience of individual incidents of violence, or isolated experiences that tragically occur in a victim or survivor's life. Gender equality must form the foundations of policy, laws, and all social programs to address structural discrimination that often manifests as individual prejudice. Beyond just addressing the harm caused, there is an obligation on the government and policy makes to reduce and prevent harm by ensuring every South African can live a life free of violence. What is required is for a comprehensive understanding of those factors entrenching structural violence in society.

There is a need to critically diagnose the differences between women and men regarding their specific activities, conditions, needs, access to and control over resources, and access to development benefits and decision-making in GBVF interventions. Such an analysis should study the linkages of these and other factors in the

---

[114] Gruber (2009).

[115] Martin (1998).

[116] Courage to Act (2022, November).

[117] *Tshabalala v The State; Ntuli v The State* [2019] ZACC 48 *Tshabalala v S; Ntuli v S*, para 91.

larger social, economic, political, and environmental context. Discriminatory practices cannot be redressed by the development of laws alone, but it should be redressed through the deconstruction of the sexist and biases of society and replaced with an egalitarian, non-sexist foundation. Addressing rape and other forms of GBVF requires a holistic and comprehensive approach that includes the effort of the executive, the legislature and the judiciary and communities.[118]

4.9 Concluding Remarks

In conclusion, the above discussion has emphasized the crucial importance of the feminist theories to highlight violence against women. A feminist perspective provides a deeper understanding of violence by analyzing how it is connected to, and embedded in, patriarchal structures of power.[119] The feminist theory acts as a useful starting point to reveal how masculine dominance asserts itself within various power structures,[120] whilst the ecological theory has proven to be deep-rooted in studying the development of violence. The ecological theory is crucial towards the reduction and elimination of risk factors at all levels. In addition, this research takes the importance of the intersection of multiple inequalities into account when addressing the complex issue of GBV. Thinking about GBV through an intersectional lens means understanding that "gender, race and class inequality shape experiences of violence," and taking into consideration "the additional barriers many poor non-white women face when attempting to address their situations of violence (e.g. the burdens of poverty and child care responsibilities) ... the failure of institutions to address these consequences of converging gender, class, and race oppression ultimately limits their ability to meaningfully intervene."[121] The feminist and intersectional understanding of gender and of violence is understood to be both a cause and consequence of gender inequalities, and as an inequality in its own right,[122] as an expression of power and structural dominance and reflective of the power relations in society as a whole.

The underlying approach to effectively addressing GBVF should be a multi-level and holistic one, and be informed by gender theory, intersectionality, and feminist violence studies. Such an approach, in turn, requires approaching gender equality and GBV from an organizational violence perspective, rather than approaching gender-based violence only from a gender equality perspective, or indeed an individualist perspective.

---

[118] *Tshabalala v The State; Ntuli v The State*, para 78.

[119] Cockburn (2004) pp. 29–30.

[120] Corradi et al. (2016).

[121] Jayasinghe and Ward (2018).

[122] Hearn et al. (2020).

The next chapter will provide a situational analysis of GBVF in the country as well as some challenges women face in reporting violence against them.

References

Agrast MD et al. (2012) The world justice project: Rule of law index 2012–2013. https://worldjusticeproject.org/sites/default/files/documents/WJP_Index_Report_2012.pdf. Accessed 12 Dec 2022

Anderson KL (2009) Gendering coercive control. Violence Against Women 15(12):1444–1457. https://doi.org/10.1177/1077801209346837

Andrews P (1999) Violence against women in South Africa: the role of culture and the limitations of the law. Temple Polit Civil Rights Law Rev 25(8)

Andrews P (2007) Striking the rock: confronting gender equality in South Africa. Mich J Race Law 3:307–335

Andrews P (2009) Who's afraid of polygamy? Exploring the boundaries of family, equality and custom in South Africa. New York Law School

Armstrong S (1994) Rape in South Africa: an invisible part of apartheid's legacy. Gend Dev 2(2): 35–39. https://doi.org/10.1080/09682869308520009

Baden S et al (1998) Country gender profile: South Africa. Institute of Development Studies, Brighton

Bandelli D, Corradi C (2021) Femicide: the notion, theories, and challenges for research. Oxford Research Encyclopaedia of Criminology and Criminal Justice. https://doi.org/10.1093/acrefore/9780190264079.013.590

Both L et al (2019) Cycle of violence in women victims of domestic violence: qualitative analysis of OPD 2 interview. Brain Behav 9(11). https://doi.org/10.1002/brb3.1430

Brankovic J (2019, April 30) What drives violence in South Africa? https://www.africaportal.org/publications/what-drives-violence-south-africa/. Accessed 4 Dec 2022

Burt MR (1980) Cultural myths and supports for rape. J Pers Soc Psychol 38(2):217

Buvinic M et al. (1999) Violence in the Americas: a framework for action (From too close to home: Domestic violence in the Americas). https://www.ojp.gov/ncjrs/virtual-library/abstracts/violence-americas-framework-action-too-close-home-domestic-violence. Accessed 19 Jan 2023

Católicas por el Derecho a Decidir (2012) Femicide and impunity in Mexico: a context of structural and generalized violence. https://www2.ohchr.org/english/bodies/cedaw/docs/ngos/cddandcmdpdh_forthesession_mexico_cedaw52.pdf. Accessed 1 Feb 2023

Centre for the Study of Violence and Reconciliation (2016) Gender-based violence (GBV) in South Africa: a brief review. https://www.csvr.org.za/pdf/Gender%20Based%20Violence%20in%20South%20Africa%20-%20A%20Brief%20Review.pdf. Accessed 26 Jan 2023

Chandhoke N (1986) Crisis of settler hegemony in South Africa. Econ Polit Wkly 21(7):291–294. https://www.epw.in/journal/1986/7/perspectives/crisis-settler-hegemony-south-africa.html

Chanock M (1991) Law, state and culture: thinking about "customary law" after apartheid. Acta Juridica 52–65

Cock J (1989) Maids and madams. Women's Press Ltd

Cockburn C (2004) The continuum of violence: a gender perspective on war and peace. Sites of Violence Gender and Conflict Zones, pp 24–44. https://doi.org/10.1525/california/9780520230729.003.0002

Corradi C (2021) Femicide, its causes and recent trends: what do we know? European Union, Brussels

Corradi C et al (2016) Theories of femicide and their significance for social research. Curr Sociol 64(7):975–995. https://doi.org/10.1177/0011392115622256

Courage to Act (2022, November) What is the socio-ecological model and how does it apply to gender-based violence work? https://www.couragetoact.ca/blog/socioecological-model. Accessed 2 Apr 2023

CRAM (n.d.) Violence. https://www.cram.com/subjects/violence. Accessed 30 Mar 2023

Crenshaw K (1989) Demarginalizing the intersection of race and sex: a black feminist critique of antidiscrimination doctrine, feminist theory and antiracist politics. Univ Chic Leg Forum 1 (Article 8):139–167

Crenshaw K (1991) Mapping the margins: intersectionality, identity politics, and violence against women of color. Stanford Law Rev 43(6):1241–1299

Deane T (2018) Sexual violence and the limits of laws' powers to alter behaviour: the case of South Africa. J Int Women's Stud 19(2):84–103

Deane T (2021) Marrying young: limiting the impact of a crisis on the high prevalence of child marriages in Niger. Laws 10(3):61. https://doi.org/10.3390/laws10030061

Department of Higher Education and Training (2020) Policy framework to address gender-based violence in the post-school education and training system. https://www.dhet.gov.za/Social%20Inclusion/Gazette%20Z95_1221889%20Policy%20Framework%20to%20Address%20GBV%20in%20the%20PSET%2. Accessed 23 Jan 2023

Farmer P (2009) On suffering and structural violence: a view from below. Race/ethnicity: multidisciplinary global. Contexts 3(1):11–28

Felson RB (2006) Is violence against women about women or about violence? Contexts 5(2): 21–25. https://doi.org/10.1525/ctx.2006.5.2.21

Ferracuti F, Wolfgang ME (2013) The subculture of violence. Routledge

Finchilescu G, Dugard J (2018) Experiences of gender-based violence at a South African university: prevalence and effect on rape myth acceptance. J Interpers Violence 36(5–6): 088626051876935. https://doi.org/10.1177/0886260518769352

Galtung J (1969) Violence, peace, and peace research. J Peace Res 6(3):167–191. https://doi.org/10.1177/002234336900600301

Gilligan J (2006) Violence: reflections on our deadliest epidemic. Jessica Kingsley Publishers

Gouws A (2016) Women's activism around gender-based violence in South Africa: recognition, redistribution and representation. Rev Afr Polit Econ 43(149):400–415. https://doi.org/10.1080/03056244.2016.1217838

Govender I (2004) Gender-based violence - an increasing epidemic in South Africa S Afr Fam Pract1;65(1):e1-e2. https://doi.org/10.4102/safp.v65i1.5729. 3 March 2023; PMID: 37042525; PMCID: PMC10091185

Grech V (2015) Gendercide and femineglect. Early Hum Dev 91(12):851–854. https://doi.org/10.1016/j.earlhumdev.2015.10.014

Gruber A (2009) Rape, feminism, and the war on crime. Wash Law Rev 85:581–660. https://scholar.law.colorado.edu/cgi/viewcontent.cgi?article=1251&context=faculty-articles. Accessed 20 Apr 2023

Hamber B (2010) Masculinity and transition: crisis or confusion in South Africa? J Peacebuild Dev 5(3):75–88. https://doi.org/10.1080/15423166.2010.121687238771

Hanson S, Patel L (2014) How theory shapes practice: approaches to woman abuse and child abuse in South Africa. Br J Soc Work 44(8):2237–2253. https://doi.org/10.1093/bjsw/bct057

Hearn J et al (2020) From gender regimes to violence regimes: re-thinking the position of violence. Soc Polit Int Stud Gend State Soc 29(2):682–705. https://doi.org/10.1093/sp/jxaa022

Heise L et al (1999) Population reports: ending violence against women. The Johns Hopkins University School of Public Health, Baltimore

Heise LL (1998) Violence against women: an integrated, ecological framework. Violence Against Women 4(3):262–290. https://doi.org/10.1177/1077801298004003002

Hooks B (1984) Feminist theory: from margin to Center. South End Press, Boston

Hooks B (2014) Feminist theory: from margin to Center. South End Press, Boston. https://funceji.files.wordpress.com/2017/08/bell_hooks_feminist_theory_from_margin_to_centebookzz-org_.pdf. Accessed 21 Dec 2023

Jayasinghe T, Ward E (2018) Responding to violence, restoring justice. https://bcrw.barnard.edu/publications/responding-to-violence-restoring-justice/. Accessed 19 Nov 2023

Jewkes R, Morrell R (2015) Hegemonic masculinity: combining theory and practice in gender interventions. Cult Health Sex 17(2):112–127. https://doi.org/10.1080/13691058.2015.1085094

Kemp A et al (1995) The dawn of a new day: redefining south African feminism. In: Basu A, Mcgrory CE (eds) The challenge of local feminisms women's movements in global perspective. Routledge, pp 131–162

Koenig MA et al (2003) Women's status and domestic violence in rural Bangladesh: individual- and community-level effects. Demography 40(2):269–288. https://doi.org/10.1353/dem.2003.0014

Koziol-Mclain J et al (2006) Risk factors for femicide-suicide in abusive relationships: results from a multisite case control study. Violence Vict 21(1):3–21. https://doi.org/10.1891/0886-6708.21.1.3

Lawson DM (2003) Incidence, explanations, and treatment of partner violence. J Couns Dev 81(1):19–32. https://doi.org/10.1002/j.1556-6678.2003.tb00221.x

Marin AJ, Russo NF (1999) Feminist perspectives on male violence against women: critiquing O'Neil and Harway's model. In: O'Neil JM, Harway M (eds) New perspectives on violence against women. Sage Publications, Thousand Oaks, CA, pp 18–35

Martin D (1998) Retribution revisited: a reconsideration of feminist criminal law reform strategies. Osgoode Hall Law J 36(1):151–188

Meger S (2016) Rape loot pillage: the political economy of sexual violence in armed conflict. Oxford Academic, New York. https://doi.org/10.1093/acprof:oso/9780190277666.003.0006

Milazzo A (2016, May 25) Gender-based violence, power and norms. https://blogs.worldbank.org/developmenttalk/gender-based-violence-power-and-norms. Accessed 31 Jan 2023

Moffett H (2006) "These women, they force us to rape them": rape as narrative of social control in post-apartheid South Africa. J South Afr Stud 32(1):129–144. https://doi.org/10.1080/03057070500493845

Montesanti SR (2015) The role of structural and interpersonal violence in the lives of women: a conceptual shift in prevention of gender-based violence. BMC Womens Health 15(93). https://doi.org/10.1186/s12905-015-0247-5

Montesanti SR, Thurston WE (2015) Mapping the role of structural and interpersonal violence in the lives of women: implications for public health interventions and policy. BMC Womens Health 15(1). https://doi.org/10.1186/s12905-015-0256-4

Moosa N (1997) The interim and final constitutions and Muslim personal law: implications for South African Muslim women. Stellenbosch Law Rev 9(2):196–206

Namy S et al (2017) Towards a feminist understanding of intersecting violence against women and children in the family. Soc Sci Med 184:40–48. https://doi.org/10.1016/j.socscimed.2017.04.042

Nowrojee B, Manby B (1995) Violence against women in South Africa: the state response to domestic violence and rape. Human Rights Watch, New York

Patil V (2013) From patriarchy to intersectionality: a transnational feminist assessment of how far we've really come. Signs J Women Cult Soc 38(4):847–867. https://doi.org/10.1086/669560

Paul F (1997) On suffering and structural violence: a view from below. In: Kleinman A et al (eds) Social suffering. University of California Press, Berkeley, pp 261–283

Radford J, Russell DEH (1992) Femicide: the politics of woman killing. Open University Press

Renzetti CM (1992) Violent Betrayal: partner abuse in lesbian relationships. SAGE Publications, Inc

Robbins SP et al (2012) Contemporary human behavior theory: a critical perspective for social work. Allyn & Bacon, Boston

Russell B, Hamel J (eds) (2022) Gender and domestic violence: contemporary legal practice and intervention reforms. Oxford University Press

Russell DEH (2012, November). Defining femicide. https://www.dianarussell.com/defining-femicide-.html. Accessed 8 Apr 2023

Russo NF, Pirlott A (2006) Gender-based violence. Ann N Y Acad Sci 1087(1):178–205

Sabri B, Granger DA (2018) Gender-based violence and trauma in marginalized populations of women: role of biological embedding and toxic stress. Health Care Women Int 39(9): 1038–1055. https://doi.org/10.1080/07399332.2018.1491046

Sachs A (1990) Judges and gender: the constitutional rights of women in a post-apartheid South Africa. Agenda 6(7):1–11. https://doi.org/10.1080/10130950.1990.9675085

Sagot M, Carcedo CA (2010) When violence against women kills: femicide in Costa Rica, 1990–99. In: Fregoso R, Bejarano C (eds) Terrorizing women: feminicide in the Americas. Duke University Press, New York, pp 138–156

Schechter S (1982) Women and male violence. South End Press, Boston

Shaw J (2013) Gender and violence: feminist theories, deadly economies and damaging discourse. https://www.e-ir.info/2017/11/03/gender-and-violence-feminist-theories-deadly-economies-and-damaging-discourse/. Accessed 6 Jan 2023

Sibanda-Moyo N et al. (2017, April 28) Violence against women in South Africa: a country in crisis 2017. https://www.africaportal.org/publications/violence-against-women-south-africa-country-crisis-2017/. Accessed 13 Apr 2023

Small J, Kompe L (1992) Organising rural women: the experience of TRAC. Agenda 12:9–19. https://doi.org/10.2307/4065469

Sokoloff NJ, Dupont I (2005) Domestic violence at the intersections of race, class, and gender. Violence Against Women 11(1):38–64. https://doi.org/10.1177/1077801204271476

South African Human Rights Commission (2017) Annual report: 2017. https://www.sahrc.org.za/home/21/files/SAHRC%20Annual%20Report%202017%20HR.PDF. Accessed 9 Aug 2023

Stats SA (2022) Unemployment rate in South Africa from Q1 2019 to Q3 2022, by age group. https://www.statista.com/statistics/1129482/unemployment-rate-by-age-group-in-south-africa/#:~:text=In%20the%20third%20quarter%20of. Accessed 6 Feb 2023

Stauffer C (2015) The sexual politics of gender-based violence in South Africa: linking public and private worlds. J Sociol Christ 5(1):1–16

Taylor R, Jasinski JL (2011) Femicide and the feminist perspective. Homicide Stud 15(4):341–362. https://doi.org/10.1177/1088767911424541

Truth Commission (1998) Special report - TRC final report - Volume 1, Section 1, Chapter 2. https://sabctrc.saha.org.za/reports/volume1/chapter2/subsection8.htm. Accessed 25 Mar 2023

United Nations High Commissioner for Refugees (2016, June 14) Report of the Special Rapporteur on violence against women, its causes and consequences on her mission to South Africa. https://www.refworld.org/docid/57d90a4b4.html. Accessed 14 Sept 2022

Verena A (2021) Violence against women: causes and consequences. https://medicamondiale.org/en/violence-against-women/causes-and-consequences#:~:text=The%20structural%20causes%20of%20violence%20against%20women%20include%20socialised%20gender. Accessed 13 Apr 2023

Walker L (1979) The battered woman. Harper and Row, New York

Wharton JJS (1848) My library my history books on Google play the law lexicon, or dictionary of jurisprudence: explaining all the technical words and phrases employed in the several departments of English law. Spettigue and Farrance

Winter DD, Leighton DC (2001) Structural violence. In: Christie DJ et al (eds) Peace, conflict, and violence: peace psychology in the 21st century. Prentice Hall, New York

World Health Organization (2005) WHO multi-country study on women's health and domestic violence against women: initial results on prevalence, health outcomes and women's responses. https://apps.who.int/iris/handle/10665/43309. Accessed 5 Feb 2003

World Health Organization (2012) Understanding and addressing violence against women: femicide. https://apps.who.int/iris/bitstream/handle/10665/77421/WHO_RHR_12.38_eng.pdf. Accessed 10 Mar 2023

Yllö K, Bograd M (1988) Feminist perspectives on wife abuse. Sage Publications, Inc

Chapter 5
Situational Analysis of Gender-Based Violence and Femicide in South Africa

5.1 An Overview

South Africa remains one of the most violent countries in the world.[1] This status is determined based on the country's levels of crime, most significantly its murder rates. The first part of this chapter looks at the concept of femicide and homicide to properly assess these rates, followed by a discussion on the importance of data and research in the fight against GBVF. This type of data is critical to providing a better understanding of the nature, magnitude, severity, and frequency of GBVF. The use of such data acts to reaffirm focus and channels momentum behind establishing a culture to address GBVF. It also provides a basis for evidence-based decision-making, which is essential for choosing interventions and policies. Statistics for some of the most prevalent types of crime perpetrated against women both globally and in South Africa will then be discussed and an assessment of the trends in, and extent of victimization of women will be analyzed. Importantly an understanding of what crime statistics can and cannot tell us is a vital starting point to tackling crime. Research and statistics remain valuable tools for developing evidence-based policies and interventions to end GBVF.

5.1.1 Femicide vs. Homicide

Femicide is internationally recognized as the most extreme and brutal manifestation of violence against women affecting all regions and countries worldwide.[2] The specific characteristics of femicide around the world include women disproportionately being killed by men, being killed in the context of intimate or family

[1] NUMBEO (2021), para 4.
[2] United Nations Office on Drugs and Crime (2022c).

T. Deane, *Gender-Based Violence and Femicide in South Africa*, Gender, Justice and Legal Feminism 5, https://doi.org/10.1007/978-3-031-61053-0_5

relationships (femicide victims have previously experienced non-lethal GBV),[3] women's social vulnerability, legal inequality[4] and low access to education.[5] Further characteristics include cultural and social factors that are subject to change on a long-term basis, impacting the rate at which women are killed.[6] In addition, stereotyped gender roles, discrimination and unequal power relations between women and men in society have seen an increase in GBVF. These factors characterize the specific context in which such killings take place and can trigger violence by perpetrators when a woman's behavior is perceived to not be in line with social norms or stereotyped gender roles.[7] In this context, the term "gender-related motivation" does not refer to the subjective intent of the perpetrator to commit the homicide, but to its underlying root causes. The subjective motive of the perpetrator to commit the crime, for example, such as a specific bias against or hatred of women, may be present in some cases alongside the "gender-related motivation."[8]

The notion of gender-related killings of women and girls is a type of killing within the broader category of intentional homicide[9] and differs from other types of homicide as it refers to homicides of women and girls that are gender-related.[10] Two of the most common forms of violence against women include: (i) intimate partner violence where violence by a husband or male intimate partner (physical, sexual or psychological) is the most widespread form of violence against women globally, and (ii) non-partner sexual violence, where sexual violence is committed by perpetrators other than a current or former husband or partner, including male relatives, friends, acquaintances or strangers.

The notion of gender-related killing, or "femicide," requires an understanding of which acts are gender related as this has been seen to be subject to a certain degree of interpretation. For example, in many cases there is a continuum of (intimate partner) violence that culminates in the killing of women even when perpetrators have no specific (misogynistic) motives.[11] Nevertheless, some aspects of gender-related killing of women are indisputable, one being that this type of homicide is part of female homicide, yet not all female homicides are gender related. Therefore, only a

---

[3]The vast majority of femicide cases occur as the final phase of interpersonal or domestic violence.

[4]Centre for the Study of Violence and Reconciliation (2016).

[5]Resulting in gender inequality, stereotypes, and social discrimination. Garcia-Vergara et al. (2022).

[6]Since femicide is context and gender specific, policies that are successful in reducing male-to-male killing do not affect femicide. Thus, as the former's rate decreases, femicide remains unchanged or increases. See Stamatel (2014).

[7]United Nations Office on Drugs and Crime (2022b).

[8]United Nations Office on Drugs and Crime (2022b), p. 5.

[9]This definition and typology are aligned to the structure and framework of the International Classification of Crime for Statistical Purposes (ICCS). See United Nations Office on Drugs and Crime (2015); United Nations Office on Drugs and Crime (2022b); United Nations Office on Drugs and Crime (2020b).

[10]United Nations Office on Drugs and Crime (2019a).

[11]Swemmer (2021), pp. 325–326.

specific, if considerable, share can be labelled "gender-related killings of women and girls," i.e., "femicide."

"Femicide" represents just a small percentage of the overall number of homicides,[12] but research analysis indicates that the drivers of this type of lethal violence require tailored responses for its elimination. Killings carried out by intimate partners are rarely spontaneous or random and should be examined as an extreme act on a continuum of gender-related violence that remains underreported and too often ignored.[13] Gender-related killings of women and girls are committed in a variety of contexts and through different mechanisms. In broader terms, such killings can be divided into those perpetrated within the family and those perpetrated outside the family sphere. Data availability at the regional and global level show that most cases of this type of crime fall into the first category.[14] In addition, studies highlight that since 2000, the number of deaths by interpersonal homicide has exceeded the number of war- and terrorism-related deaths.[15]

Data further indicates that most violence against women is perpetrated by current or former husbands or intimate partners.[16] Among the many documents that draw attention to the alarming proportions reached by this phenomenon in all its different manifestations, is the 2013 United Nations General Assembly resolution on "Taking Action against Gender Related Killing of Women and Girls," where concern was specifically expressed over the fact "that the global prevalence of different manifestations of the gender-related killing of women and girls is reaching alarming proportions . . ."[17]

It also noted that gender related killing of women and girls had been criminalized in some countries as "femicide" or "feminicide" and has been incorporated as such into national legislation in those countries.[18] In other countries however femicide is not different from homicide in criminal law.[19] While the majority of intentional homicide victims are male, the majority of the victims of intimate partner/family-related homicide are women.[20] Therefore, understanding the extent and patterns of

---

[12] Stöckl et al. (2013).

[13] Vatnar et al. (2022).

[14] United Nations Office on Drugs and Crime (2019a).

[15] Matias et al. (2020); Vatnar et al. (2022).

[16] United Nations Office on Drugs and Crime (2019a).

[17] Resolution 68/191, specifically, in the preamble of the resolution. On 18 December 2013, the United Nations General Assembly adopted resolution 68/191 which expressed a deep international concern about the gender-related killing of women and girls, while recognizing efforts made to address that form of violence in different regions, including in countries where the concept of femicide or feminicide has been incorporated into national legislation. See United Nations General Assembly (2013).

[18] United Nations ECLAC Statistics Division (2020).

[19] Only a handful of countries legally recognise femicide as distinctly different from homicide; most of which are in Latin America where 16 countries have included femicide as a specific crime. For more information, see Gourley (2017).

[20] Vatnar et al. (2022); United Nations Office on Drugs and Crime (2019a).

the killing of women and girls requires a dedicated analysis of this type of violence. To achieve this, the need for accurate and reliable statistics on the extent of violence against women cannot be over-emphasized.

5.2 The Importance of Data and Research in the Fight Against GBVF

Solutions to the GBVF issue will be challenging but the growing international recognition of these violations create opportunities for the elimination thereof. As a starting point an assessment of the extent of the problem through data is critical. The collection and dissemination of data on the prevalence and incidence of various forms of GBV, as well as on the causes and consequences of such violence, is a starting point for developing effective mechanisms at policy level and for eradicating this phenomenon. The analysis and reporting on GBVF data will allow for a better understanding of service demand, including gaps, and policy and program implementation and outcomes. Estimating service gaps and unmet needs based on service data can also contribute to ensuring an inclusive approach towards prevention and elimination of GBVF. Furthermore, the analysis and data are vital to understanding the full scope and scale of femicide and provides the foundation for a sound and sustainable public policy response.

Without a full understanding of the scope and dimensions of violence against women, it is not possible to design suitable responses aimed at appropriately addressing or preventing such violence at any level of government or civil society.[21] In this regard, accurate and comprehensive data serves to increase societal awareness of GBV and call attention to the accountability of States to act against such violence. Importantly, the lack of an informed estimate of the prevalence of violence against women impacts costing and cost calculations.

Administrative data is also a powerful tool for dialogue and advocacy with governments to improve violence against women prevention and response. The goal is to ultimately inform GBVF prevention, improve services for survivors and increase the accountability of perpetrators. A discussion on the scope of gender-related killing of women and girls will also form a key part of this discussion. Such a discussion provides an analysis of killings perpetrated within the family sphere and explores the scale of intimate partner/family-related killings of women and girls.

Indeed, information needed by policymakers and advocates for GBVF may include the number of women affected by various types of violence and the short- and long-term consequences thereof, the personal characteristics that leave certain women particularly vulnerable to victimization, the barriers to seeking help and the responses of criminal justice, health and social services to women who seek help. Detailed data is required to gauge the magnitude and dimensions of the problem, to

[21] United Nations Department of Economic and Social Affairs Statistics Division (2014).

establish baselines, to identify groups at considerable risk, to focus intervention and prevention efforts where they are needed most, to monitor change over time, to assess the effectiveness of interventions and to address the harm to victims of violence. In the absence of accurate information, efforts to track progress in terms of policy responses to the problem are severely compromised.[22]

5.2.1 Data Collection

For countries to be held accountable, effective solutions must be informed by data, and data collection based on globally agreed standards on both national and international level. The problem is that in many countries including in South Africa, GBVF, while it remains a serious crime, is not categorized as a crime on its own. It is identified through other crimes. In addition, both globally and nationally, the availability of data on intimate partner/family-related homicide means that such killings of females are analyzed in greater depth than other forms of femicide and much more prevalence data is identifiable. It should be noted that where reference is made to global statistics caution is necessary when comparing data on crime, as variations between legal definitions[23] and methods of collection can differ across countries.[24] With this caveat in mind, where data is available, however, it is clear that intimate partner/family-related homicide covers most of the killings categorized as "femicide."[25]

In addition, while the disaggregation of homicide data at the country level has improved over the years, regional and global estimates are based on a limited

[22] Breiding et al. (2015).

[23] Evidence shows that criminal justice recording and investigating practices vary significantly across countries, leading to possible misinterpretations and underestimations when only data resulting from specific gender- related killings legislation is considered. See United Nations Office on Drugs and Crime (2022b) and United Nations Office on Drugs and Crime (2019a).

[24] Calculating the exact prevalence of femicide is challenging. Mainly because not all countries regularly collect data and send it to the United Nations Office on Drugs and Crime (UNODC) international database (under the headings "women intentionally killed" and "female victims intentionally killed by intimate partner/family member"), nor do they proceed in a comparable and systematic way. Different local agencies may collect data using broader as well as more limited notions, or a legal definition which does not apply in other penal codes. Gaps across time are also very common, as not all countries submit statistics on an annual basis and for many the latest data available is not recent. See United Nations Office on Drugs and Crime (2019a).

[25] UNODC collects data from Member States on intimate partner/family-related homicide as a proxy for gender-related killings of women and the broad concept evolving around the notion of "femicide." This indicator covers female victims of homicide perpetrated by current or former intimate partners, or other family members. General sex-disaggregated homicide data are collected through regular UNODC data collection on crime. Using the framework of the ICCS, homicide data can be categorized and analysed to define gender-related killings and quantify intimate partner/ family-related homicide. More information is available at United Nations Office on Drugs and Crime (2017, September).

number of countries, with Africa and Asia accounting for most of the gaps.[26] Where available then, the data presented in this chapter is based on homicide statistics produced by national statistical systems in which the relationship between the victim and perpetrator and/or the motive are reported as well as from literature studies. This chapter draws on the two most common methods for counting crime in South Africa,[27] police statistics and victim surveys, to explore crime trends and related perceptions and feelings.

An analysis of available prevalence data from surveys and from smaller scale national and international research and other studies conducted over the years will be referred to. This information has been obtained through a systematic and comprehensive review of available data on the prevalence of the two forms of violence against women. In addition, the author has read an overview of the literature on the topic of GBVF, examining accredited journals, websites (especially those related to crime statistics, for example, the SAPS, Africa Check, Institute for Security Studies (ISS) and WHO websites) as well as reviewing the major newspapers on crime statistics and related issues. References are made to the *BBC News, News24, IOL News* and various other newspaper articles. This chapter shows that whilst some categories of crime have declined significantly since the early nineties, other categories like violent crime and murder have spiked. The chapter ends by exploring what the data, combined with recent evidence on violence and crime prevention, tell us about crime in South Africa's near future.

5.3 A Brief Commentary on the Limitations of GBVF Statistics

Research and statistics would go a long way to empowering communities to better understand and respond to safety issues as they emerge rather than relying on out-of-date information that can only provide information on long-term trends. Access to information would promote a more active citizenry to become involved in contributing to public safety. As mentioned previously, effective solutions must be informed by data, and data collection based on globally agreed standards is high on international and government agendas. While the availability of data on violence against women and girls and on the prevalence of intimate partner violence has in recent years improved quite substantially[28] there remains a significant gap of comprehensive, reliable, comparable, and up-to-date data on GBV.

---

[26] United Nations Office on Drugs and Crime (2022a).

[27] Newburn (2017), p. 45.

[28] In recent decades, significant advances have been made to develop globally agreed-upon indicators and standards for the generation of violence against women data. This includes work done by the WHO as part of the multi-country study on women's health and domestic violence against women, (García-Moreno et al. (2005)) a methodology that has been replicated in countries across

Though countries are increasingly using similar definitions and approaches, gaps remain in the availability of data on some forms of violence, such as femicide, sexual harassment, and online violence. In South Africa whilst availability of data on violence against women and girls has increased significantly in recent years,[29] there remain limitations. Limitations must be noted as they affect data trustworthiness, validity, and reliability.[30] Indeed, several limitations have been identified including that crime statistics released annually by SAPS do not provide much information about GBVF specifically. As mentioned previously, they do provide information about sexual offenses, but questions have been raised about their reliability[31] and whether the problem is being overestimated or underestimated.[32]

Therefore and for example, although the crime rate, in general, has reportedly decreased between 2013/14 and 2016/17,[33] violent crimes against women, such as sexual assault, increased drastically between 2015/16 and 2016/17[34] to 2021/2022.[35] A major concern is that official police statistics are fraught with problems of under-reporting,[36] codification of crimes and the lack of disaggregated data.[37] This is largely because whilst there are gendered statistics there is no specific GBVF crime category. Therefore, the situation remains that the exact prevalence of violence against women and girls in South Africa remains unverifiable.

---

different regions to generate data on violence against women; the inclusion of an optional domestic violence module in the Demographic and Health Survey (DHS) that is being implemented by a growing number of countries; the core set of nine violence against women indicators proposed by the Friends of the Chair of the United Nations (UN Secretary-General & UN Statistical Commission (2008)); and the United Nations (2014), among others. These indicators and standards, including those identified in the SDG framework, refer to the prevalence of violence against women and need to be generated through population-based surveys. Population-level surveys based on reports from survivors provide the most accurate estimates of the prevalence of intimate partner violence and sexual violence. See Kendall (2020).

[29] In South Africa there are several stakeholders that also collect data on femicide and other forms of violence against women. These include the South African Medical Research Council (MRC); the Human Sciences Research Council (HSRC), other research institutions and bodies as well as different civil society structures and organisations.

[30] Commission for Gender Equality (2022).

[31] Commission for Gender Equality (2022).

[32] Deane (2018).

[33] Stats SA (2017, September 28).

[34] Stats SA (2018).

[35] Excluding the period of lockdown during the COVID-19 pandemic. This is because reporting of crimes on all levels were not accurate given the lockdown measures implemented. This will be discussed in greater detail below. For the 2021/2022 reporting period, see South African Government (2021, November 19).

[36] The statistics and figures exclude the vast number of incidents that go unreported, as well as the incident of violence that are not "overt" or those considered "violent," and the normalised and pervasive gendered violence and discrimination experienced daily, particularly by women. Sowetan Live (2022, February 21).

[37] Stats SA (2017, September 28); Machisa (2011).

In addition, SA has no centralized statistics on incidents and types of violence against women, beyond the recording of sexual offences crimes under the *Sexual Offences Act*[38] in SAPS, which statistics are released annually. In addition, statistics are in no way conclusive of the real prevalence of violence against women and girls as it is an unchallenged fact that there is massive under-reporting of all forms of GBV crimes. To this end SAPS has recently committed to ensuring that its crime statistics are in line with international best practice.[39] This is being done with the aim of enhancing the quality and integrity of the South African crime statistics.[40] It is important to note that whilst it may be that the crime statistics are not particularly reliable, various studies indicate that they are accurate enough to provide some indication of the crime levels in South Africa.

In addition, women face various challenges in reporting violence against them, which impacts data collection. For example, the literature on GBVF identifies that whilst the theoretical development of the GBVF concept has enabled scholars, activists, and policy-makers around the world to develop policies and analyze behavior related to violence in multiple ways, some women are simply unaware of what constitutes GBV or they do not know about their rights or the help that is available.[41] For example, due to strong cultural attitudes and social norms[42] that legitimize violent behavior, many women do not consider wife beating or stalking, psychological violence, female genital mutilation, harassment, etc., as violence.[43] The evidence demonstrates a consistent underreporting and a failure to seek help worldwide.[44] Furthermore, there is a strong association between norms and attitudes condoning male authority and endorsing wife beating and the perpetration of violence.

Additional barriers to reporting or seeking care from formal sources include women simply not believing that the violence is serious enough to report,[45] for fear that no one will believe that the abuse happened,[46] the fear of bringing shame to their families, wanting to save face[47] or the shame and stigma attached to the

---

[38] *The Criminal Law (Sexual Offences and Related Matters) Amendment Act* 32 of *2007, as amended by Act 13 of 2021.*

[39] Which will reportedly be achieved through a Memorandum of Understanding with Statistics South Africa.

[40] For more information, see SAPS (2018).

[41] Gurm et al. (2020).

[42] Murphy et al. (2020).

[43] Paluck et al. (2010).

[44] Palermo et al. (2014).

[45] Prochuck (2018).

[46] Gurm et al. (2020).

[47] Holmes and Hunt (2017).

violence,[48] financial barriers,[49] perceived impunity for perpetrators,[50] lack of awareness of available services or access to such services,[51] fear of retaliation[52] or being blamed for the violence,[53] discriminatory and stereotypical attitudes toward victims in courts and law enforcement settings.[54] In a study conducted by Burnes et al.[55] the authors estimate that only 15.4% of older adults report violence to police. Some of the reasons include the fear of revictimization, which is the most prevalent reason, embarrassment, fear, denial, isolation, lack of resources and a general lack of knowledge about reporting procedures.

A study conducted by Prochuck[56] succinctly identifies the various barriers to the reporting of sexual violence that women may experience. These barriers and challenges may include inter alia women considering the crime as minor and not worth reporting (71%), the incident was a "private or personal" matter and was handled informally (67%), not wanting the inconvenience of dealing with the police (45%) a lack of evidence (43%), a strong belief that the offender would not be convicted or adequately punished (40%)[57] or the belief that the offender did not intend to cause harm (39%), fear of the court process or not wanting to go to court (34%), not wanting to get the offender in trouble (30%), not wanting others to know about the assault (30%), a belief that police would not have been effective (26%), the fear of retaliation by the offender (22%), a belief that the police would not have located the offender (21%), past experiences with police had been unsatisfactory (13%), believe that police would be biased (13%) and feelings that reporting would bring shame and dishonor to the family (12%).

Appropriate and effective policy responses to prevent and address the effects of GBV depend on an accurate and complete understanding of the prevalence, dynamics, and root causes. Such evidence would assist in the development of targeted interventions. However, reliable data is a major cause for concern and remains lacking due to these various factors and challenges.

---

[48] Ssanyu (2022).
[49] Umubyeyi et al. (2016).
[50] Jody-Ann et al. (2022).
[51] Van der Heijden et al. (2020).
[52] Siziba et al. (2022), p. 154.
[53] Perrin et al. (2019).
[54] Palermo et al. (2014).
[55] Burnes et al. (2019), p. 891.
[56] Prochuck (2018).
[57] Dobbin and Kalev (2016), p. 2.

5.4 GBV During Times of Crisis

At this point, for various reasons, it becomes relevant to discuss, in brief, the issue of GBV during times of crisis like the COVID-19 pandemic. First, the COVID-19 pandemic and the backlash against women's sexual and reproductive health and rights are diminishing the outlook for gender equality severely impacting the attainment of SDGs relating to gender.[58]

Second, since this book covers a period during which the COVID-19 pandemic is often referred to and its impact has consequently affected both data collection and rates of GBV it becomes particularly relevant. In addition, while all crisis-affected settings are associated with an increased risk of GBV, there are unique factors about COVID-19 that make it particularly alarming.[59] Measures like lockdown and restrictions taken to reduce the risk of such exposure impacted rates of GBV and data collection. Considering the large number of cases that go unreported the exact prevalence of GBV during such times is even more of a challenge to determine. Additionally, the limited resources often in place for gathering this type of evidence in such contexts is compromised.[60]

Third, while the depth and severity of the COVID-19 pandemic is still uncertain, reports do indicate that during times of crisis, women and girls face an increased risk of exposure to GBV.[61] Quarantines and other social distancing measures limit both physical mobility and potentially increase economic vulnerability among women experiencing interpersonal violence. During pandemics, women may worry about their physical safety or experience additional mental or emotional distress, making it even more difficult to create necessary space in the relationship and mitigate immediate risk for violence. In fact, the regional or global nature and associated fear and uncertainty of pandemics provide an enabling environment that may exacerbate or spark diverse forms of GBV.

While rigorous studies estimating increases in reporting of GBV during or post-pandemic are scarce, media reports and anecdotal evidence are widespread.[62] Although GBV is known to be pervasive in all settings, emergencies like COVID-19 disrupt existing protective structures and create multiple circumstances than can lead to various forms of violence, abuse, and exploitation.[63] Literature suggests that women's interest and ability to leave abusive partners is complex.[64] Women may opt to stay with abusive partners for a host of reasons, ranging from emotional attachment, psychological distress, financial dependence, or fear that separation will

58 United Nations (2022).

59 Wenham et al. (2020).

60 Stark and Ager (2011).

61 Deane (2021); Stark and Landis (2016).

62 Peterman et al. (2020).

63 Heise and Kotsadam (2015).

64 Peterman et al. (2020).

elevate harm, to personal physical safety or the safety of their children.[65] Each of these are compounded in pandemic settings.

The evidence is that in many countries, especially in low to middle income countries, the poor economic and social conditions coupled with the lockdown measures exacerbated existing abuse.[66] Indeed, during the COVID-19 pandemic, lockdown measures and their socio-economic effects have increased the vulnerability of women when faced with abusive partners, while limiting their access to services.[67] In light of the quarantines and movement restrictions that have been put in place across the world to curb the pandemic, women and girls faced an increased risk of experiencing violence at the hands of family members, intimate partners or others living within their homes.[68]

Indeed, the risks of experiencing household violence during times of crisis are often exacerbated by factors such as emotional stress, economic strain, and shifting roles and responsibilities among family members.[69] For instance, according to one study conducted in Nigeria[70] the number of reported cases of GBV, following the introduction of lockdowns at the end of March 2020, increased from 300 in March to more than 700 in April. This amounted to a monthly increase of 149% in cases of GBV.[71] The reports of domestic violence in Nigeria followed a similar trend to elsewhere in the world. In Croatia, for example, rape cases increased by 228% during the first five months of 2020 in comparison to 2019, and the percentage of attempted rapes rose by 175%;[72] in China, police reports of domestic violence were three times higher in February 2020 compared to reports from the previous year.[73]

Outside of personal and familial constraints, women's access to legal systems and safety support services have been severely limited during the pandemic. The lockdown measures exacerbated the pre-existing, significant challenges that prevent legal systems from responding efficiently and effectively to the needs of intimate partner violence survivors. The increased vulnerability of women during this time also became more apparent when the lockdown compromised access to what was

[65] Rajah and Osborn (2020); Ciurria (2018); St. Vil et al. (2016); First et al. (2017).

[66] Peterman et al. (2020).

[67] World Health Organization (2021b). *Violence against women*.

[68] Peterman et al. (2020).

[69] Gibbs et al. (2020).

[70] International Growth Centre (2020, May 19).

[71] United Nations (2020, May 4).

[72] International Growth Centre (2020, May 19).

[73] United Nations (2020, May 4). In Argentina, Canada, France, Germany, Spain, the United Kingdom and the United States, government authorities, women's rights activists and civil society partners flagged reports of increased domestic violence during the crisis and heightened demand for emergency shelter.

considered life-saving services and justice.[74] Many one-stop centers[75] and domestic abuse shelters were forced to close or provide limited services. As resources were diverted towards the pandemic response, access to justice and other forms of legal redress for survivors became increasingly challenging to access.[76] For example, it was noted that due to the various restrictions in place, it impacted how the police responded to acts of interpersonal violence specifically. For example, in an effort to limit prisoners' exposure to the disease police officers were less likely to assess cases of interpersonal violence as high-priority for arrest and detainment.[77] Such action would be consistent with and compound many police officers' decision to leave issues of interpersonal violence as a "personal" or "family" matter even outside of pandemic contexts.[78] Additionally, the strict movement restrictions meant that survivors became unable to access centers and shelters, having to rely on hotlines to receive any kind of support. With key services and justice mechanisms compromised, the reports of increased domestic violence and heightened risk of other forms of GBV constituted a key challenge to addressing the high rates of GBV and it severely impacted the collection of data on GBV during this period.[79]

5.5 Comparing of Trends in Femicide Rates

A comparison of trends in femicide rates in South Africa and around the globe is important. First, because South Africa has constantly been reported has having the highest rates of violence in the world, and despite the issue around availability and credibility of statistics[80] it becomes important to try and quantify this in some actual figures, notwithstanding the concerns around such data. Second, since murder is seen as the crime trend with the highest degree of validity and reliability (a high degree of data-integrity) globally, it would greatly assist in quantifying femicide murder. This is done not without an understanding that crime statistics do not tell us everything and can be incredibly misleading.[81] It is acknowledged that too many victims of femicide still go uncounted. For example, for approximately four in ten

[74]Due to restrictions in movement, survivors could not access critical life-saving services such as post-exposure prophylaxis and psychosocial support, having to rely on telephone calls to manage the violent situations they face. See United Nations Office on Drugs and Crime (2020a).

[75]One-Stop Centres give access to holistic services (health, psychosocial support, legal and police services) to survivors of GBV under one roof and free of charge. See United Nations Women: Africa (2011).

[76]United Nations Women: Africa (2020, April 10).

[77]American Civil Liberties Union (2020).

[78]Wolf et al. (2003).

[79]United Nations (2020, May 4).

[80]Deane (2018).

[81]Stats SA (2014, December 4). While the VOCS cannot replace police statistics, it can be a rich source of information which will assist in the planning of crime prevention as well as providing a

intentional murders of women and girls in 2021, there is not enough information to identify them as gender-related killings because of national variation in criminal justice recordings and investigation practices.[82]

In addition, the likelihood of victims reporting crime, and the police recording them, is not the same in every country.[83] Crime victims are less likely to report crime in a country with an oppressive or incompetent police force than in a country where the police are helpful and trustworthy. In addition, the distances people must travel to the nearest police station, and the availability of transport to get there, is another factor which can affect crime reporting rates.[84] Multiple offences are not recorded uniformly in all countries. In some countries only the most serious offence reported in a single incident is recorded while in others all offences reported are recorded.[85] As mentioned above, differences in data quality between countries is also a factor. In developed countries, recorded crimes are entered into a computerized database and channeled to a central point for analysis.[86] In many less developed countries, crime statistics are recorded only on paper which can easily result in the loss of some of the statistics.[87] There is therefore no global, standardized or consistently recorded data on femicide.[88]

It has however become increasingly acknowledged that despite the heterogeneity of national approaches, the need for accurate and timely data collection has garnered ever more relevance.[89] This has more recently led to the adoption of a new global framework for measuring gender-related killings of women and girls, developed by the United Nations Office on Drugs and Crime (UNODC) and UN Women.[90] The framework will enable more precise measuring of the extent of femicide and assess worldwide risk factors associated with this atrocious manifestation of violence against women.

---

more holistic picture of crime in South Africa. The data can be used for the development of policies and strategies, as well as for crime prevention and public education programmes.

[82] United Nations Women (2022, November 25).

[83] Mc Cafferty (2003).

[84] Africa Check (2015).

[85] Masuku (2016).

[86] UNODC collects data on intimate partner/family-related homicide through the United Nations Survey of Crime Trends and Operations of Criminal Justice Systems.

[87] Mc Cafferty (2003).

[88] CNN (2021, August 30).

[89] United Nations General Assembly (2013).

[90] United Nations Office on Drugs and Crime (2022c).

5.6 Femicide in Numbers

5.6.1 Global Trends

Like all forms of GBV, femicide is a problem that affects every country and territory across the world.[91] Globally, it is estimated that approximately 736 million[92] or nearly one in three women, have in their lifetime been subjected to either physical and/or sexual intimate partner violence, non-partner violence, or both.[93] The global rate of female homicide was estimated at 2.3 per 100,000 of the female population and approximately 90% of suspects were found to be male with most of the violence against women being perpetrated by current or former husbands or intimate partners.[94] Looking at available statistics, the Global Homicide Report by the UNODC[95] estimates that in 2017 approximately 87,000 women were intentionally killed and during the 2021 reporting period an estimated 81,100 women and girls were killed intentionally.[96] When one looks at the total number of female victims, almost five to six out of ten women were victims of intentional homicide.[97] On average approximately 137 women are reportedly killed every day and who were killed by a member of their own family,[98] and 82% of women were reportedly victims of all homicides carried out by intimate partners.

Looking at the number of women (approximately 30,000), killed entirely by their intimate partners, bearing in mind that this figure does not include other family members, this translates to more than one-third (34%) of all women and girls being intentionally killed worldwide, or 82 women being killed daily by someone whom they are or have been intimate with.

Importantly, according to data accompanying the 2019 Global Homicide Report by the UNODC,[99] when South Africa is compared with other countries where stats are available, like the Central and South American countries including Venezuela,

---

[91] UN Women (2022, November 25).

[92] This amounts to approximately 30% of women aged 15 and older. This figure does not include sexual harassment. The rates of depression, anxiety disorders, unplanned pregnancies, sexually transmitted infections, and HIV are higher in women who have experienced violence compared to women who have not, as well as many other health problems that can last even after the violence has ended. World Health Organization (2021a).

[93] World Health Organization (2021a).

[94] More than 640 million women aged 15 and older have been subjected to intimate partner violence (26% of women aged 15 and older). World Health Organization (2021b).

See also United Nations Office on Drugs and Crime (2022a).

[95] United Nations Office on Drugs and Crime (2019a).

[96] United Nations Office on Drugs and Crime (2022a).

[97] United Nations Office on Drugs and Crime (2019a).

[98] Mail & Guardian (2021a, June 22).

[99] The UNODC collects data primarily from criminal justice sources. Other sources of homicide data, for example, the World Health Organisation, collect data from public health sources. The UNODC therefore uses the same statistics as SAPS.

Honduras and El Salvador, South Africa ranks among the five countries with the highest rates of female homicide.[100] The 2019 report[101] indicates that the largest number (approximately 20,000) of all women killed worldwide by intimate partners or other family members was in Asia, followed by Africa (19,000), the Americas (8000), Europe (3000), and Oceania (300). With an intimate partner/family-related homicide rate of 3.1 per 100,000 female population, Africa remains the region where women have the highest risk of being killed by an intimate partner or other family member, whilst Europe (with 0.7 per 100,000 female population) is the region where the risk is lowest.

More than two-thirds of all women (69%) killed in Africa during the reporting period were killed by intimate partners or other family members. In Africa, South Africa has the highest rate (9.46 per 100,000), while Algeria has the lowest (0.37).[102] Even though Europe is seen as the lowest risk region, more than a third (38%) of women were killed by intimate partners or other family members, which is a major cause for concern.[103] The intimate partner/family-related homicide rate was also high in the Americas at 1.6 per 100,000 female population, as well as Oceania at 1.3 and Asia at 0.9.[104]

Looking at the total global rate of female total homicide in 2017, it was estimated to be 2.3 per 100,000 female population, the global female intimate partner/family-related homicide rate was 1.3 and the female intimate partner homicide rate was estimated at 0.8 per 100,000 female population. In comparison, South Africa's rate for that year was 10.1 per 100,000.

In 2018, South Africa's rate dropped slightly to 9.5 per 100,000, but, in comparison, the United States' rate was 2.2 per 100,000 and India's was 2.7 per 100,000.[105] The WHO estimates that while this may be true for the 2018 figures, 12.1 in every 100,000 women are victims of femicide in South Africa each year—a figure which is over 100 times worse than Italy in their newly-announced "state of crisis"—and five times worse than the global average of 2.6.[106] However, the actual murder rate of women is even higher.[107] Noteworthy is that not every case can be defined under the blanket term of "femicide." Subsequently, when one includes other factors (provided by SAPS), one can see that there are 15.2 female victims in every 100,000. By those calculations, a woman is murdered every three hours in South Africa.[108]

[100] United Nations Office on Drugs and Crime (2019b).

[101] United Nations Office on Drugs and Crime (2019a).

[102] Corradi (2021).

[103] Between 2009 and 2018 a woman is killed by a man every three days in the United Kingdom. See Femicide Census (2018).

[104] United Nations Office on Drugs and Crime (2019a).

[105] Mail & Guardian (2021b, April 14).

[106] For a bit of context, France is said to be among the countries with the highest rate of women killed by their partner with 0.18 victims per 100,000 women. See BBC News (2019a, September 3).

[107] Head (2019, September 4).

[108] Wilkinson (2019).

During the same year, 2018, the regions with the largest number of females killed purely by intimate partners (not including other family members) were Asia and Africa (with 11,000 each), followed by the Americas (6000), Europe (2000), and Oceania (200) which accounts for the largest share of all the regions in terms of women killed exclusively by intimate partners, at 42%. Africa was also the region with the highest rate of females killed purely by intimate partners in 2017 (1.7 per 100,000 female population). The Americas had the second-highest rate (1.2), Oceania the third (0.9), Europe the fourth (0.6), and at 29% Asia had the fifth-highest rate (0.5 per 100,000 female population).

An over-time trends analyses between 2010 and 2021 saw Europe witness an average reduction in the number of female intimate partner/family-related homicides (by approximately 19%), albeit with differences across sub-regions and with signs of trend reversals since 2020 in some sub-regions such as Western and Southern Europe. By contrast, the Americas recorded an average increase over the same period (by approximately 6%), with the exclusion of the South American sub-region which saw a slight decrease in femicide. Estimating the global number of gender-related killings of women and girls is challenging as data gaps persist. During the research it was noted that limited data availability meant that the estimation of over-time trends is not possible in Africa, Asia, and Oceania.[109]

During 2020, in Northern America, and to a lesser extent in Western and Southern Europe, the gender-related killings of women and girls in the private sphere was particularly concerning. The main reason for the increase of femicide in the private sphere has been attributed to the impact of COVID-19 confinement measures, although other contributing factors cannot be ruled out.[110] Other sub-regions in Europe and the Americas recorded negligible changes or decreases in the number of killings between 2019 and the end of 2020, which suggests that the onset of the COVID-19 pandemic had heterogeneous impacts. The decreases in some sub-regions may reflect delays in recording due to COVID-19 rather than reductions in the number of killings. During the period disaggregated trend data from 25 countries in Europe and the Americas indicate that increases in female homicides in the private sphere at the onset of the COVID-19 pandemic were driven primarily by increases in killings perpetrated by family members other than intimate partners. The increases in female family-related homicides at the onset of the COVID-19 pandemic were larger than any yearly variations observed since 2015. The overall number of female homicides has remained largely unchanged over the past few years and decade.[111]

[109] United Nations Office on Drugs and Crime (2022a).

[110] For example, COVID-19 related food-insecurity and economic instability, are some other factors associated with an increase in GBV. See Sherwood et al. (2022). Also, job losses, alcohol abuse, confined in small spaces for too long increasing tensions have led to the increase in GBV. See News24 (2020, April 5); and Daily Maverick: ISS Today. (2020, April 6).

[111] United Nations Office on Drugs and Crime (2022a).

Looking at South Africa, it is a country that faces very different challenges to Western and other countries that had implemented lockdowns to prevent the spread of the virus. Considered to be one of the most unequal countries in the world,[112] millions of people live in single rooms and cramped conditions in informal settlements or crowded inner-city buildings,[113] increasing its specific challenges and making it difficult to allow for substantial adjustments to their lives to mitigate the spread of the virus. This impacts all aspect of citizens lives. While confining every person to his or her residence was intended to contain the epidemic, it also had the unintended effect of making the household the most likely site of violence during this period—households that were already home to a great deal of conflict.[114] The harsh and rapid confinement measures took place in the country within a context that forced together individuals whose relationships with one another may have already been conflictual and/or abusive, while simultaneously isolating them from help.[115] These problems are exacerbated by chronic alcohol and drug abuse and well as high unemployment rates.

The exact extent of GVB in South Africa during the lockdown period remains an issue. At the start of lockdown in March 2020, 87,000 cases of GBV and interpersonal violence was reported in the country,[116] which indicated a significant increase compared to pre-COVID-19.[117] However, subsequently three issues with this figure should be noted.

First, On 2 April 2020 whilst the Minister announced that 87,000 cases related to GBV had been made to the police in the first week of the lockdown,[118] it must be noted that on 5 April, three days after this announcement, the Minister corrected himself and indicated that the figure of 87,000, referred to the total number of calls made to the GBVCC for all of 2019.[119] However, despite this anomaly, the number of cases reported by grassroots organizations for 2020 were higher than the previous year.[120] In figures, approximately 2230 GBV cases had been reported during the first week of the national lockdown.[121] This figure was supplemented by the national Gender-Based Violence Command Centre (GBVCC)[122] which reported triple the

---

[112]Where 30.4 million people or 56% of the population lived on R1 227 or less a month in 2019 (BusinessTechSA (2017), while the top 10% of earners took home 65% of all income (Mail & Guardian (2019, November 19).

[113]See, also, Daily Maverick: ISS Today (2020, April 6).

[114]Vetten (2021).

[115]Vetten (2021).

[116]The South African (2020, April 3).

[117]Leburu-Masigo and Kgadima (2020).

[118]IOL News (2020b, April 2); Vetten (2021).

[119]News24 (2020, April 5).

[120]Corradi (2021).

[121]Daily Maverick: ISS Today (2020, April 6).

[122]The GBVCC, along with Lifeline's "Stop GBV" helpline, was one of the two national tollfree helplines in operation during the lockdown.

usual number of calls.[123] In contrast, in 2017 the GBVCC received a total of 182,354 calls, where 1047 (or 0.6%) calls amounted to GBV cases.[124] In 2018/19 the GBVCC received 102,286 calls where 6905 (or 6.8%) of these were actual cases, of which 2257 were GBV cases.[125] What is important to note is that this figure represented 2.2% of all calls and 32.7% of all cases. In recognition and confirmation of the seriousness of GBVF in South Africa President Ramaphosa indicated in one of his addresses to the nation that every three hours, a woman loses her life due to GBV in the country.[126]

Second, the reports did not provide disaggregated data as to the gender of the aggressor nor did it specify the types of interpersonal violence and GBV reported, although it has been widely reported that most interpersonal violence is perpetrated by males.[127] The lack of disaggregated data reduces policy effectiveness and does not allow for progress towards the protection of the rights of women and girls to be monitored.[128] It also impacts on the ability of members of the public to effectively monitor whether perpetrators have been held accountable for their actions through the criminal justice system. The creation and maintenance of an effective database, which also ensures that the details of crimes committed against such individuals are comprehensively captured, should be a priority for government.[129]

Third, whilst some reports indicated an increase in GBV others revealed a decline of about 69% in the number of cases reported to SAPS in March and April 2020.[130] Administration data reported by SAPS does not represent the prevalence of GBV in South Africa, as there is a possibility of underreporting by the victims of violence during this period.[131] The decline in reporting or underreporting to SAPS during the COVID-19 pandemic could be partly due to fear of going to a police station during the lockdown, fear of repercussions of reporting an aggressor whom the victim is in lockdown with, or lack of privacy to report to the incident during the lockdown.

In 2021, Asia recorded the largest number of female intimate partner and family related killings with an estimated 17,800 victims, followed by 17,200 in Africa, 7500 in the Americas 2500 in Europe, and 300 in Oceania. Adjusted for total population size, the available data shows that, in 2021, 2.5 women and girls per 100,000 were killed by an intimate partner or family member in Africa, compared with 1.4 in the Americas, 1.2 in Oceania, 0.8 in Asia, and 0.6 in Europe.[132] Once

[123] IOL News (2020a, April 2). For more information, see Department of Justice and Constitutional Development (2019).

[124] Department of Justice and Constitutional Development (2019).

[125] Department of Justice and Constitutional Development (2019).

[126] News24 (2022a, November 1).

[127] Nduna and Tshona (2021).

[128] South African Human Rights Commission (2018)

[129] South African Human Rights Commission (2017).

[130] ISS Africa (2020, June 26).

[131] Vetten (2021).

[132] United Nations Office on Drugs and Crime (2022a).

again it must be noted that while Asia is the region with the largest absolute number of killings, Africa is the region with the highest level of violence relative to the size of its female population.[133] The finding of this 2021 report shows that in 2021 more than five women or girls are killed every hour by someone in their own family. This year's figures also show that over the past decade, the overall number of female homicides have remained largely unchanged, underscoring the urgency to prevent and respond to this scourge with stronger actions. While these numbers are alarmingly high, the true scale of femicide may be much higher. In many cases, only gender related killings perpetrated by an intimate partner or family member are counted as femicides. However, the evidence shows that gender-related killings take place in many contexts beyond the private sphere.[134]

Of the estimated 81,100 female homicides in 2021, roughly four in ten have no contextual information to allow them to be identified and counted as gender-related killings or femicide. During the same year, it is reported that approximately 45,000 women and girls worldwide were killed by intimate partners or other family members.[135] The availability and accuracy of data on gender-related killings committed in the public sphere are particularly scarce, making it difficult to quantify and inform prevention policies for these types of killings. The large share of female homicides worldwide where no contextual information is available highlights the urgent need for national authorities to move beyond a crime statistics approach where homicide events are simply counted, to an approach where contextual characteristics of homicides (such as the victim-perpetrator relationship) are recorded on a routine basis.

To strengthen the collection and harmonization of data on gender-related killings of women and girls globally, UNODC and UN Women recently developed the Statistical framework for measuring the gender-related killings or femicide, which was approved by the United Nation's Statistical Commission in March 2022.[136] The lack of sufficient contextual information also highlights why it is difficult to obtain a precise estimate of the global number of gender-related killings of women and girls. For several countries and for many years, gender-related female homicides can be estimated only through statistical modelling and based on information from neighboring countries or other years. Regional estimates therefore also come with intervals of uncertainty, which are relatively wider in regions with limited data such as Africa, Asia, and Oceania.[137]

[133] Differences in absolute numbers between world regions are also a reflection of differences in the size of the regional populations, so it is important to also examine the extent of the problem in terms of rates (per 100,000 female population).

[134] They can be related to rape or sexual violence by someone unknown to the victim; linked to harmful practices such as female genital mutilation or so-called "honor"-based violence; a result of hate crimes linked to sexual orientation or gender identity; or connected with armed conflict, gangs, human trafficking, and other forms of organized crime.

[135] See United Nations Office on Drugs and Crime (2022a).

[136] United Nations Office on Drugs and Crime (2022b).

[137] United Nations Office on Drugs and Crime (2022a).

Whilst only one in five homicides at the global level are perpetrated by an intimate partner or other family member, women and girls make up most of those deaths. Looking at victim/perpetrator disaggregation of 36% male versus 64% female victims, the large disparity in the share of male and female victims of homicide committed by intimate partners or other family members is clear. While many intentional homicide victims are male, many of the victims of intimate partner/family-related homicide are women.[138] Additionally, women continue to bear the greatest burden in terms of intimate partner violence. The disparity between the share of male and female victims of homicide perpetrated exclusively by an intimate partner is substantially larger than for victims of homicide perpetrated by intimate partners or other family members. Approximately 82% were female victims and 18% were male victims.[139]

A study conducted by Africa Check,[140] using the WHO[141] female homicide data to highlight the magnitude of femicide in South Africa, compared to the world average contained important data on male homicides in South Africa. Unsurprisingly at 36.4 per 100,000 people, South Africa has one of the world's highest murder rates.[142] It was found that most murders result from conflict between young adult men who made up 81% of the 21,022 murder victims recorded by the police in 2018/19.[143] Looking at the global rates of homicide in 2020, the figures also indicate that the vast majority of all homicide victims worldwide (approximately 80%)[144] were men or boys, but the sex composition of homicide victims differs markedly depending on the context. It was highlighted in the study that women and girls account for only one tenth of all homicide victims perpetrated in the public sphere, yet they bear a disproportionate burden of lethal violence perpetrated in the home. In 58% of all killings perpetrated by intimate partners or other family members, a woman or girl was the victim.[145]

In comparison, South Africa's homicide rate for men consistently stood at more than three times the rate of women during the period 2000–2015.[146] The data suggests that men are three times more likely to be victims of murder in South Africa compared to women. The most recent global database on the murder

138 Minello and Dalla-Zuanna (2019).

139 United Nations Office on Drugs and Crime (2019a).

140 Makou (2017).

141 The WHO calculates a femicide rate based on deaths from interpersonal violence for the whole female population—including women and girls. Their latest estimate is a female interpersonal violence death rate of 12.1 per 100 000 in 2016.

142 BBC News (2019b, September 12).

143 SAPS (2020a).

144 Corradi (2021).

145 United Nations Office on Drugs and Crime (2020b).

146 On the day of their release, these statistics were already at least six months out of date. That means that the crime situation at the relevant date, particularly at local level, could be very different to that described by these statistics.

of females (including adult women and girls) is from the WHO.[147] In 2016, the age-standardized interpersonal violence death rate for the female population in South Africa was 12.5 per 100,000. This was 4.8 times the global average rate of 2.6. South Africa had the fourth highest female interpersonal violence death rate out of the 183 countries listed by the WHO in 2016.

While the number of murders committed each year is an important indicator, it does not provide insight into the relative risk faced by a group. To determine whether risk is increasing or decreasing you must calculate the murder rate.[148] The murder rate for adult women is calculated using the number of victims from the police and population estimates from Statistics South Africa (Stas SA). Based on these figures, the adult women murder rate was 15.2 in 2017/18. This means that there were 15.2 murders for every 100,000 adult women in South Africa. In 2019/20, a total of 2695 women were murdered in South Africa—down from 2771 in 2018/19.[149] This confirms the estimation that a woman is murdered every three hours,[150] which is almost five times the global average.

These findings show that while the overwhelming majority of male homicides occur outside the private sphere, for women and girls the most dangerous place is the home.[151] Many of the victims of femicide are killed by their current and former partners, but they are also killed by fathers, brothers, mothers, sisters, and other family members because of prejudices, expected roles and status as women. The death of those killed by intimate partners does not usually result from random or spontaneous acts, but rather from the culmination of prior gender-related violence.[152] Of importance, it is jealousy and fear of abandonment which remain the main motives of these killings.[153] The prevention and elimination of gender-related killings of women and girls require grasping the full dimension of this crime and disentangling its complexity. Gender-related killings are often not recorded as such and where they are, they lack consistency and completeness. Improving the quality, availability, and timeliness of data on this phenomenon helps to assess progress or

---

[147] The WHO advises using "age-standardised rates" for global comparisons. This rate adjusts for differences in the age distribution of the population, assuming a standard population for all countries.

[148] Wilkinson (2019).

[149] SAPS (2020a).

[150] eNCA (2020, July 31). Police Minister Bheki Cele presented the annual crime statistics to Parliament, from April 2019 to March 2020. This period falls just outside the country's national lockdown period. Most noteworthy is the rise in sexual offenses crimes, including rape and sexual assault.

[151] Although intimate partner/family-related homicide is the most important factor in understanding the magnitude of female deaths resulting from intentional homicide, this form of homicide only accounts for a relatively small proportion of all (male and female) homicides recorded globally. Bagwell-Gray et al. (2015).

[152] United Nations Office on Drugs and Crime (2019a).

[153] Johnson et al. (2020). See, also, Belknap et al. (2012).

setbacks and support evidence-based policy making and an effective criminal justice response.

5.7 Trends in South Africa

5.7.1 *Study from South Africa's National Femicide Study and Police Statistics*

5.7.1.1 National Studies

In 2017, South Africa's third national femicide study[154] was conducted. The study examined medical and police investigation data from a random sample of 81 urban and rural settings across the country. It compared results with the 1999 and 2009 studies, the first two national femicide[155] studies conducted. This evidence examined women murdered in 2017 and compares these findings with those of the 1999 and 2009 studies. In so doing, it sought to address the key question of if there is any evidence that the national efforts to combat GBV in South Africa are having any impact on the problem of femicide?

Looking at the statistics, the 2017 results showed that 2407 women aged 14 and above were murdered in South Africa, averaging almost 7 women a day, and 1029 were murdered by an intimate partner.[156] This is similar to figures in 2009 where 2363 aged 14 and above were murdered in South Africa. The 2009 figure of 3793, was however significantly lower than the number of women killed in 1999. The study found that the rate of intimate partner femicide declined from 8.8/100,000 population in 1999 to 4.8/100,000 population. South Africa's overall femicide rate for women and girls 14 years and older has declined over 18 years.[157] From a high of 24.7 per 100,000 population in 1999 South Africa's femicide rate almost halved to 12.9 in 2009,[158] and the overall femicide dropped even further in 2017 to 11.2 / 100,000 population which is less than half the estimated rate for 1999 of 24.7/

[154]The Gender & Health Research Unit (GHRU) of the South African MRC has been studying femicide in South Africa for more than 20 years, with previous research showing that in 1999 four women, and in 2009 three women were killed every day by their husband or boyfriend (intimate partner). This evidence brief summarises the findings of the third National Femicide Study, which examined women murdered in 2017 and compares these findings with those of the 1999 and 2009 studies. In so doing, it seeks to address the key question: *Is there any evidence that the national efforts to combat GBV in South Africa are having any impact on the problem of femicide?* See Abrahams et al. (2022, March 8).

[155]The study considered femicide rates because it was the best statistics for comparison across the study years as population growth is taken into account in calculating rates.

[156]Firearms Control Briefing (2021).

[157]Abrahams et al. (2022, March 8).

[158]To contextualise these figures, SA's national murder rate declined from 38.4 per 100,000 population in 2009 to 34.5 in 2017. Prinsloo et al. (2021, September).

100,000. Similarly, the intimate partner femicide rate halved from 9.1/100,000 in 1999 to 4.6/100,000 in 2017. An even larger decline is seen for non-intimate partner femicide over the 18 years from 11.5/10,000 to 4.5/100,000 in 2017.[159]

When a comparison is made between the proportion of intimate partner femicide and non-intimate partner femicide, intimate partner femicide remains the leading cause of murder of women in South Africa. The number of women and girls aged 14 years and older that were killed by an intimate partner in 2017 remained unchanged from 2009. In both years, 3 women were murdered per day by an intimate partner, down from 4 a day in 1999.[160] The same age[161] pattern was observed across the three studies.[162] In 2017 the mean age of all femicide was 37 years (interquartile range 26–51). Women murdered by intimate partners were younger (mean age 30 years: interquartile range: 24–37) than those murdered by non-intimate partners (mean age 35 years: interquartile range: 26–54).

South Africa's overall femicide rate has more than halved since 1999, dropping from 24.7 per 100,000 that year to 12.9 in 2009 and 11.2 in 1999. This continual decline is mirrored in South Africa's intimate partner femicide rate, which dropped from 8.8 per 100,000 (1999) to 5.6 (2009) to 4.8 (2017). In contrast, non-intimate partner femicide increased from 4.2 per 100,000 in 2009 to 4.4 in 2017, after halving from 8.6 in 1999.[163] Femicides reported in 2017 stood at 2407, a significant drop from the 3793 total recorded in 1999. While intimate partner femicide dropped from 57.1% in 2009 to 52.3% in 2017, women and girls aged 14 and older were still more likely to be killed by an intimate partner than a non-intimate family member, friend, acquaintance, or stranger.[164] For example, statistics showed that of the 2407 deaths in 2017, 1033 were killed by an intimate partner.[165]

The study also looked at each province's femicide rates. When compared to national rates, in 2017 the Eastern Cape reported higher intimate and non-intimate partner femicide rates. The Western Cape, Northern Cape, Free State and KwaZulu-Natal also had much higher rates of overall femicide and intimate partner femicide rates compared to national and other provincial rates. The two provinces with the lowest overall femicide rates were Limpopo and Mpumalanga which were significantly lower than the overall South African femicide rate. Looking at the rape-murders the study indicated an overall decline in the proportion of suspected rape-murders between the three studies. In 2009 there was a substantial increase from

[159] Abrahams et al. (2022, March 8).

[160] Firearms Control Briefing (2021).

[161] The mean age of all femicide cases is 37.7 years. Women murdered by intimate partners were younger (mean age 32.3) than those murdered by non-intimate partners (mean age 40.7).

[162] Abrahams et al. (2022, March 8). It must be noted that one of the major limitations identified is that across the three studies the intimate partner femicide and non-intimate partner femicide rates do not add up to the overall Femicide rate because of missing South African Police data. Police dockets could not be located for 502 femicides in 1999, 38 in 2009 and 379 in 2017.

[163] Abrahams et al. (2022, March 8).

[164] Firearms Control Briefing (2021).

[165] News24 (2022a, November 1).

1999 in suspected rape-murders among non-intimate partner femicides, but in the 2017 study, the levels of suspected rape-murders decreased to the same level of 1999, i.e., 13.2% in 1999 and 13.6% in 2017.

GBVF does not occur in a vacuum and the statistics need to be read alongside other relevant data to understand its causes as well as the reasons behind changes in the number of cases. The reports in decline must be considered in light of the limitations relating to data discussed above and the fact that the study in question noted with concern that across the three studies the intimate partner femicide and non-intimate partner femicide rates do not add up to the overall femicide rate because of missing SAPS data as well as the fact that police dockets could not be located for 502 femicides in 1999, 38 in 2009 and 379 in 2017.[166] The 2017 study also showed an increase in missing information related to the police investigation, highlighting that the missing dockets increased from 1.6% in 2009 to 9.1% in 2017.

Police interviews during COVID-19 challenges resulted in police interviews not being completed. Another key finding of the study was that there was an increase in cases where the perpetrators were not identified during the investigation. These findings are indicative of a decline in the quality of police investigations of femicide cases.[167]

The findings in this report provide evidence that South Africa is reaping the rewards from community-based activism and the government's policy and practice measures aimed at reducing GBV. It is particularly interesting, as it has shown a greater decline in intimate than non-intimate partner femicides. However, despite this decline, South Africa's femicide rate is still five-six times the global average, indicating the continued urgency of interventions to address widespread violence against women. It is imperative that there must be a strengthening of institutional capacity, such as police services, to prevent and appropriately respond to femicide in the country. The fourth Femicide study data collection started in November 2021 and will review Femicide during COVID-19. It is therefore still uncertain if the hard lock-down conditions increased femicide, or if the trend of decreasing interpersonal violence overall will be seen for femicide in the country as well. What is important is that the research conducted over three decades by the SA MRC can be used to understand and prevent GBVF.

5.7.1.2 Police Statistics

In an attempt to prioritize GBVF,[168] the 2019/2020 crime statistics, released by SAPS highlighted the relationship between the victims and their killers in the cases recorded that year.[169] The relationship was known in only one in five of the total

---

[166] South African Medical Research Council (2022, March 8).

[167] South African Medical Research Council (2022, March 8).

[168] SAPS (2021b).

[169] SAPS (2019).

murders—of both males and females—that year. Of the 3790 cases where the relationship was known, 16% of the victims were murdered by a boyfriend or girlfriend, 10% by a family member, 4% by a spouse and 2% by an ex-boyfriend or girlfriend. Specifically, SAPS reported that 1 482 (6.9%) of the murder cases for 2019/2020 were domestic related.

Furthermore, reported sexual offences increased to 53,293 in 2019/20 from 52,420 in 2018/19. Most of these were cases of rape. The rate of sexual offences decreased slightly from 90.9 per 100,000 in 2018/19 to 90.8 in 2019/20.[170] In 2020, SAPS started to release crime statistics on a quarterly basis. During April to June 2020,[171] SAPS reported that 55% of domestic violence-related murders[172] were perpetrated by husbands or boyfriends.

Looking at first quarter of 2021, SAPS recorded that 558 women were murdered but this number increased in the first quarter of 2022, with 855 women being murdered.[173] Between July and September 2021, 897 women were murdered in South Africa.[174] For the same period in 2022, that number increased to 989, an increase of 10.3%.[175] The statistics show that more than 1200 women were victims of attempted murder between July and September 2022. Attempted murder of women went up from 1155 to 1277, indicating an increase of 10.6%. Alarmingly, 13,701 women were victims of assault with intent to cause grievous bodily harm (GBH) between July and September 2022, an increase of 1877 incidents from the same period in 2021. This marks an increase of 15.9%.[176] A substantial percentage increase was accordingly recorded for murder, attempted murder, and assault GBH against women.[177]

During the third quarter of the 2020/2021 reporting period, more than 9500 cases of GBV and 13,000 cases of domestic violence were reported. Over the same period, 897 women were murdered (an increase of 7.7% compared to the same period in

[170] SAPS (2019).

[171] SAPS (2020b).

[172] Even though SAPS did not separate the gender of the murder victims for their analysis, the breakdown is similar to the relationships found in the media reports about women murdered: where there was a known relationship between the victim and the killer, the highest proportion of victims were murdered by their current intimate partner. See Mail & Guardian (2021b, April 14).

[173] Police Minister General Bheki Cele released the quarter two crime statistics of the 2022/2023 season on Wednesday, 23 November 2022. See South African Government (2022, November 23). The numbers released are worrying as there has been a significant increase in crimes against women and children. The report indicated that within the three months, over 13,000 women were victims of assault with intent to cause grievous bodily harm. See, also, SAPS (2022b, September).

[174] The statistics cover the second quarter of 2022/23—between 1 July and 30 September. During a presentation of these figures, it was noted by Police Commissioner Cele that the figures were in comparison with the same period in 2021 when South Africa was still under COVID-19 lockdown levels 2, 3, and 4.

[175] SAPS (2022a, April). See, also, Mail & Guardian (2022, November 29); SAPS (2022b, September).

[176] SAPS (2022b, September).

[177] South African Government (2022, November 23).

2020), while sexual offence cases increased by 4.7% and incidents of rape rose by 7.1% compared to the second quarter of 2020.[178]

Importantly, it should be noted that were decreases are indicated it does not mean that these crime figures are indicative of a reduction in the crime rate. The figures remain skewed due to the comparing of figures from a period of no lockdown restrictions to a period where the country was placed under hard lockdown. For example, between January and March 2021, it was reported that there was an overall decline of 8.5% in contact crimes including assault, sexual offences,[179] common assault and robbery, with only two criminal types in this category recording an increase.[180] These were murder and attempted murder, which recorded an 8.4% and 8.7% increase, respectively. A sample of 6893 of the rape incidents revealed that 4 130 of such incidents took place at the home of the victim or the home of the alleged rapist.[181] Once again, this decrease needs to be considered critically since the country was in a higher level of lockdown at the start of the year.

During the first quarter of 2022 alone SAPS reported that there were 10 818 rape cases.[182] In addition, 1 895 cases of sexual assault were reported to police between July and September 2022. This is an increase of 142 reported cases (8.1%) compared to the same period last year, which was 1753.[183] It was also determined from a sample of 8 227 rape incidents that 5 083 (62%) of these incidents occurred at the residence of the victims or perpetrators, that 1651 of the rape incidents occurred at public places such as streets, parks, and beaches and 69 people were raped at abandoned buildings.

In addition, it must be noted that not all forms of sexual violence are defined as crimes in South Africa. Much sexual harassment, for example, falls within the ambit of behavior treated as misconduct and is dealt with in terms of labor law and institutions' disciplinary codes. This location of sexual violence within different laws means that it is difficult to get a comprehensive overview of the nature and extent of reported sexual victimization in South Africa.[184] Although SAPS provides figures for some sexual offences, educational institutions and workplaces are not compelled to report on their disciplinary proceedings. As a result, some cases of sexual victimization will be hidden. Very little research has been undertaken to explore these gaps. There is also very little nationally representative data on all types of sexual offences, and in some instances, there is no information at all regarding the experiences of particular categories of victims.

[178] South African Government (2021, November 19).

[179] 9518 people were allegedly raped between that period.

[180] SAPS (2021a).

[181] SAPS (2021a).

[182] News24 (2022b, December 2).

[183] SAPS (2022b, September).

[184] Vetten (2014, November 13).

5.8 Concluding Remarks

This chapter provides a situational analysis of GBVF in South Africa because it is acknowledged that preventing and ending gender-related killings of women and girls require grasping the full dimension of this crime and disentangling its complexity. The research has found that improving the quality, availability, and timeliness of data on this phenomenon helps to assess progress or setbacks and support evidence-based policy making and an effective criminal justice response. Such data will make it easier to evaluate governments' approaches to GBV and to assess whether they are seriously attempting to combat the problem. In addition, the information provided herein is useful for those wishing to understand trends in GBVF to inform their study designs, programs, interventions, and policy implementation.

The next chapter will analyze the perceptions of crime and the fear of crime since incidences of violence and harassment are notoriously underreported, which makes official crime and police data a poor reflection of actual extent of the problem. It has been reported that the best estimates of the incidence of GBV thus come from household surveys that probe respondents' experiences.[185] The most sophisticated of these surveys ask about experiences across types of violence and in multiple spheres, such as at home and at work, on the street, with family members and with strangers, in the past year and over the course of a lifetime. Such surveys will better allow for a comprehensive overview of the experiences of differently situated women.

References

Abrahams N et al. (2022, March 8) Research brief: Decrease in femicide in South Africa: three national studies across 18 years. https://www.samrc.ac.za/reports/research-brief-decrease-femicide-south-africa-three-national-studies-across-18-years. Accessed on 25 Nov 2022

Africa Check (2015) Factsheet: South Africa's 2014/15 assault and sexual crime statistics. https://africacheck.org/fact-checks/factsheets/factsheet-south-africas-201415-assault-and-sexual-crime-statistics. Accessed on 2 Jan 2023

American Civil Liberties Union (2020) ACLU follow up letter urging COVID-19 voting legislation. https://www.aclu.org/letter/aclu-follow-letter-urging-covid-19-voting-legislation-3222020 . Accessed on 23 Apr 2023

Bagwell-Gray ME et al (2015) Intimate partner sexual violence. Trauma Violence Abuse 16(3): 316–335. https://doi.org/10.1177/1524838014557290

BBC News (2019a, September 3) France announces anti-femicide measures as 100th killing recorded. https://www.bbc.com/news/world-europe-49571327?ocid=socialflow_twitter. Accessed on 22 Feb 2023

BBC News (2019b, September 12) South Africa crime: police figures show rising murder and sexual offences. https://www.bbc.com/news/world-africa-49673944. Accessed on 3 Mar 2023

Belknap J et al (2012) Types of intimate partner homicides committed by women. Homicide Stud 16(4):359–379. https://doi.org/10.1177/1088767912461444

[185] Htun and Jensenius (2020).

Breiding MJ et al. (2015) Intimate partner violence surveillance: uniform definitions and recommended data elements. https://www.cdc.gov/violenceprevention/pdf/ipv/intimatepartnerviolence.pdf. Accessed on 28 Dec 2022

Burnes D et al (2019) Help-seeking among victims of elder abuse: findings from the national elder mistreatment study. J Gerontol Ser B 74(5):891–896. https://doi-org.ezproxy.kpu.ca:2443/10.1093/geronb/gby122

BusinessTechSA (2017) This is how much money the poorest are living on each month in South Africa. https://businesstech.co.za/news/finance/332553/this-is-how-much-money-the-poorest-are-living-on-each-month-in-south-africa/. Accessed on 8 Jan 2023

Centre for the Study of Violence and Reconciliation (2016) Gender-based violence (GBV) in South Africa: A brief review. https://www.csvr.org.za/pdf/Gender%20Based%20Violence%20in%20South%20Africa%20-%20A%20Brief%20Review.pdf. Accessed on 26 Jan 2023

Ciurria M (2018) The loss of autonomy in abused persons: psychological, moral, and legal dimensions. Humanities 7(2):48. https://doi.org/10.3390/h7020048

CNN (2021, August 30) Explainer: what is femicide and how bad is it globally? https://edition.cnn.com/2021/09/30/world/femicide-explainer-as-equals-intl-cmd/index.html. Accessed on 29 Nov 2022

Commission for Gender Equality (2022) Bi-annual SAPS report March – September 2021. https://cge.org.za/wp-content/uploads/2022/07/CGE-SAPS-REPORT.pdf. Accessed on 12 Nov 2022

Corradi C (2021) Femicide, its causes and recent trends: what do we know? European Union, Brussels

Daily Maverick: ISS Today (2020, April 6) How might the Covid-19 lockdown affect public safety in SA? https://www.dailymaverick.co.za/article/2020-04-06-how-might-the-covid-19-lockdown-affect-public-safety-in-sa/. Accessed on 7 Mar 2023

Deane T (2018) Sexual violence and the limits of laws' powers to alter behaviour: the case of South Africa. J Int Women's Stud 19(2):84–103

Deane T (2021) Marrying young: limiting the impact of a crisis on the high prevalence of child marriages in Niger. Laws 10(3):61. https://doi.org/10.3390/laws10030061

Department of Justice and Constitutional Development (2019) Annual Reports Implementation of the Criminal Law (Sexual Offences and Related Matters) Amendment Act, 2007 (Act No. 32 of 2007). https://www.justice.gov.za/vg/sxo/SORMA-Report-2019-2020.pdf. Accessed on 4 Jan 2023

Dobbin F, Kalev A (2016) Why diversity programs fail. Harv Bus Rev 94(7–8):1–15

eNCA (2020, July 31) Police Minister Bheki Cele briefs media on the latest crime stats. https://www.youtube.com/watch?v=eN5vvTCYhAQ. Accessed on 16 Mar 2023

Femicide Census (2018) Reports – Femicide census. https://www.femicidecensus.org/reports/. Accessed on 28 Nov 2022

Firearms Control Briefing (2021) Briefing 1 of 2022: Femicide in South Africa over 18 years. https://gfsa.org.za/2022/03/30/briefing-1-of-2022-femicide-in-south-africa-over-18-years/. Accessed on 27 Nov 2022

First J et al (2017) Intimate partner violence and disasters. Affilia 32(3):390–403. https://doi.org/10.1177/0886109917706338

García-Moreno C et al. (2005) WHO multi-country study on women's health and domestic violence against women initial results on prevalence, health outcomes and women's responses. https://apps.who.int/iris/handle/10665/43309. Accessed on 4 Aug 2023

Garcia-Vergara E et al (2022) A comprehensive analysis of factors associated with intimate partner femicide: a systematic review. Int J Environ Res Public Health 19(12):7336. https://doi.org/10.3390/ijerph19127336

Gibbs A et al (2020) New learnings on drivers of men's physical and/or sexual violence against their female partners, and women's experiences of this, and the implications for prevention interventions. Glob Health Action 13(1):1739845. https://doi.org/10.1080/16549716.2020.1739845

Gourley R (2017) Femicide and international women's rights. https://theglobalamericans.org/reports/femicide-international-womens-rights/. Accessed on 30 Nov 2022

Gurm B et al (2020) Making sense of a global pandemic: relationship violence & working together towards a violence free society. Kwantlen Polytechnic University, Surrey BC

Head T (2019, September 4). Femicide rates: South Africa vs the rest of the world. https://www.thesouthafrican.com/news/how-many-women-killed-south-africa-femicide/. Accessed on 26 Nov 2022

Heise LL, Kotsadam A (2015) Cross-national and multilevel correlates of partner violence: an analysis of data from population-based surveys. Lancet Glob Health 3(6):e332–e340. https://doi.org/10.1016/s2214-109x(15)00013-3

Holmes C, Hunt S (2017) Indigenous communities and family violence: changing the conversation. https://www.ccnsa-nccah.ca/docs/emerging/RPT-FamilyViolence-Holmes-Hunt-EN.pdf. Accessed on 14 Dec 2023

Htun M, Jensenius FR (2020) Fighting violence against women: laws, norms & challenges ahead. Daedalus 149(1):144–159. https://doi.org/10.1162/daed_a_01779

International Growth Centre (2020, May 19) The shadow pandemic: gender-based violence and COVID-19. https://www.theigc.org/blogs/covid-19/shadow-pandemic-gender-based-violence-and-covid-19. Accessed on 22 Apr 2023

IOL News (2020a, April 2) GBV Centre calls triple during lockdown, 1st for Women steps up to help. https://www.iol.co.za/news/south-africa/western-cape/gbv-centre-calls-triple-during-lockdown-1st-for-women-steps-up-to-help-45995727. Accessed on 5 Mar 2023

IOL News (2020b, April 2) SAPS received 87 000 gender-based violence calls during first week of lockdown - Cele. https://www.iol.co.za/news/south-africa/saps-received-87-000-gender-based-violence-calls-during-first-week-of-lockdown-cele-46024648. Accessed on 8 Mar 2023

ISS Africa (2020, June 26) Domestic violence during COVID-19: are we asking the right questions? https://issafrica.org/iss-today/domestic-violence-during-covid-19-are-we-asking-the-right-questions. Accessed on 10 Mar 2023

Jody-Ann R et al (2022) Jamaica case study: gender-based violence impunity in gang-affected contexts. University of Chicago, Agency for International Development

Johnson L et al (2020) Do you believe your partner is capable of killing you? An examination of female IPV survivors' perceptions of fatality risk indicators. J Interp Viol 37(1–2): 088626052091627. https://doi.org/10.1177/0886260520916273

Kendall T (2020) A synthesis of evidence on the collection and use of administrative data on violence against women: background paper for the development of global guidance. https://giwps.georgetown.edu/resource/a-synthesis-of-evidence-on-the-collection-and-use-of-administrative-data-on-violence-against-women-background-paper-for-the-development-of-global-guidance/. Accessed on 4 Oct 2022

Leburu-Masigo GE, Kgadima NP (2020) Gender-based violence during the covid-19 pandemic in South Africa: guidelines for social work practice. Gend Behav 18(4):16618–16629

Machisa MT (2011) The war at home: the Gauteng GBV indicators research study: gender Links and the South African Medical Research Council. https://www.researchgate.net/publication/299627061_The_War_at_Home_The_Gauteng_GBV_Indicators_Research_Study_Gender_Links_and_the_South_African_Medical_Research_Council. Accessed on 16 Nov 2022

Mail & Guardian (2019, November 19) Why South Africa is the world's most unequal society. https://mg.co.za/article/2019-11-19-why-sa-is-the-worlds-most-unequal-society/. Accessed on 8 Mar 2023

Mail & Guardian (2021a, June 22) Facts and figures: global domestic violence numbers. https://mg.co.za/news/2021-06-22-facts-and-figures-global-domestic-violence-numbers/#:~:text=Some%2016%25%20of%20women%20aged. Accessed on 22 Nov 2022

Mail & Guardian (2021b, April 14) #SayHerName: the faces of South Africa's femicide epidemic. https://mg.co.za/health/2021-04-14-sayhername-the-faces-of-south-africas-femicide-epidemic/. Accessed on 24 Feb 2023

Mail & Guardian (2022, November 29) Good, bad & ugly: how SA's fight against GBV & femicide is going. https://mg.co.za/news/2022-11-29-good-bad-ugly-how-sas-fight-against-gbv-femicide-is-going/#:~:text=Between%20April%202020%20and%20September. Accessed on 4 Jan 2023

Makou G (2017) Femicide in South Africa: 3 numbers about the murdering of women investigated. https://africacheck.org/fact-checks/reports/femicide-south-africa-3-numbers-about-murdering-women-investigated. Accessed on 13 Oct 2022

Masuku S (2016) For better and for worse: South African crime trends in 2002. South African Crime Quarterly 3. https://doi.org/10.17159/2413-3108/2003/i3a1073

Matias A et al (2020) Intimate partner homicide: a meta-analysis of risk factors. Aggress Violent Behav 50:101358. https://doi.org/10.1016/J.AVB.2019.101358

Mc Cafferty R (2003) Murder in South Africa: a comparison of past and present. https://www.gunowners.org/fs0304/. Accessed on 4 Jan 2023

Minello A, Dalla-Zuanna G (2019) A gender geography of intentional homicide within and outside of the family: male and female murders in Europe, the US and Canada (2003–15). Eur J Criminol 18(6):147737081988425. https://doi.org/10.1177/1477370819884251

Murphy M et al (2020) Nowhere to go: disclosure and help-seeking behaviors for survivors of violence against women and girls in South Sudan. Confl Health 14(6). https://doi.org/10.1186/s13031-020-0257-2

Nduna M, Tshona SO (2021) Domesticated poly-violence against women during the 2020 Covid-19 lockdown in South Africa. Psychol Stud 66. https://doi.org/10.1007/s12646-021-00616-9

Newburn T (2017) Criminology, 3rd edn. Routledge

News24 (2020, April 5) Bheki Cele: "I wish alcohol ban could be extended beyond lockdown." https://www.news24.com/citypress/News/bheki-cele-i-wish-alcohol-ban-could-be-extended-beyond-lockdown-20200405?isapp=true. Accessed on 6 Mar 2023

News24 (2022a, November 1) SA's crime stats tell a story of a nation at war with its women, children – Ramaphosa. https://www.news24.com/news24/politics/government/sas-crime-stats-tell-a-story-of-a-nation-at-war-with-its-women-children-ramaphosa-20221101. Accessed on 9 Jan 2023

News24 (2022b, December 2) Violence against women is staggeringly high in South Africa. https://www.news24.com/w24/selfcare/love/her_story/violence-against-women-is-staggeringly-high-in-south-africa-20221202. Accessed on 4 Jan 2023

NUMBEO (2021) Crime index by country 2021 mid-year. https://www.numbeo.com/crime/rankings_by_country.jsp?title=2021-mid. Accessed on 12 Dec 2022

Palermo T et al (2014) Tip of the iceberg: reporting and gender-based violence in developing countries. Am J Epidemiol 179(5):602–612. https://doi.org/10.1093/aje/kwt295

Paluck EL et al (2010) Social norms marketing aimed at gender based violence: a literature review and critical assessment. International Rescue Committee, New York

Perrin N et al (2019) Social norms and beliefs about gender based violence scale: a measure for use with gender based violence prevention programs in low-resource and humanitarian settings. Confl Health 13(6). https://doi.org/10.1186/s13031-019-0189-x

Peterman A et al. (2020) Pandemics and violence against women and children. https://www.cgdev.org/sites/default/files/pandemics-and-vawg-april2.pdf. Accessed on 24 Apr 2023

Prinsloo M et al. (2021, September). The 2nd injury mortality survey: a national study of injury mortality levels and causes in South Africa in 2017. https://www.samrc.ac.za/research-reports/2nd-injury-mortality-survey-national-study-injury-mortality-levels-and-causes. Accessed on 23 Nov 2022

Prochuck A (2018) We are here: women's experiences of the barriers to reporting sexual assault. http://www.westcoastleaf.org/wp-content/uploads/2018/10/West-Coast-Leaf-dismantling-web-final.pdf. Accessed on 22 Dec 2023

Rajah V, Osborn M (2020) Understanding women's resistance to intimate partner violence: a scoping review. Trauma Viol Abuse 23(5):152483801989734. https://doi.org/10.1177/1524838019897345

SAPS (2018) Crime statistics: integrity. https://www.saps.gov.za/services/crimestats.php. Accessed on 8 Jan 2023

SAPS (2019) Crime situation in Republic of South Africa twelve (12) months (April to March 2019-20) https://www.saps.gov.za/services/april_to_march_2019_20_presentation.pdf. Accessed on 25 Feb 2023

SAPS (2020a) Crime situation in the Republic of South Africa twelve (12) months (April to March 2018-19). https://static.pmg.org.za/190919saps.pdf. Accessed on 4 Mar 2023

SAPS (2020b) Crime situation in Republic of South Africa three months (April to June 2020-21). https://www.saps.gov.za/services/April_June%202020_2021.pdf. Accessed on 25 Feb 2023

SAPS (2021a) Crime statistics Republic of South Africa: Fourth quarter 2020/2021 (January to March 2021). https://www.saps.gov.za/services/fourth_quarter_2020_21_crimestats.pdf. Accessed on 4 Jan 2023

SAPS (2021b) Speaking notes delivered by Police Minister at the release of quarter 2 crime statistics 2022/2023. https://www.saps.gov.za/newsroom/msspeechdetail.php?nid=43497. Accessed on 13 Aug 2023

SAPS (2022a, April) Police recorded crime statistics Republic of South Africa: First quarter of 2022/2023 financial year (April and June 2022). https://www.saps.gov.za/services/downloads/April-2022_23-presentation.pdf. Accessed on 9 Jan 2023

SAPS (2022b, September) Police recorded crime statistics Republic of South Africa: Second quarter of 2022/2023 financial year (July to September 2022). https://www.saps.gov.za/services/downloads/July-to-September-2022-Presentation.pdf. Accessed on 9 Jan 2023

Sherwood J et al. (2022) A rapid assessment of violence crisis services during COVID-19 lockdowns in South Africa. https://www.ohchr.org/sites/default/files/2022-01/south-afri-gbv-rapid-assess.pdf. Accessed on 8 Mar 2023

Siziba E et al (2022) In their own voices- understanding GBV in Zimbabwe: evidence from a survivor's perspective. J Afr Stud Dev 14(4):154–159. https://doi.org/10.5897/JASD2022.0665

South African Government (2021, November 19) Minister Bheki Cele: quarter two crime statistics 2021/2022. https://www.gov.za/speeches/speaking-notes-delivered-police-minister-general%C2%A0bheki-cele-mp-occasion-release-%C2%A0quarter. Accessed on 21 Nov 2022

South African Government (2022, November 23) Minister General Bheki Cele: quarter two crime statistics 2022/23. https://www.gov.za/speeches/minister-general-bheki-cele-quarter-two-crime-statistics-20222023-23-nov-2022-0000#:~:text=7%20004%20people%20were%20killed,Lockdown%20four%2C%20three%20and%20two. Accessed on 6 Aug 2023

South African Human Rights Commission (2017) SAHRC Submission to DOJCS regarding Hate Crimes & Hate Speech Bill. https://www.sahrc.org.za/home/21/files/SAHRC%20Submission%20to%20DOJCS%20re.%20Hate%20Crimes%20&%20Hate%20Speech%20Bill-31.1.17%20FINAL.pdf. Accessed on 13 Feb 2023

South African Human Rights Commission (2018) Unpacking the gaps and challenges in addressing gender-based violence in South Africa. https://www.sahrc.org.za/home/21/files/SAHRC%20GBV%20Research%20Brief%20Publication.pdf. Accessed on 15 Feb 2023

South African Medical Research Council (2022, March 8) Research of nearly two decades reveals that intimate partner femicide is declining in South Africa. https://www.samrc.ac.za/media-release/research-nearly-two-decades-reveals-intimate-partner-femicide-declining-south-africa. Accessed on 25 Nov 2022

Sowetan Live (2022, February 21) Latest GBV and femicide crime stats not "accurate," says Powa. https://www.sowetanlive.co.za/news/south-africa/2022-02-21-latest-gbv-and-femicide-crime-stats-not-accurate-says-powa/. Accessed on 13 Nov 2022

Ssanyu JM et al (2022) Reporting of sexual and gender-based violence and associated factors among survivors in Mayuge, Uganda. Afr Health Sci 22(1):62–68. https://doi.org/10.4314/ahs.v22i1.8

St. Vil NM et al (2016) A qualitative study of survival strategies used by low-income black women who experience intimate partner violence. Soc Work 62(1):63–71. https://doi.org/10.1093/sw/sww080

Stamatel JP (2014) Explaining variations in female homicide victimization rates across Europe. Eur J Criminol 11(5):578–600. https://doi.org/10.1177/1477370814537941
Stark L, Ager A (2011) A systematic review of prevalence studies of gender-based violence in complex emergencies. Trauma Viol Abuse 12(3):127–134. https://doi.org/10.1177/1524838011404252
Stark L, Landis D (2016) Violence against children in humanitarian settings: a literature review of population-based approaches. Soc Sci Med 152:125–137. https://doi.org/10.1016/j.socscimed.2016.01.052
Stats SA (2014, December 4) Victims of crime survey 2013/14. http://beta2.statssa.gov.za/publications/P0341/P03412013.pdf. Accessed on 9 Jan 2023
Stats SA (2017, September 28) Victims of crime survey, release 2016/17. https://www.statssa.gov.za/publications/P0341/P03412016.pdf. Accessed on 4 Nov 2022
Stats SA (2018) Crime statistics series Volume V crime against women in South Africa: an in-depth analysis of the victims of crime survey data 2018. https://www.statssa.gov.za/publications/Report-03-40-05/Report-03-40-05June2018.pdf. Accessed on 6 Nov 2022
Stöckl H et al (2013) The global prevalence of intimate partner homicide: a systematic review. The Lancet 382(9895):859–865. https://doi.org/10.1016/S0140-6736(13)61030-2
Swemmer S (2021) Femicide and the continuum of gender-based violence. In: Filho L et al (eds) Gender equality. Encyclopedia of the UN sustainable development goals. Springer, Cham, pp 325–336. https://doi.org/10.1007/978-3-319-95687-9_44
The South African (2020, April 3) Lockdown: 87 000 cases of gender-based violence reported. https://www.thesouthafrican.com/news/gender-based-violence-reported-during-lockdown-cele/. Accessed on 8 Mar 2023
Umubyeyi A et al (2016) Gender inequality prevents abused women from seeking care despite protection given in gender-based violence legislation: a qualitative study from Rwanda. Plos One 11:5
UN Secretary-General & UN Statistical Commission (2008) Friends of the Chair Friends of the Chair of the United Nations Statistical Commission on the indicators on violence against women: Note / by the Secretary-General. https://digitallibrary.un.org/record/645656#record-files-collapse-header. Accessed on 8 Aug 2023
United Nations (2014) Guidelines on producing statistics on violence against women: statistical surveys. https://unstats.un.org/unsd/gender/docs/Guidelines_Statistics_VAW.pdf. Accessed on 5 Aug 2023
United Nations (4 May 2020) Gender-based violence in Nigeria during the Covid-19 crisis: the shadow pandemic. https://nigeria.un.org/sites/default/files/2020-05/Gender%20Based%20Violence%20in%20Nigeria%20During%20COVID%2019%20Crisis_The%20Shadow%20Pandemic.pdf. Accessed on 24 Apr 2023
United Nations (2022) The progress on the sustainable development goals: the gender snapshot 2022. https://unstats.un.org/sdgs/report/2022/. Accessed on 20 Apr 2023
United Nations Department of Economic and Social Affairs Statistics Division (2014) Guidelines on producing statistics on violence against women: statistical surveys. https://www.un.org/development/desa/cdpmo/tools/2020/guidelines-producing-statistics-violence-against-women-statistical-surveys. Accessed on 18 Dec 2022
United Nations ECLAC Statistics Division (2020) Technical sheet: number of femicide and feminicide. https://statistics.cepal.org/portal/cepalstat/technical-sheet.html?lang=en&indicator_id=2780&area_id=222. Accessed on 23 Nov 2022
United Nations General Assembly (2013) Taking action against gender-related killing of women and girls: note by the secretariat: (A/RES/68/191). https://digitallibrary.un.org/record/758374?ln=en. Accessed on 19 Dec 2022
United Nations Office on Drugs and Crime (2015) International classification of crime for statistical purposes. https://www.unodc.org/documents/data-and-analysis/statistics/crime/ICCS/ICCS_English_2016_web.pdf. Accessed on 24 Nov 2022

United Nations Office on Drugs and Crime (2017, September) ICCS Briefing note: measuring violence against women and other gender issues through ICCS lenses. https://www.unodc.org/documents/data-and-analysis/statistics/crime/ICCS/Gender_and_the_ICCS.pdf. Accessed on 23 Nov 2022

United Nations Office on Drugs and Crime (2019a) Global study on homicide. https://www.unodc.org/documents/data-and-analysis/gsh/Booklet1.pdf. Accessed on 30 Nov 2022

United Nations Office on Drugs and Crime (2019b) Homicide rate by sex. https://dataunodc.un.org/data/homicide/Homicide%20rate%20by%20sex. Accessed on 24 Feb 2023

United Nations Office on Drugs and Crime (2020a) Coronavirus Disease (COVID-19) response: thematic brief on gender-based violence against women and girls. https://www.unodc.org/documents/Advocacy-Section/GBVAW_and_UNODC_in_COVID19_final_7Apr2020.pdf. Accessed on 23 Apr 2023

United Nations Office on Drugs and Crime (2020b) Killings of women and girls by their intimate partner or other family members: global estimates 2020. https://www.unodc.org/documents/data-and-analysis/statistics/crime/UN_BriefFem_251121.pdf. Accessed on 26 Nov 2022

United Nations Office on Drugs and Crime (2022a) Gender-related killings of women and girls (femicide/feminicide): global estimates of gender-related killings of women and girls in the private sphere in 2021 improving data to improve responses. https://www.unodc.org/documents/data-and-analysis/briefs/Femicide_brief_Nov2022.pdf. Accessed on 4 Mar 2023

United Nations Office on Drugs and Crime (2022b) Statistical framework for measuring the gender-related killing of women and girls. https://www.unodc.org/documents/data-and-analysis/statistics/Statistical_framework_femicide_2022.pdf. Accessed on 6 Aug 2023

United Nations Office on Drugs and Crime (2022c) UN approves new statistical framework to measure and characterize femicide for more effective prevention measures. https://www.unodc.org/unodc/en/press/releases/2022/March/un-approves-new-statistical-framework-to-measure-and-characterize-femicide-for-more-effective-prevention-measures.html. Accessed on 23 Nov 2022

United Nations Women (2022, November 25) Five essential facts to know about femicide. https://www.unwomen.org/en/news-stories/feature-story/2022/11/five-essential-facts-to-know-about-femicide. Accessed on 4 Mar 2023

United Nations Women: Africa (2011) One-stop center for survivors of gender-based violence. https://evaw-global-database.unwomen.org/en/countries/africa/zimbabwe/2011/one-stop-center-for-survivors-of-gender-based-violence#:~:text=Brief%20Description. Accessed on 19 Apr 2023

United Nations Women: Africa (2020, April 10) COVID-19 and the link to violence against women and girls. https://africa.unwomen.org/en/news-and-events/stories/2020/04/covid-19-and-the-link-to-violence-against-women-and-girls. Accessed on 20 Apr 2023

Van der Heijden I et al (2020) Barriers to gender-based violence services and support for women with disabilities in Cape Town, South Africa. Disabil Soc 35(9):1398–1418. https://doi.org/10.1080/09687599.2019.1690429

Vatnar SKB et al (2022) Intimate Partner homicides in Norway 1990–2020: an analysis of incidence and characteristics. J Interpers Viol 37(23–24):NP21599–NP21625. https://doi.org/10.1177/08862605211063508

Vetten L (2014, November 13) Rape and other forms of sexual violence in South Africa. https://issafrica.org/research/policy-brief/rape-and-other-forms-of-sexual-violence-in-south-africa. Accessed on 6 Jan 2023

Vetten L (2021) Care and support in a time of epidemic - the impact of the covid-19 lockdown on domestic violence in South Africa: what do we know? Research Brief (1). Heinrich Böll Foundation, Cape Town

Wenham C et al. (2020) COVID-19: the gendered impacts of the outbreak. The Lancet 395(10227). https://doi.org/10.1016/s0140-6736(20)30526-2

Wilkinson K (2019) Five facts: femicide in South Africa. https://africacheck.org/fact-checks/reports/five-facts-femicide-south-africa. Accessed on 27 Nov 2022

Wolf ME et al (2003) Barriers to seeking police help for intimate partner violence. J Family Viol 18(2):121–129. https://doi.org/10.1023/a:1022893231951

World Health Organization (2021a) Violence against women prevalence estimates, 2018: global, regional and national prevalence estimates for intimate partner violence against women and global and regional prevalence estimates for non-partner sexual violence against women. https://www.who.int/publications/i/item/9789240022256. Accessed on 18 Mar 2023

World Health Organization (2021b) Violence against women. https://www.who.int/news-room/fact-sheets/detail/violence-against-women. Accessed on 9 Mar 2023

Chapter 6
Perceptions of Crime and the Fear of Crime

6.1 An Overview: Why the Fear of Crime Is a Serious Problem

The previous chapter indicates that violence against women is endemic. The statistics on femicide, rape and domestic violence demonstrate unprecedented prevalence rates. Women's quality of life the world over and particularly in South Africa has long been observed as being curtailed by the balance of social power. The literature reviewed for this research confirms that GBVF is a significant aspect of women's experiences where this can be felt in South Africa. Fear of crime is a very important phenomenon because it constrains behavior and lifestyles, increases anxiety, decreases social engagement, and increases the cost of criminal justice and security measures.[1]

However, the fear or perception of crime was not always considered to be a serious concern. The fear of crime first emerged as an issue of serious concern around the time of racial and economic conflict during the 1960s.[2] Before that not much attention was given to the public's opinion or reaction to crime.[3] The perception of crime is an important area that warrants investigation as it influences attitudes and impacts the quality of one's life. Attitudes towards and perceptions of crime play a very important role in shaping human behavior, including criminal activity and vulnerability to crime.[4] Indeed, perceptions of whether crime is increasing or decreasing, for example, and the level of fear of crime associated with these perceptions are important matters that need to be understood to inform interventions and policy.[5]

[1] Pleggenkuhle and Schafer (2019).

[2] Furstenberg (1971).

[3] Hale (1996).

[4] Stats SA (2018).

[5] Stats SA (2018).

T. Deane, *Gender-Based Violence and Femicide in South Africa*, Gender, Justice and Legal Feminism 5, https://doi.org/10.1007/978-3-031-61053-0_6

Over the last 20 years or so, the phenomenon of fear of crime has become a popular research topic, especially in the United States and European countries.[6] Over time, the fear of crime has become a more important consideration than crime itself because the fear of crime not only directly affects one's quality of life but public security and psychosocial health.[7] Fear of crime is also related to living areas because the physical characteristics of a living area, the socioeconomic status of occupants, security status, social support networks and so on affect individual perceptions of fear of crime.[8]

In South Africa too, perceptions are regarded as so important that the first half of the NDP[9] on crime and safety is stated in terms of perceptions and feelings of safety rather than the actual experience of crime. The NDP envisages that "in 2030, people living in South Africa feel safe at home, at school and at work, and they enjoy a community life free of fear. Women walk freely in the streets and children play safely outside."[10] Specifically, Chapter 12 of the NDP stipulates that "gender-based violence in South Africa is unacceptably high" and that the fear of crime "has consequences for women and girls and their ability to achieve their potential in every sphere of social and productive life. Gender-based violence in all its forms denies women and girls the opportunity to achieve equality and freedoms enshrined in the Constitution."[11] In the discussion to follow below data is used to explore how crime impacts the lives of women and to analyze how the freedoms enshrined in the South African *Constitution* are compromised due to fears and perceptions of crime.

6.2 Attitudes and Perceptions of Crime and Its Impact on Gender-Based Violence and Femicide

6.2.1 Overview

Public safety governance cannot be based on police statistics alone since police crime statistics provide only a limited insight into the nature of crime and violence. This is not a uniquely South African problem.[12] The same is true of all police data around the world.[13] For a range of reasons, a lot of crime and violence is never reported to the police. This limits the use of relying on police statistics alone to develop interventions to improve public safety. Fortunately, complementary

[6]Chadee et al. (2017).

[7]Köseoglu (2021).

[8]Siegel (2012).

[9]National Planning Commission: The Presidency of South Africa (2012).

[10]National Planning Commission (2011), p. 349.

[11]National Planning Commission: The Presidency of South Africa (2012), pp. 395–396.

[12]Perrin et al. (2019).

[13]Van Dijk (2007).

methods for understanding crime and violence exist. One of these methods, a victim survey,[14] is well established in South Africa. The annual Victims of Crime Survey (VoCS) provides a potentially useful source of complementary data to bolster vital registration and police crime statistics. It has the "potential" because it may not provide data that are sufficiently accurate and reliable to inform prevention efforts.[15] However the VoCS have been known to complement official crime statistics.[16] In passing it is interesting to note that a second complementary method for understanding crime and violence has been utilized, the Cardiff Model.[17] This model draws on health data, and is still in its infancy but developing.[18]

For this section, the statistical information is largely based on data from the VoCS, as it relates to the South African context, specifically. It also includes some administrative data, to a lesser extent, from the Institute for Security Studies (ISS) to highlight the gendered impact of crime in South Africa, with particular emphasis on the impact of crime on women. This includes the impact of crime on households headed by women. The statistical evidence provided potentially assists policy makers, law enforcement agencies and civil society to gauge progress and plan interventions for protecting women and girls.

Two limitations are noted that prevent the researcher from delving deeper and providing information normally sought by researchers, policy makers and civil society. First, the VoCS questionnaire that has been in use for the past few (approximately seven) years, does not go into much detail on crimes that mostly affect women such as sexual offenses. This limitation has, to some extent, been addressed

---

[14] Over the past few decades, the advent of victim surveys has facilitated a broader understanding of the crime problem as well as a better assessment of its burden on citizens at the international level. While in the past only police and criminal justice data were used to measure crime, it is now widely acknowledged that such information alone is not sufficient and should be integrated with victim surveys results. Surveys of victims of crime are a more comparable tool to assess risks across countries and world regions.

[15] Matzopoulos et al. (2019).

[16] Daily Maverick (2022).

[17] Shepard (2007).

The Cardiff Model, a programme on violence prevention, was created by Jonathan Shepard, professor at Cardiff University in Wales, United Kingdom. The Cardiff Model is an excellent example of cross-sectoral collaboration—the strategic use of information from the health sector to improve policing. Shepard found a disconnect between, on one hand, the casualty data and violent acts known to police and, on the other hand, the violent acts that the emergency room departments (EDs) recorded. For example, it was more likely that the police would know about an elderly person being attacked than about a young person presenting with injuries in the emergency room. This disconnect in information led to less efficient policing of areas of concentrated violence. To address this gap, the core aspect of the Cardiff Model utilises the sharing of anonymous health-sector information from EDs with the police in real time. Crime and Disorder Reduction Partnerships have been created between the ED staffs and the police to share information about the location and time of violent acts, weapons used and other relevant demographic information. This information helps the police target violence prevention efforts. Police have new information on where they should be patrolling, and which bars and nightclubs are hotbeds for assault injuries.

[18] Jabar et al. (2017).

by the new survey called Governance, Public Safety and Justice (GPSJ) which has more details on sexual offenses. South Africa's first Victims of Crime—Governance, Public Safety, and Justice Survey)[19] was published on 1 December 2020.[20] This survey also explores experiences and perceptions of crime among South Africa's population.[21] Unlike police statistics, which only represent crimes reported to and recorded by police, this survey allows one to estimate the percentage of all households and individuals older than 16 who experience crime. It also gauges the rate at which victims report the crimes to police and asks questions related to perceptions of safety or how safe people actually feel.

Second, the effective sample size for certain types of crime such as murder and sexual offense is a challenge. While the VoCS sample size of approximately 30,000 households is reasonably large, the number of cases for individuals or households that experience these crimes is often very small, to the extent that the potential for sampling error for population estimates is typically very high. However, notwithstanding the limitations mentioned, this section still provides useful information about crime against women and the fear and perceptions related to these crimes.

6.2.2 *Surveys*

In several victim surveys conducted in South Africa since 1996, rape was described as one of the most widely feared crimes, second only to murder.[22] What was noted with concern is that a disjuncture exists between perceptions of crime and the actual levels of recorded crime. For example, the 2012/2013 crime statistics released by SAPS reveal an overall decrease in serious crime between 2002/2003 and 2012/2013. Yet, during this period, suspicions lingered among the public and media that

[19] The Governance, Public Safety, and Justice Survey (GPSJS) is a countrywide household-based survey that aims to bridge the statistical information gaps in the field of governance statistics by conducting interviews with households and individuals and collecting the data items needed for planning and monitoring. The GPSJS was conducted for the first time in South Africa in 2018/2019 as an updated version of the long-running VOCS to include themes on governance. The rule of law and control of corruption were the only themes or sub-themes covered by VOCS before 2018. To achieve a reasonable balance between questionnaire length and depth of questions, a three-year rotation regime was adopted where the five themes are spread over three years. Once in three years, the GPSJS will measure, in detail, the general experience (including perceptions) of crime experienced by households and individuals in the country.

[20] Stats SA (2020).

[21] It has been reported that the surveys provide information on crime and victimization through a standard questionnaire, the results of which are nationally and internationally comparable.

[22] Mc Cafferty (2003).

crime was actually increasing.[23] The VoCS data indicate notable declines in victims' reporting of overall crime to police over the years.[24]

According to the 2018 in-dept analysis of VoCS,[25] attitudes and perceptions continue to play a very important role in shaping human behavior, including criminal activity and vulnerability to crime. Attitudes towards women which is driven mostly by cultural and religious beliefs, determine how women are treated in society.[26] This includes attitudes of women about themselves. Indicators related to perceptions of wife-beating aim to test women's attitudes towards gender roles and gender equality. Some questions were accordingly included in the VoCS questionnaire to capture the attitudes and perceptions of both men and women concerning violence against women and crime trends in South Africa. The first question on attitudes asked respondents if it is generally acceptable for a man to hit a woman. Approximately 3.3% of men and 2.3% of women in South Africa believe that it is acceptable for a man to hit a woman.

Whilst it is encouraging to see that these percentages are small, the problem is that it becomes near impossible to eliminate violence against women when women themselves believe it may be acceptable to be hit by a man.

The second question asked respondents whether it is acceptable for a husband to hit his wife in various situations, for example, if she goes out without telling him, if she neglects the children, if she argues with him, if she refuses to have sex with him, or if she burns the food or cooks the wrong type of food. Given these possible "wrongs" committed by a wife, the percentage of those who thought it is acceptable for a man (husband) to hit a woman (wife) increased. Looking at the percentages by gender 5.2% of women think it is acceptable to do so if she goes out without informing the husband whilst 6% of men think that it is acceptable to hit their wife in these circumstances; 6.5% and 6.8% of women respectively believe that it is acceptable for their husbands to hit them if they either neglect the children or argue with the husband, and 7.6% and 7.7% of men believe that it is acceptable to do so in these circumstances. Regarding whether it is acceptable for a husband to hit his wife where she refuses to have sex with him or where she burns the food, 3.1% of women and 2.6% of men think that it is acceptable to hit or get hit if there is a refusal of sex and 1.3% of both men and women believe that it is okay to hit and be hit if they burn the food.

It is interesting to note that the pattern of responses for men and women is quite similar, the only difference being that the percentages for women are slightly lower than those for men. Both groups think in the same way concerning the seriousness of the issues. Neglecting the children and arguing with the husband are considered by

---

[23] Govender (2016).

[24] For example, in 2013/2014, 90% of victims reported their stolen vehicles to police but by 2019/2020 only 79% did so. Similar declines are found in hijacking (100% to 78%) and assault (67% to 41%), with less pronounced but important dips in reports of house robbery (62% to 54%).

[25] Stats SA (2018).

[26] Stats SA (2018).

both men and women to be the most serious issue, while burning the food is a minor issue. What is clear is that women are still expected to endure being beaten based on ingrained social conditioning about the status of a wife. The strength and weight of traditions is such that many women even find it justifiable to be physically punished in certain circumstances.

The survey further explored the correlation, if any, between the responses to the first question and those to the second question. For those who replied that in general it is acceptable for a man to hit a woman in question 1, 51.1% of men and 33.8% of women responded that it is acceptable for a husband to hit his wife if the wife is guilty of one or more of the five so-called "wrongs." For those who answered "no" to the first question, the percentage of those who said it is acceptable for a husband to hit his wife if the wife is guilty of one or more of the five "wrongs" was 10.4% for men and 9.4% for women. The summation is therefore that even those who think that it is not acceptable to hit a woman, also think that in certain circumstances a husband has the right to hit his wife. Even if the numbers may seem small, the attitudes of women regarding the violence to which they are exposed in their marriages and other intimate relationships is still largely based on concepts and constructs that heavily favor inequity and dominance of men.

The patterns of opinions for male and female-headed households are similar, however, the percentage of women who thought that crime increased was greater than that of men. A four-year data graph on the percentage of South Africans who thought that crime had increased was plotted to determine the trends in the perceptions of both men and women.[27] The percentage of women who thought that crime increased were consistent over a four-year period and the percentage of women was greater than the corresponding percentage for men. The trends, however, exhibit similar patterns with percentages declining between 2014/2015 and 2016/2017, showing that people are becoming more positive about crime trends but 40.9% of women were less positive compared to 37.9% of men.

Although its accuracy was affected by the coronavirus pandemic,[28] the findings on experiences of crime and perceptions of safety and GBV in the 2020/2021 VoCS[29] remain valuable. What was of major concern was that during this period (2021) trust in the police fell to an all-time low of 27%.[30] The pandemic may also

[27] See Stats SA (2018).

[28] As a result of the COVID-19 pandemic and restricted movement some of the challenges experienced included the suspension of face-to-face data collection for all its surveys; the mode of data collection changed from face-to-face CAPI (Computer Assister Personal Interviews) to CATI (Computer Assisted Telephonic Interviews) to facilitate data collection during successive phases of COVID; Households that provided usable telephone numbers in 2019 were called. The sample, therefore, excluded households that were out-of-scope, or who could not participate in 2019, as well as those where telephone numbers were incorrect or have changed, or where households have moved. Stats SA (2021).

[29] Stats SA (2021).

[30] The VoCS remain one of the best ways to determine how this loss of confidence impacts the reporting of crime to police.

have affected the VoCS valuable perception data, such as questions exploring feelings of safety. Looking over a five-year trend, it suggests a notable increase from 29% of people feeling safe at night in 2016/2017 to 40% in 2020/2021.

The 2020/2021 period saw 84.8% of the population indicating that they felt safe walking alone in their neighborhood during the day while 40% felt safe walking alone in their neighborhood during the night. The increase could be attributed to the fact that some may have felt safer in their residential area if interviewed during a hard lockdown in 2020 when streets were busier, and surveillance was persistent. However, it should be noted that when one looks specifically at the data during the 2019/2020 period it shows that people felt safer during this period than the period of 2020/2021.[31]

In the 2020/2021 survey, when respondents were asked if they had taken measures to protect themselves against crime, a mere one third of them responded in the affirmative whilst most of those respondents indicated that they felt safer after changing their habits. Some of these changes included walking during "safer hours" (45%) and being "more alert of my own surroundings" (22%). It is once again noted that the nature of public spaces dramatically changed during various phases of the pandemic, which would have affected these responses.

Specifically on the issue of GBV, the 2020/2021 VoCS showed that approximately 91% of respondents had been exposed to campaigns related to violence against women and children; between 83% to 88% of respondents said they "were aware of" services available to victims of GBV such as medical care, protection orders and counselling, but only 47% of them knew of shelters and places of safety. Importantly, the survey only elicited information related to the "awareness of services" and not whether people knew how to access them or if they had indeed accessed it.

The survey further highlights that both males (88.3%) and females (87.3%) understand that spouses or intimate partners are the ones primarily responsible for committing the most acts of GBV. This is followed by those who think a former partner, relative or family member that is part of the household commits the most acts of GBV, followed by unknown persons or strangers The data indicates that the three leading groups/categories of perpetrators of acts of GBV are usually persons known to the victim. In addition, 99% believed that all violence against women and children should be reported, and 93% thought people should call the police if they witnessed violence at a neighbor or friend's residence. On the other hand, only 65% believed that people should intervene in such violence themselves. This discrepancy could imply a disconnect between how South Africans think and feel about violence and how they should act when faced with it. Regarding how they would respond in the face of a male friend "insulting or verbally abusing a woman he was in a relationship with," most said that they would feel uncomfortable but probably not say or do anything.

[31] Stats SA (2022).

Perceptions around equality reveal that most respondents believed that women and men should have the same chance of "being elected to political office" and that "having an income is the best way for a woman to be an independent person." However, 55% perceived that if a woman earns more money than their male partner, it was certain to cause problems. This perception clearly undermines the sentiment of gender equality implied in the previous responses of the respondents. It should however be noted that there was an overall decrease in the perception, from 2019/2020 to 2020/2021, that if a woman earns more than her man, it is almost certain to cause problems. Biasness was also apparent when questions were posed on whether it was acceptable "for a man/husband to hit or beat his woman/wife." Nearly 10% of respondents indicated that such violence was acceptable in specific contexts, such as sexual infidelity.[32] In general, there has been a decrease in the percentage between 2019/2020 and 2020/2021 for those who believe that it is justifiable for a man to beat his woman/wife for any reason.

Looking at the gendered nature of the violence, overall, most victims and perpetrators of all types of violence are men.[33] These statistics provide a clear indication that despite some of the promising findings discussed above, for as long as there is a belief by boys and men, as well as by women themselves, that violence is a legitimate means to express authority and solve problems, it is unlikely that violence against women or children will decrease.[34]

It is noted that public safety governance cannot be based on police statistics alone, and the investment in a crime and violence measurement tool like the VoCS's is commendable. However, the VoCS, like police data, should be interpreted and acted on with caution, especially considering the period of reporting, i.e., during the pandemic. Ideally, police and VoCS data should be compared to violence-related injury data from health facilities, bank and insurance data on property and financial crime, and other quality perception surveys. Looking to only one crime and violence measurement tool is not sufficient as alone, none of these data sets reveals "the truth" about crime, violence, or risk. As a set of tools that may be referenced together it provides a clearer picture of the extent of crime and perceptions on safety and fears in the country.[35]

The surveys highlight that many factors influence citizens perceptions and attitudes towards crime in the country. The following discussion focuses on some of these factors.

---

[32] It is noted that by framing the question in only one form and direction, i.e., a man assaulting a woman, it entrenches assumptions about domestic violence, intimate partnerships (that they are heterosexual) and sexual identity (that all people with male bodies identify as "man").

[33] ISS Africa (2021).

[34] ISS Africa (2017).

[35] Daily Maverick (2022).

6.3 The Criminal Justice System's Response to GBVF

An overall approach to eliminate GBVF is to address all facets of society that cause and condone such behavior. Among other remedies, an effective criminal justice system (CJS) is needed to address GBVF where and when it occurs.[36] Within the CJS, public safety and confidence is a necessary and critical step in preventing crime and increasing levels of safety. The likelihood of crimes being committed is increased if the system is regarded as being incompetent and inefficient. Public confidence is eroded by perceptions that criminals act with impunity and will escape the law, arrests do not lead to convictions, or the convictions are not commensurate with the serious nature of the offense committed or that prisoners escape easily from courtrooms or correctional facilities. The most effective deterrent to criminality is consequently an efficient and effective CJS.[37]

What follows is a discussion on some of the most serious failings of the CJS in responding to GBVF.

6.3.1 Lack of Documented History of Violence

In the 2017 national femicide study[38] it was highlighted that only 29% of SAPS dockets in the study had information on past partner violence among intimate partner femicide cases (compared to 30% in 1999 and 2009) and 23 of the women killed by an intimate partner had a protection order issued at the time of her death. This failure is of a significant concern as one of the most frequently observed risk factor at an interpersonal level is a couple's history of prior violence, which also includes the perpetrator's obsessive jealousy and coercive control over a partner (on money, behavior, contacts with friends) and the victim's estrangement or divorce from her abusive partner.[39] The 2017 national femicide study also highlighted that with so many femicide cases remaining unsolved, a documented history of intimate-partner violence would be helpful in identifying suspects. This is based on the research that murder is seldom the first act of violence by an intimate partner.

---

[36] National Planning Commission: The Presidency of South Africa (2012).

[37] National Planning Commission (2011), p. 351.

[38] Abrahams et al. (2022).

[39] World Health Organization (2012).

6.3.2 *Low Conviction Rates*

The National Prosecuting Authority (NPA) only started to report on murder convictions and intimate partner femicides in its 2017 annual reports.[40] In 2017, the NPA also started to include some case studies of murders by intimate partners in its reports. Prior to 2017, its reports had focused on issues such as sexual offenses, organized crime, cybercrime, and property crimes.

In its report the NPA reports that its conviction rate for intimate partner homicide cases is 98.7%. However, it gives no indication of how many of the murder cases reported to SAPS make it to court. For example, SAPS reported 62,683 murders between April 2017 and March 2020, and the NPA reported 10,284 murder convictions during the same period.

It needs to be highlighted that while there was no improvement in the proportion of convictions among intimate partner femicide cases over 18 years (37.4% in 1999 and 37.7% in 2017), there was an improvement in convictions among non-intimate partner femicides since 2009 (from 23.1% in 2009 to 31.8% in 2017). However, conviction rates remain worryingly low.

During its 2021/2022 reporting period[41] the NPA once again reported conviction rate in femicide prosecution of 94.3%; a conviction rate in murder intimate partner femicide prosecutions at 93.8%, an increase from the previous 2020/2021 reporting period of 93.1% but a decrease (97.7%) from the 2019/2020 reporting period. However, these statistics do not paint an accurate picture as once again it does not indicate how many of the reported cases finally make it to court.

Of concern during the reporting period of 2022/2023, it was reported that the NPA achieved a conviction rate of only 74.8%.[42] The NPA did provide a breakdown of these rates and indicate that a conviction rate of 91.9% (475 convictions from 517 verdict cases) was obtained for femicide and 356 convictions for intimate partner femicide[43] were obtained from 386 verdict cases, representing a 92.2% conviction rate. However, looking at the statistics, the conviction rates for all gender-based violence crimes decreased between the 2021/2022 and 2022/2023 reporting period.[44]

---

[40] National Prosecuting Authority (2018).

[41] National Prosecuting Authority (2021).

[42] National Prosecuting Authority (2023).

[43] The NPA indicated that intimate partner femicide is defined as femicide committed by a current or former husband (divorced or separated), boyfriend (dating or cohabiting), ex-boyfriend or rejected would-be lover.

[44] The conviction rates in numbers included:

Conviction rate in femicide prosecutions: 2019/2020 no statistics; 2020/2021 94.3% (231/245); 2021/2022 94.3% (396/420); 2022/2023 91.9% (475/517); *Conviction rate in intimate partner femicide prosecutions*: 2019/2020 no statistics; 2020/2021 93.1% (190/204); 2021/2022 93.8% (316/337); 2022/2023 92.2% (356/386); Conviction rate in sexual offenses: 2019/2020 75.2% (4098/5 451); 2020/2021 75.8% (2539/3 349); 2021/2022 74.2% (3402/4584); 2022/2023 74.8% (3460/4627). See National Prosecuting Authority (2023). *Annual report 2022/23*.

6.3.3 *Missing Data and Police Inefficiencies*

Apart from COVID-19 impacting on the data collection process, two additional factors associated with poor quality policing has contributed to incomplete information, (1) missing dockets and (2) no suspect identified.

Regarding the non-identification of suspects, between 2009 and 2017, it was reported that there was an increased from 22.9% to 30.1% in 2017.[45] Cases with unidentified perpetrators was a concern in all provinces with some provinces recording more than others. For example, KwaZulu-Natal saw 27.3% of unidentified perpetrators, Eastern Cape 28% and Gauteng with 16% had the largest number of missing perpetrator information, with the lowest being in Northern Cape (0.3%), North West Province (3.5%) and Mpumalanga (3.9%).[46]

Regarding missing dockets, for many years, media reports have continuously highlighted the seriousness of stolen and lost case dockets plaguing SAPS.[47] Between, 2009 and 2017 missing dockets increased from 1.6% to 9.1% in 2017.

More recently, the Western Cape Department of Community Safety (WCDCS) reported that between April and June 2022, 198 cases serving before the court were withdrawn as a result of police inefficiencies by SAPS.[48] Of these 36 GBV cases had been withdrawn or struck off the roll due to systemic failures,[49] 25 cases had been withdrawn because the dockets were not brought to court, and eight because the investigation was incomplete.[50] The quality of investigations is crucial in securing positive convictions and this responsibility falls on SAPS. However serious mistakes such as missing information from dockets, inadequate collection of evidence or investigations and missing signatures from complainant statements have led to the non-prosecution of cases,[51] seriously impacting reporting by the community.

During its second quarter report (July–September 2022) the WCDCS reported that its Court Watching Brief[52] showed that 208 cases monitored during this period at 15 courts across the province were struck off the court roll due to police inefficiencies.[53] The Court Watching Brief Unit is tasked with monitoring cases of GBVF and domestic violence. The report by the unit indicated that of the 208 cases, 64 cases (30%) were GBV matters while 144 involved murder, aggravated robbery,

---

[45] This information is taken from an analysis of the MRC's 1999, 2009, and 2017 femicide studies. National Prosecuting Authority (2023).

[46] Abrahams et al. (2022).

[47] ISS Africa (2009).

[48] These statistics are drawn from the quarterly report of the Department of Community Safety's Court Watching Brief team. See Western Cape Government (2019).

[49] Western Cape Department (2021).

[50] EWN (2022).

[51] Amnesty International (2021).

[52] The Court Watching Brief (CWB) unit is a Department of Community Safety initiative to enhance the ability to perform oversight of the police as mandated by Section 2016(3) of the *Constitution*.

[53] IOL News (2022).

possession and dealing in drugs and possession of firearms and ammunition. Of the 144 cases, 74 (51%) were withdrawn because the investigations were incomplete, while 53 cases (36.8%) were withdrawn as the dockets were not in court. In the GBV cases, 32 cases (50%) were withdrawn as the dockets were not in court, while 29 cases (45%) were withdrawn because of incomplete investigation.

In 2021, it was reported that the conviction rate for crimes of reported rape is a mere 8.6% due to a high number of cases dropping out of the CJS, and most reported cases never being prosecuted.[54] In 2020 the Court Watching Brief Unit reported on the period of 1 July to 30 September 2020. It was further reported that missing dockets and ineffective policing result in an average of 22 cases of GBV, including rape and murder, being thrown out of Western Cape courts every month.[55] In addition, a total of 92 cases were struck off the court roll during this period, 52 as a result of dockets not being present at the court, and 40 due to investigations not being completed.

The constant failures to deal with contraventions of protection orders and dockets going missing is a widespread problem in South Africa and the CJS is consequently failing victims of GBV.[56] These failures by the state and police in particular have been reported as being secondary victimization and exacerbating the trauma for victims.[57] In addition, missing dockets, and incomplete investigations hamper justice. During 2018/2019 the survey results indicated that there was an ever-increasing gulf in household satisfaction between police services (54.2% were satisfied) and how courts generally deal with perpetrators of crime (41.1% were satisfied).[58] There is a general feeling that there is no sense in bringing cases forward as justice is being denied them.[59] This has remained the trend over the years. The way the SAPS handled the cases which were struck off the court rolls was part of the reason why communities were losing trust in the system.[60]

6.3.4 DNA Backlog

The prosecution of crimes like murder and rape, is being undermined because of various challenges around the management of forensic DNA. Shortages of essential chemicals required for the DNA analysis[61] and the SAPSs delay in processing DNA

[54] Amnesty International (2021).
[55] Daily Maverick (2020).
[56] Amnesty International (2021).
[57] IOL News (2022).
[58] Stats SA (2019).
[59] Gontsana (2022).
[60] News24 (2022).
[61] National Prosecuting Authority (2021).

samples is a major concern.[62] This has resulted in a national backlog of those cases being prosecuted in courts. Currently there is a multi-year backlog at the National Forensic Science Laboratories which is delaying the prosecution of cases,[63] impacting and frustrating efforts to fast-track criminal cases especially murder and sexual assault. This also leads to a low conviction rate of GBVF-related cases, which is less than 14%.[64] As of February 2022, there were between 200,000–215,000[65] outstanding DNA cases that were not analyzed. It has been reported that the challenge is not only the delays in the DNA sampling, but the entire police service infrastructure which remains in a compromised state.

In South Africa, prisoners convicted of serious offenses are required to give compulsory DNA samples under the *Criminal Law (Forensic Procedures) Amendment Bill*.[66] As of 31 January 2022, a suspect arrested and charged with a Schedule 8 offense[67] is required to provide a DNA sample which will be uploaded onto the National Forensics DNA database to enable law enforcement to link perpetrators to cold cases, identify repeat offenders and get more perpetrators prosecuted. The idea is that the taking of a DNA sample of a suspected perpetrator, even before a court date is set, is expected to massively increase the successful prosecution rate, and assist law enforcement in clamping down on perpetrators. It is intended to give the country's law enforcement additional tools around DNA collection and usage in capturing and prosecuting criminals. The regulations will better allow authorities to develop a database of violent offenders in the country[68] and DNA-taking will be mandatory, with prisoners required to give a sample while they serve their prison term or before their release.

---

[62] Business Insider (2021).

[63] The Citizen (2022a) and BusinessTech (2022).

[64] Between April to June 2022, 855 women and 243 children were killed in South Africa, and 9516 rape cases were reported.

[65] The Citizen (2022b).

[66] B25-2021. The Bill was intended to empower SAPS to take buccal samples containing the DNA of persons serving prison sentences for offenses listed in Schedule 8 of the Criminal Procedure Act, 1977. These cover violent crimes including rape, murder, human trafficking, robbery, and culpable homicide. Amendments to the principal Act (the *Criminal Law (Forensic Procedures) Amendment Act, 2013* (Act No. 37 of 2013)) promulgated in 2015 had empowered SAPS to take buccal samples, but only for a two-year transitional period that had expired in January 2017. The Bill removed this limitation, empowering SAPS to take buccal samples indefinitely. The Bill also placed the National Commissioner of Police under an obligation to report on progress made in collecting buccal samples from Schedule 8 offenders and provided for the use of minimum force against offenders who resisted having a sample taken.

[67] Schedule 8 offenses include some of the country's most serious violent crimes—including murder and rape.

[68] South African Government (2022).

While existing legislation had given powers to law enforcement to take DNA (buccal samples),[69] there has been "significant obstacles" as prisoners simply refused to have buccal samples taken.[70] It was reported that the refusal to give buccal samples is as a result of the fear that prisoners could be linked with other unsolved cases where their DNA samples have not been taken before. However, the new *Bill* will address this obstacle.[71] Authorities are now permitted to lodge a court application to obtain the samples and are permitted to use "minimal force" in retrieving them.

However, it should be noted with some degree of concern that making alleged perpetrators of crime provide DNA samples will not help victims if the national backlog of DNA results is not dealt with.[72] Therefore, whilst DNA remains the most effective crime-fighting tool and the sampling of Schedule 8 arrestees has the potential to make a huge impact in solving cold cases, identifying repeat offenders and assisting in successful prosecutions of rapists and murderers, SAPS will have to ensure that their stations are equipped with the necessary consumables to do the sampling.[73]

What is clear is that the existing DNA backlog at the Forensic Science Laboratories affects the survivors as their cases are being withdrawn from court pending DNA results.[74] This is effectively denying victims of GBVF access to justice.[75] If the massive DNA backlog is not addressed and, if law enforcement agencies are not allocated more resources for the collection of DNA samples this new legislation will be futile. Where this is allowed to continue there will be no deterrent to committing sexual offenses and GBVF perpetrators will continue to act with impunity. It therefore becomes imperative to strengthen the CJS.

6.4 Concluding Remarks

This chapter analyses the perceptions of crime and the fear of crime since incidences of violence and harassment are notoriously underreported, which makes official crime and police data a poor reflection of the actual extent of the problem. The best estimates of the incidence of GBV thus come from household surveys that probe respondents' experiences.[76] These surveys ask about experiences across types of violence and in multiple spheres, such as at home and at work, on the street, with

[69] *Criminal Law (Forensic Procedures) Amendment Act, 2013* (Act No. 37 of 2013).

[70] BusinessTech (2022).

[71] South African Government (2022).

[72] The Citizen (2022a).

[73] Independent OnLine (2022).

[74] The Citizen (2022b).

[75] Amnesty International (2022).

[76] Htun and Jensenius (2020), p. 144.

family members and with strangers, in the past year and over the course of a lifetime allowing for a more comprehensive overview of the experiences of differently situated women.

Finally, activists and scholars have long argued that GBV is attributable not only to individual-level factors such as aggression, alcohol and drug use, or family history, but also to cultural attitudes and social norms that legitimize violent behavior, and above all to the gender structure of society, which tends to subordinate women and render them vulnerable to men's economic and social power. The use of VoCs and other tools can therefore provide a more accurate measure and evaluation of the social contexts that enable violence and impunity and the varied factors that influence citizens perceptions and attitudes towards crime in the country.

The next chapter will analyze South Africa's legal responses to GBVF. This is to provide a broad understanding of the policy and legislative frameworks regarding GBV in the country and to look at the country's international obligations in terms of various human rights instruments.

References

Abrahams N et al. (2022, March 8) Research brief: decrease in femicide in South Africa: three national studies across 18 years. https://www.samrc.ac.za/reports/research-brief-decrease-femicide-south-africa-three-national-studies-across-18-years. Accessed 25 Nov 2022

Amnesty International (2021) Gender-based violence: call on the South African Police Service to care. https://amnesty.org.za/action/gender-based-violence-call-on-the-south-african-police-service-to-care/. Accessed 11 Mar 2023

Amnesty International (2022, October 3) An open letter to Bheki Cele: the DNA backlog is an untenable situation. https://ewn.co.za/2022/10/03/an-open-letter-to-bheki-cele-the-dna-backlog-is-an-untenable-situation. Accessed 1 Dec 2022

Business Insider (2021, August 25) SA's DNA backlog won't be cleared before 2023, at the current processing rate. https://www.businessinsider.co.za/south-africa-dna-backlog-wont-be-cleared-by-2023-2021. Accessed 3 Dec 2022

BusinessTech (2022, February 17) New DNA laws for SA – how they work. https://businesstech.co.za/news/government/559744/new-dna-laws-for-south-africa-how-they-work/#:~:text=From%2031%20January%2C%20a%20suspect,crimes%20%E2%80%93%20including%20murder%20and%20rape. Accessed 4 Dec 2022

Chadee D et al (2017) Fear of crime and community concerns: mediating effect of risk and pragmatic fear. J Commun Appl Soc Psychol 27(6):450–462. https://doi.org/10.1002/casp.2326

Daily Maverick (2020, November 25) Stop gender-based violence and femicide. https://www.dailymaverick.co.za/article/2020-11-25-missing-dockets-and-incomplete-investigations-hamper-justice-in-western-cape-gbv-cases/. Accessed 12 Mar 2023

Daily Maverick (2022, March 28) South Africa's latest crime victim survey leaves readers and analysts with more questions than answers. https://www.dailymaverick.co.za/article/2022-03-28-south-africas-latest-crime-victim-survey-leaves-readers-and-analysts-with-more-questions-than-answers/. Accessed 16 Jan 2023

EWN (2022, August 2) GBV cases being thrown out of court due to missing dockets a concern for WC dept. https://ewn.co.za/2022/08/02/gbv-cases-being-thrown-out-of-court-due-to-missing-dockets-a-concern-for-wc-dept. Accessed 9 Mar 2023

Furstenberg FN (1971) Public reactions to crime in the streets. Am Sch 11(Autumn):601–610

Gontsana MA (2022, August 4) 200 cases dropped in three months because of police inefficiency, report finds. https://www.groundup.org.za/article/gbv-docket-goes-missing-at-delft-police-station-this-is-not-unusual-says-activist/. Accessed 8 Mar 2023

Govender M (2016) The paradox of crime perceptions: SAPS Crime Statistics, Victims of Crime Surveys and the media. S Afr Crim Q 46. https://doi.org/10.17159/2413-3108/2013/v0i46a807

Hale C (1996) Fear of crime: a review of the literature. Int Rev Victimology 4(2):79–150. https://doi.org/10.1177/026975809600400201

Htun M, Jensenius FR (2020) Fighting violence against women: laws, norms & challenges ahead. Daedalus 149(1):144–159. https://doi.org/10.1162/daed_a_01779

Independent OnLine (2022, January 15) New DNA law to fight violent crime but experts are concerned that it will overburden SAPS. https://www.iol.co.za/saturday-star/news/new-dna-law-to-fight-violent-crime-but-experts-are-concerned-that-it-will-overburden-saps-8164a33b-7af4-4677-9ccf-56755b66c641. Accessed 4 Dec 2022

IOL News (2022, December 8) SAPS inefficiency leads to 64 GBV cases struck off court roll in Western Cape. https://www.iol.co.za/news/south-africa/western-cape/saps-inefficiency-leads-to-64-gbv-cases-struck-off-court-roll-in-western-cape-b42d1e07-ae75-43c1-b15f-8bb5dc8c5e05. Accessed 7 Mar 2023

ISS Africa (2009, August 21) The SAPS e-Docket system. https://issafrica.org/iss-today/the-saps-e-docket-system. Accessed 12 Mar 2023

ISS Africa (2017, October 6) Violent homes breed violent societies. https://issafrica.org/iss-today/violent-homes-breed-violent-societies. Accessed 2 Mar 2023

ISS Africa (2021, October 27) The gendered nature of violence. https://issafrica.org/crimehub/multimedia/the-gendered-nature-of-violence. Accessed 2 Mar 2023

Jabar A et al (2017) Rationale and design of the Violence, Injury and Trauma Observatory (VITO): The Cape Town VITO pilot studies protocol. BMJ Open 7(12):e016485. https://doi.org/10.1136/bmjopen-2017-016485

Köseoglu M (2021) Fear of crime perceptions of university students. Sociologia, Problemas E Práticas 96:41–57. https://journals.openedition.org/spp/9017

Matzopoulos R et al (2019) Utility of crime surveys for sustainable development goals monitoring and violence prevention using a public health approach. S Afr Med J 109(6):382. https://doi.org/10.7196/samj.2019.v109i6.13806

Mc Cafferty R (2003) Murder in South Africa: a comparison of past and present. https://www.gunowners.org/fs0304/. Accessed 4 Jan 2023

National Planning Commission (2011) Chapter 12: building safer communities. https://www.nationalplanningcommission.org.za/assets/Documents/NDP_Chapters/devplan_ch12_0.pdf. Accessed 10 Nov 2022

National Planning Commission: The Presidency of South Africa (2012) National Development Plan 2030: our future - make it work. https://www.gov.za/documents/national-development-plan-2030-our-future-make-it-work. Accessed 12 Aug 2023

National Prosecuting Authority (2018) Annual report 2017/18. https://www.npa.gov.za/sites/default/files/annual-reports/NDPP%20Annual%20Report-%202017-18.pdf. Accessed 24 Feb 2023

National Prosecuting Authority (2021) Annual report 2021/2022. https://www.npa.gov.za/sites/default/files/uploads/NPA%20Annual%20Report%202022_web.pdf. Accessed 24 Feb 2023

National Prosecuting Authority (2023) Annual report 2022/23. https://www.npa.gov.za/sites/default/files/uploads/NPA%20Annual%20Report%202022-23.pdf. Accessed 12 Aug 2023

News24 (2022, August 10) "I feel like my trauma was belittled": Cape Town woman says cops didn't take GBV claims seriously. https://www.news24.com/news24/southafrica/news/i-feel-like-my-trauma-was-belittled-cape-town-woman-says-cops-didnt-take-gbv-claims-seriously-20220810. Accessed 11 Mar 2023

Perrin N et al (2019) Social norms and beliefs about gender-based violence scale: a measure for use with gender-based violence prevention programs in low-resource and humanitarian settings. Confl Heal 13(1). https://doi.org/10.1186/s13031-019-0189-x

Pleggenkuhle B, Schafer JA (2019) Fear of crime among residents of rural counties: an analysis by gender. J Crim Justice 41(4):383–397. https://doi.org/10.1080/0735648X.2017.1391109

Shepard J (2007, October) The Cardiff model for violence prevention. Cardiff University

Siegel LJ (2012) Criminology. Belmont West/Wadsworth

South African Government (2022, May 24) Minister Bheki Cele: Police, IPID and Civilian Secretariat for Police Service Dept budget vote 2022/23. https://www.gov.za/speeches/minister-bheki-cele-police-ipid-and-civilian-secretariat-police-service-dept-budget-vote-2. Accessed 4 Dec 2022

Stats SA (2018) Crime statistics series volume V crime against women in South Africa: an in-depth analysis of the victims of crime survey data 2018. https://www.statssa.gov.za/publications/Report-03-40-05/Report-03-40-05June2018.pdf. Accessed 6 Nov 2022

Stats SA (2019, August 14) Governance, public safety and justice survey 2018/19. http://www.statssa.gov.za/publications/P0340/P03402019.pdf. Accessed 26 Dec 2022

Stats SA (2020, December 1) Governance, public safety, and justice survey GPSJS 2019/20. http://www.statssa.gov.za/publications/P0341/P03412019.pdf. Accessed 28 Feb 2023

Stats SA (2021) Governance, public safety and justice survey (GPSJS) victims of crime 2020/21. https://www.statssa.gov.za/publications/P0341/GPSJS%202020_21%20presentation.pdf. Accessed 15 Feb 2023

Stats SA (2022) Key findings: P0341 - victims of crime release, 2021. https://www.statssa.gov.za/?page_id=1856&PPN=P0341&SCH=73252. Accessed 3 Mar 2023

The Citizen (2022a, January 24) SA's DNA testing backlog must be dealt with, says NPO. https://www.citizen.co.za/witness/news/kzn/sas-dna-testing-backlog-must-be-dealt-with-says-npo-20220124/. Accessed 4 Dec 2022

The Citizen (2022b, April 13) "Demoralising" DNA backlog slows criminal cases. https://www.citizen.co.za/witness/news/demoralising-dna-backlog-slows-criminal-cases-20220413/. Accessed 2 Dec 2022

Van Dijk J (2007) The world of crime. SAGE Publications

Western Cape Department (2021) Annual report 2021/22. https://www.westerncape.gov.za/sites/www.westerncape.gov.za/files/docs_annual_report_2021-22.pdf. Accessed 10 Mar 2023

Western Cape Government (2019) Court watching briefs. https://www.westerncape.gov.za/assets/02_11_2019_hod_forum_3_-_watching_brief_z_fold.pdf. Accessed 9 Mar 2023

World Health Organization (2012) Understanding and addressing violence against women: femicide. https://apps.who.int/iris/bitstream/handle/10665/77421/WHO_RHR_12.38_eng.pdf. Accessed 10 Mar 2023

Chapter 7
Legal Responses to Gender-Based Violence and Femicide

7.1 Overview

South Africa has placed the right to equality and the right to be free from all forms of violence as a constitutional right in its *Bill of Rights*. Consequently, the *Constitution*[1] has placed a *legal obligation* on the government to realize these rights. Such an obligation requires different action to a moral, economic, or political obligation.[2] Since achieving democracy, South Africa has made substantive advancements towards a constitutional framework and domestic policy that is empowering, progressive and transformative in nature.[3] The political and social transformation that has happened in South Africa since the inception of democracy means that the country must take urgent and robust action to eliminate violence against women and girls. The foundational principles underpinning South Africa's democracy require the full protection of human rights for all. In order to comply with their constitutional mandate, the government has enacted policies, legislation, strategies, and institutions to manage and respond to the scourge of GBVF. This chapter is situated within this context and aims to explore the countries legal responses to GBVF in various sections below.

In addition, a brief synopsis on the country's international obligations in terms of key treaties, conventions, declarations, resolutions, and international norms related to GBV will be mentioned. This is important as the purpose of international human rights law is to create due diligence and obligations on member states to comply with and implement specific rights. This means that the international obligation to exercise due diligence requires States to establish effective measures to prevent, investigate and prosecute cases of violence against women. This includes effective means to respond to each case of violence, as well as address the structural causes of

---

[1] Act 108 of 1996.

[2] Pejan et al. (2007).

[3] Deane (2018).

T. Deane, *Gender-Based Violence and Femicide in South Africa*, Gender, Justice and Legal Feminism 5, https://doi.org/10.1007/978-3-031-61053-0_7

violence by ensuring comprehensive legal and policy frameworks, gender sensitive justice systems and police, available health and social services and awareness raising activities.[4]

7.2 Key National and International Legal and Policy Frameworks Related to Gender-Based Violence in South Africa

7.2.1 Domestic Legal Framework

South Africa's progressive laws and policies related to GBV and sexual-related violence, includes, inter alia, the *Constitution of the Republic of South Africa* adopted in 1996, and amended in 2012, which contains various guarantees and protections against GBV in South Africa.[5] The *Constitution* is considered to be one of the most progressive and inclusive constitutions in the world, with a *Bill of Rights* proclaimed to be the cornerstone of democracy. GBVF contravenes numerous constitutionally guaranteed rights, most significantly, the right to be free from discrimination,[6] the right to equality, which provides for equality before the law and the right to equal benefit and protection of the law.[7] The reality and threat of infringements impinge on women's rights to inherent dignity, the right to have that

[4]UN Office on Drugs and Crime (2017), para 2.

[5]See, inter alia, section 9 of the *Constitution*: The right to equality including equality before the law, and equal protection and benefit before the law for everyone, and the prohibition of unfair discrimination by the state and individuals on many grounds, including gender; section 10: The right to human dignity, while the right to life is guaranteed in section 11; section 12: Guarantees the right to freedom and security of the person, which includes the right of everyone to be free from all forms of violence. (1) Everyone has the right to freedom and security of the person, which includes the right—(c) to be free from all forms of violence from either public or private sources; (d) not to be tortured in any way; and (e) not to be treated or punished in a cruel, inhuman or degrading way. (2) Everyone has the right to bodily and psychological integrity, which includes the right – (a) to make decisions concerning reproduction; (b) to security in and control over their body; (c) not to be subjected to medical or scientific experiments without their informed consent.

[6]Section 9.3 of the *Constitution* states that: "the state must not unfairly discriminate directly or indirectly against anyone on one or more grounds, including race, gender, sex, pregnancy, marital status, ethnic or social origin, colour, sexual orientation, age, disability, religion, conscience, belief, language and birth."

Section 9.4 further states that: "No person may unfairly discriminate directly or indirectly against anyone on one or more grounds in terms of subsection (3). National legislation must be enacted to prevent or prohibit unfair discrimination."

Not only is discrimination unconstitutional, and therefore also unlawful, it is also something that the Constitution says must be prevented in terms of more specific laws.

[7]Section 9(1) of the *Constitution* states that: "Everyone is equal before the law and has the right to equal protection and benefit of the law."

dignity respected and protected,[8] the right to life,[9] the right to freedom and security of the person[10] and the right to bodily and psychological integrity.[11]

In addition, the *Constitution* makes provision for six Chapter 9 institutions, which institutions are meant to safeguard and promote democracy in the country.[12] Specifically, section 181 of the *Constitution* provides for the independence and impartiality of these institutions, whilst other organs of state are obliged to assist and protect these institutions to ensure their continued independence, impartiality, dignity and effectiveness.[13] Two of the most relevant of these institutions for the purposes of GBV are the South African Human Rights Commission (SAHRC),[14] which is meant to uphold and monitor human rights in the country and the Commission for Gender Equality (CGE),[15] who has a mandate to investigate gender equality disputes. The Constitutional Court has specifically acknowledged the distinctive role of the SAHRC and other Chapter 9 institutions in creating a new constitutional culture.[16] In addition, the Court endorsed a significant monitoring role for the SAHRC and mandates it to adopt a supervisory role to ensure governments compliance with its constitutional obligations.[17]

---

[8] Section 10 of the *Constitution* states that: "Everyone has inherent dignity and the right to have their dignity respected and protected."

[9] Section 11 of the *Constitution.*

[10] Section 12(1) of the *Constitution.*

[11] Section 12(2) of the *Constitution.*

[12] The six Chapter 9 Institutions were created to be independent, impartial bodies with the purpose of keeping government accountable. South Africa's history of discrimination, oppression and lack of accountability was one of the primary reasons for the establishment of these institutions. These institutions are essential in the democracy of South Africa. They assist organs of state in adhering to the new constitutional dispensation and include the following: "(a) The Public Protector. (b) The South African Human Rights Commission. (c) The Commission for the Promotion and Protection of the Rights of Cultural, Religious and Linguistic Communities. (d) The Commission for Gender Equality. (e) The Auditor-General. (f) The Electoral Commission."

[13] Sections 181(2) and (3) of the *Constitution.* No person or organ of state may interfere with the functioning of the institutions.

[14] *South African Human Rights Commission Act, 2013.*

[15] *The Commission on Gender Equality Act, 1996* sets out in detail the commission's functions and powers including, inter alia, the right to monitor (a watchdog function), to educate, to investigate and settle complaints, to conduct research, to advocate for gender equality, to report, advise and make recommendations, and to litigate. Section 11 of the *Act.*

[16] For example, in *New National Party of South Africa v Government of the Republic of South Africa & others* 1999 (3) SA 191 (CC), 1999 (5) BCLR 489 (CC) at para 78, it was stated that: "[t]he establishment of the Commission and the other institutions under Chapter 9 of the Constitution are a new development on the South African scene. They are a product of the new constitutionalism, and their advent inevitably has important implications for other organs of State who must understand and recognise their respective roles in the new constitutional arrangement. The Constitution places a constitutional obligation on those organs of State to assist and protect the Commission in order to ensure its independence, impartiality, dignity and effectiveness."

[17] *Government of the Republic of South Africa and Others v Grootboom and Others* (CCT11/00) [2000] ZACC 19; 2001 (1) SA 46; 2000 (11) BCLR 1169 (4 October 2000), para 97.

Furthermore, to give expression to the constitutional rights to equality, human dignity, life, and freedom and security of the person, South Africa has adopted the *Employment Equity Act 55 of 1998* (*EEA*).[18] The *EEA* is accompanied by an amended Code of Good Practice on the Handling of Sexual Harassment Cases in the Workplace.[19] In addition, the *Labour Relations Act* Schedule[20] includes a code of good practice on dismissals (Schedule 8) and guides, employers, on the various aspects of dismissal, fair procedure, and substantive fairness. It becomes critical in sexual harassment cases if a sanction of dismissal is effected against someone accused of sexual harassment. The *Promotion of Equality and Prevention of Unfair Discrimination Act, 4 of 2000* (*PEPUDA*) gives expression to the right to equality.[21] The *Protection from Harassment Act, 17 of 2011* was passed in December 2011 which intends to provide for the issuing of protection orders against harassment, to effect consequential amendments to the *Firearms Control Act, 2000* and to provide for matters connected therewith.[22]

Of particular importance is the *Domestic Violence Act, 116 of 1998* (*DVA*) which provides women with the highest form of protection from domestic violence. It places the responsibility on state organs and in particular SAPS to ensure that survivors of domestic violence can apply for protection orders to prevent abusers from entering a mutual home or the survivor's home or place of work. The *DVA* includes an expansive definition of domestic violence that includes physical, sexual, emotional, verbal, psychological and economic abuse as well as intimidation, harassment, stalking and controlling behaviors.

---

[18] Where Sections 2, 3, 5, 6, 50(2), and 60 are pertinent to sexual harassment in the workplace. Section 2 in particular sets out the purpose of the legislation which is to achieve equity in the workplace by promoting equal opportunity and fair treatment in employment through the elimination of unfair discrimination.

[19] The Code is the legislative framework that defines sexual harassment in the workplace, placing it firmly within the ambit of employment law. Its objective is to "eliminate sexual harassment in the workplace" and it "provides appropriate procedures to deal with sexual harassment and prevent its recurrence." The Code states that sexual harassment in the workplace is a form of unfair discrimination, which is prohibited on the grounds of sex and/or gender and/or sexual orientation. Harassment on any of the grounds, referred to in section 6(3) of the *EEA*, constitutes unfair discrimination.

[20] As amended by section 57 of *Act No. 42 of 1996* and by section 56 of *Act No. 12 of 2002*.

[21] Section 8 of *PEPUDA* stipulates that no person may be unfairly discriminated against on the grounds of gender, expressly including GBV. It further prohibits any limitation of women's access to social services, such as health or education, and the denial of systemic inequality of access to opportunities.

[22] Section 1 provides that sexual harassment means: (a) unwelcome sexual attention from a person who knows or ought reasonably to know that such attention is unwelcome; (b) unwelcome explicit or implicit behavior, suggestions, messages, or remarks of a sexual nature that have the effect of offending, intimidating or humiliating the complainant or a related person in circumstances, which a reasonable person having regard to all the circumstances would have anticipated that the complainant or related person would be offended, humiliated or intimidated; (c) implied or expressed promise of reward for complying with a sexually-oriented request; or (d) implied or expressed threat of reprisal or actual reprisal for refusal to comply with a sexually-oriented request.

Additionally, the *Criminal Law (Sexual Offences and Related Matters) Amendment Act, 32 of 2007 (Sexual Offences Act)* (*SOA*) provides the framework for the provision of adequate and effective protection to all victims of sexual offenses and makes express mention of vulnerable groups such as women, children, and mentally handicapped persons.[23]

More recently, three new laws aimed at creating a more robust legislative framework which governs the prohibition of acts of violence against women and children was signed by the President.[24] First, on 28 January 2022, the *Domestic Violence Amendment Act 14 of 2021* (*DVAA*) was signed into law. The purpose of the *DVAA* is to amend its predecessor, the *DVA*, and introduces significant changes to it,[25] by expanding the scope of the Act to apply to forms of harm that occur through the use of electronic communication, including unreasonably and repeatedly contacting a person online monitoring or tracking a person's movements or activities without their consent, or disclosing an electronic message that is abusive, degrading, offensive or humiliating, or violates or offends the sexual integrity or dignity of a person. The *DVAA* expands on existing definitions, such as "domestic violence," to include spiritual abuse, elder abuse, coercive behavior, controlling behavior, and subjecting children to certain listed coercive and controlling behavior. Another significant change is that victims of domestic violence can now apply for protection orders electronically.[26] The *DVAA* also imposes obligations on the Departments of Health and Social Development to provide certain services to survivors of domestic violence.

Second, the *Criminal and Related Matters Amendment Act, 12 of 2021* was also signed into law. The purpose of Act is to amend the *Magistrates' Courts Act, 1944*, to provide for the appointment of intermediaries and the giving of evidence through intermediaries in proceedings other than criminal proceedings, the oath and competency of intermediaries, and the giving of evidence through audio-visual link in proceedings other than criminal proceedings. It also amends the *Criminal Procedure Act, 1977*, so as to further regulate the granting and cancellation of bail, the giving of evidence by means of closed-circuit television or similar electronic media, the giving of evidence by a witness with physical, psychological or mental disability, the appointment, oath and competency of intermediaries, and the right of a complainant

---

[23] Article 56(1) of the *SOA* states that whenever an accused person is charged with an offense under section 3, 4, 5, 6, or 7 it is not a valid defence for that accused person to contend that a marital or other relationship exists or existed between him or her and the complainant. The *Act* also contains provisions on trafficking (Chapter 7, Part 6).

[24] South African Government (2022).

[25] The *DVAA* also amends provisions of the *Criminal Procedure Act 51 of 1977, Firearms Control Act 60 of 2000, Protection from Harassment Act 17 of 2011* and the *Superior Courts Act 10 of 2013.*

[26] Section 4(1)(bb) of the *DVAA* provides that any complainant may, on an ex parte basis, apply to a court for a protection order. The application must be lodged to the clerk or can be submitted by sending the application to an electronic address (email address) of the court who has jurisdiction to hear the matter. This change will undoubtedly lessen the burden on complainants who are seeking urgent protection.

in a domestic related offense to participate in parole proceedings. The *Criminal Law Amendment Act, 1997*, is amended to further regulate sentences in respect of offenses that have been committed against vulnerable persons, and the *Superior Courts Act, 2013*, is amended to provide for the appointment of intermediaries and the giving of evidence through intermediaries in proceedings other than criminal proceedings, the oath and competency of intermediaries, and the giving of evidence through audio-visual link in proceedings other than criminal proceedings, and to provide for matters connected therewith.

The third law that was adopted includes the *Criminal Law (Sexual Offences and Related Matters) Amendment Act, Amendment Act 13 of* 2021. The purpose of this new law is to amend the *SOA*, and it extends the ambit of the offense of incest, introduces a new offense of sexual intimidation, expands the list of people who are to be protected to include other vulnerable people, such as women under the age of 25 who are studying or living in student residence, people with physical, mental or intellectual disabilities, and people over the age of 60 who, for example, receive community-based care and support services. The Act further regulates the inclusion *and* removal of particulars of persons in the National Register for Sex Offenders. It also extends the list of persons who are to be protected in terms of Chapter 6 of the Act and persons who are entitled to submit applications to the Registrar of the National Register for Sex Offenders. Other amendments include regulating the reporting duty of persons who are aware that sexual offenses have been committed against persons who are vulnerable, and to provide for matters connected therewith.

7.2.2 International Legal Framework

These laws discussed above give expression to the constitutional rights to equality, human dignity, life and freedom and security of the person. These human rights find further expression in international and regional human rights frameworks, including, inter alia, the 1948 *Universal Declaration of Human Rights* (*UDHR*)[27] which forms the most basic international foundation for combating violence against women. The *UDHR*[28] lays out the rights and principles of equality, security, liberty, integrity, and dignity of all people, including women. Though it does not have specific provisions

[27] UN General Assembly, *Universal Declaration of Human Rights, 1948.*

[28] The *UDHR* represents the first comprehensive statement to articulate a series of alienable rights for both men and women. It is important to note that the *UDHR* is not a treaty, and this means that it is not directly binding on member states. Treaties are typically binding on those member states who elect to be bound by their obligations. Notwithstanding that the *UDHR* is not a treaty, it has however been invoked on several key international human rights matters and has therefore become a binding force through international customary law. Moreover, certain provisions of the *UDHR* have been incorporated or elaborated upon in a number of international treaties, regional human rights instruments, national constitutions and law.

relating to women, it takes a more gender-neutral approach to promoting and protecting human rights.

The 1989 *United Nations Convention on the Rights of the Child* (*CRC*) seeks to promote and protect the rights of children.[29] It serves as a yard stick in which member states are to be guided by and in the development of laws and any other efforts in promoting the rights of children. The *CRC* has had a major influence in the South African legislative framework relating to children's rights.[30]

Other frameworks include the *International Covenant on Civil and Political Rights, 1966* (*ICCPR*),[31] the *International Covenant on Economic, Social and Cultural Rights, 1966* (*ICESCR*)[32] and the 1979 *Convention on the Elimination of All Forms of Discrimination against Women* (*CEDAW*). *CEDAW* was a major step forward in establishing key rights for women and was the first document to "comprehensively address women's basic human rights within political, cultural, economic, social, and family life."[33] It obliges states "to take all appropriate measures, including legislation, to modify or abolish existing laws, regulations, customs, and practices, which constitute discrimination against women."[34] The original *CEDAW*

---

[29]Multiple edited collections have been published providing a wealth of analysis on the Convention's implementation. See, for example, Tobin (2019); Kilkelly and Liefaard (2018); Ruck et al. (2017) and Vandenhole et al. (2015)

[30]Following South Africa's ratification of the *CRC* on 16 June 1995, the new *Constitution* was adopted in 1996, with a dedicated and detailed section on children's rights (section 28). Situated in Chapter 2 of the *Constitution*, (the *Bill of Rights* chapter), the children's rights provision sits alongside a number of other provisions—including section 26 on housing, section 27 on healthcare and section 29 on education—which also apply to children. Section 28 on children's rights is a unique constitutional provision. It recognises the child's rights: to name and nationality (section 28(1)(a)), family and alternative care (section 28(1)(b)), basic nutrition and healthcare (section 28(1)(c), protection from exploitation and abuse (section 28(1)(e)–(f)) and protection from the arbitrary detention (section 28(1)(g)). In line with Article 1 of the *CRC*, section 28(3) defines a child as a person under 18 years and in requiring that a child's best interests are of "paramount importance in every matter concerning the child," section 28(2) of the *Constitution* goes beyond the *CRC* standard (Article 3(1) of which requires that a child's best interests are "a primary consideration"). Significantly, Section 28(1)(h) provides children with the additional safeguard of the right to be assigned a legal practitioner at state expense in civil proceedings affecting the child, if substantial injustice would otherwise result. This is a unique provision which reinforces the child as a legal actor and in contemplating the child's participation in civil proceedings, reflects an early and progressive understanding of children's access to justice. See Skelton (2015), p. 14; Kilkelly and Liefaard (2019), p. 521.

[31]The *ICCPR* prohibits discrimination based on sex. The prohibition against "inhuman or degrading treatment" in the *ICCPR* should be interpreted as a prohibition of violence against women.

[32]The *ICSCR* was adopted by the United Nations General Assembly on 16 December 1966. The treaty enshrines the universal right to social, economic and cultural rights. The treaty basically binds member states to working towards the social, economic and cultural rights of their citizens. These rights include the right to an adequate standard of living, the right to free education, the right to social security and the right to health.

[33]Rana and Perrie (2019), p. 111.

[34]Article 2 (f) of *CEDAW*.

did not explicitly prohibit violence against women, but rather outlawed "discrimination against women in all its forms." Subsequent recommendations issued by the *CEDAW* Committee,[35] which oversees states' compliance with the *Convention*, have explicitly defined "discrimination" to include violence against women.

Specifically, the Committee's *General Recommendation 19*[36] broadly defines discrimination to incorporate GBV including physical, mental, or sexual harm or suffering, threats of such acts, coercion, and other deprivations of liberty. This recommendation also clarifies that states may also "be responsible for private acts if they fail to act with due diligence to prevent violations of rights or to investigate and punish acts of violence, and for providing compensation."[37] This implies that states are responsible for inaction in preventing acts of GBV and discriminatory practices.

General Recommendation 35 elaborates on the gender-based nature of the forms of violence mentioned in *General Recommendation 19. General Recommendation 35* builds on the work of the *CEDAW* Committee and other international human rights mechanisms, as well as developments at national, regional, and international levels. It provides a more comprehensive guidance to accelerate the elimination of GBV. *General Recommendation 35* is also a milestone as it:

- Recognizes that the prohibition of GBV has become a norm of international customary law;
- Expands the understanding of violence to include violations of sexual and reproductive health rights;
- Stresses the need to change social norms and stereotypes that support violence, in the context of a resurgence of narratives threatening the concept of gender equality in the name of culture, tradition or religion;
- Clearly defines different levels of liability of the State for acts and omissions committed by its agents or those acting under its authority—in the territory of the State or abroad—and for failing to act with due diligence to prevent violence at the hands of private individuals and companies, protect women and girls from it, and ensure access to remedies for survivors;
- Unequivocally calls for the repeal of all laws and policies that directly and indirectly excuse, condone and facilitate violence; and

[35] *CEDAW* is monitored by a group of independent experts: the Committee for the Elimination of Discrimination Against Women, hereinafter referred to as the CEDAW Committee under its Article 17(1).

[36] UN Committee on the Elimination of Discrimination Against Women (CEDAW) (1992) *CEDAW General Recommendation No. 19: Violence against women. General Recommendation No. 19* was historic as it clearly framed violence against women as a form and manifestation of gender-based discrimination, used to subordinate and oppress women. It unequivocally brought violence outside of the private sphere and into the realm of human rights.

[37] UN Committee on the Elimination of All Forms of Violence Against Women (CEDAW), Violence Against Women, *General Recommendation no. 19* (eleventh session, 1992), U.N. Document CEDAW/C/1992/L.1/Add.15. (*General Recommendation 19: Violence against women*), Comment (9).

- Emphasizes the need for approaches that promote and respect women's autonomy and decision-making in all spheres of life.

The Fourth World Conference on Women in September 1995[38] represented a remarkable and unprecedented global and diverse plurality of perspectives on gender equality and the empowerment of all women in what has become subsequently known as the *Beijing Declaration and Platform for Action* (*Beijing Platform for Action*).[39] The *Beijing Platform for Action* is an agenda for women's empowerment which is aimed at removing all the obstacles to women's active participation in all spheres of public and private life through a full and equal share in economic, social, cultural and political decision-making. More importantly, it is aimed at establishing the principle of shared power and responsibility between women and men at home, in the workplace and in the wider national and international communities. Lastly, it emphasizes that gender equality can only be addressed by women and men working together and in partnership around the world.[40]

As a defining framework for change, the *Platform for Action* made comprehensive commitments under twelve critical areas of concern each of which is broken down into its Strategic Objectives and Actions.[41] The twelve "critical areas of concern" which are to be addressed in order to achieve gender equality and women's empowerment include:

- The persistent and increasing burden of poverty on women;
- Inequalities and inadequacies in and unequal access to education and training;
- Inequalities and inadequacies in and unequal access to healthcare and related services;
- Violence against women;
- The effects of armed and other types of conflict on women, including those living under foreign occupation;

---

[38] In recognising that violence against women is an obstacle to the achievement of equality, development and peace, that various forms of violence are perpetrated and/or condoned by the state and that there is routine failure by states to protect and promote the fundamental human rights and freedoms of women, governments at the Fourth World Conference on Women in Beijing committed to three significant strategic objectives: "1. To take integrated measures to prevent and eliminate violence against women; 2. To study the causes and consequences of violence against women and the effectiveness of preventative measures; and 3. To eliminate trafficking in women and assist victims of violence due to prostitution and trafficking."

These strategic objectives are accompanied by a set of actions to be taken by governments in order to comply with the undertakings and commitments made in terms of the Beijing Declaration and Platform for Action.

See People Opposing Women Abuse (POWA) (2010).

[39] United Nations (1995) *Fourth World Conference on Women: Beijing Declaration and Platform for Action* is considered the most progressive blueprint ever for advancing women's rights.

[40] UN Women (2015).

[41] The 1995 Beijing Platform for Action flagged 12 key areas where urgent action was needed to ensure greater equality and opportunities for women and men, girls and boys. It also laid out concrete ways for countries to bring about change. See United Nations (1995).

- Inequality in economic structures and policies, in all forms of productive activities and in access to resources;
- Inequality between men and women in the sharing of power and decision-making at all levels;
- Insufficient mechanisms at all levels to promote the advancement of women;
- Lack of respect for and inadequate promotion and protection of the human rights of women;
- Stereotyping of women and inequality in women's access to and participation in all communication systems, especially in the media;
- Gender inequalities in the management of natural resources and in the safe guarding of the environment; and
- Persistent discrimination against and violation of the rights of the girl child.

Although the *Beijing Platform for Action* is not a binding treaty, it is a consensus document and probably constitutes the most comprehensive statement about the issues concerning women. It further reaffirms important agreements reached at world summits and conferences which are aimed at enhancing the participation of women in power and decision-making. The *Beijing Platform for Action* consequently calls on governments to enact and enforce penal, civil, labor, and administrative sanctions to punish and redress the wrongs done to victims. It also calls on governments to adopt, implement and review legislation to ensure its effectiveness in eliminating violence against women, emphasizing the prevention of violence and the prosecution of offenders.

7.2.3 Regional Framework

On a regional level there is the *African Charter on Human and People's Rights, 1981* (*African Charter*),[42] the 2003 *Protocol to the African Charter on Human and Peoples Rights on the Rights of Women in Africa (Maputo Protocol)*, and the 2008 *Southern African Development Community (SADC) Protocol on Gender and Development* (*SADC Protocol*).[43] The *Maputo Protocol*, is hailed as one of the most progressive home-grown instruments relating to the promotion of the rights of women in Africa. It encompasses the provisions of *CEDAW* and further expands on various women's human rights such as those relating to sexual and reproductive health rights and violence against women. Article 14 of the *Protocol* expands on

[42] Article 4 of the *African Charter* places absolute legal requirements in that it requires States to take appropriate and effective measures to, inter alia, enact and enforce laws to prohibit and punish all forms of violence against women, establish mechanisms and accessible services for effective information, rehabilitation, and reparation for victims of violence, and provide adequate budgetary and other resources for the implementation and monitoring of actions aimed at preventing and eradicating violence against women.

[43] SADC (2023).

women's sexual and reproductive health rights to include the right to control fertility and spacing of children, authorizing medical abortion in cases of sexual assault, rape, and incest.[44] As a critical document on the protection of the rights women in Africa, the *Maputo Protocol* requires member states to eliminate all forms of discrimination against women through appropriate legislative and institutional measures. The *Maputo Protocol* directs member states to, if they have not already done so, include in their national constitutions and other legislative instruments principles of equality between men and women and ensure the effective application of these principles. Also of importance, the *Maputo Protocol* requires member states to integrate a gender perspective in their policy decisions, legislation, development plans, programs, and activities.

The *SADC Protocol* (revised in 2016)[45] emphasizes the need to address all forms of GBV. It illustrates the integration and mainstreaming of gender issues into the Southern African Development Community Programme of Action and community building initiatives which are key to sustainable development.[46] The objective of the *SADC Protocol* is to provide for the empowerment of women to eliminate discrimination and to achieve gender equality and equity through the development and implementation of gender responsive legislation, policies, programs, and projects. The *SADC Protocol*, through Articles 20–25, identifies several measures to address GBV including legal measures, social, economic, cultural and political practices, support services, measures against sexual harassment, training of service providers, and the adoption of integrated approaches.

Part Six of the *SADC Protocol* has set the following key requirements for Member States to eliminate GBV at every level:

- Enact and enforce legislation prohibiting all forms of gender-based violence;
- Develop strategies to prevent and eliminate all harmful social and cultural practices;
- Ensure that perpetrators of all forms of gender-based violence are tried by a court of competent jurisdiction;
- Ensure that the laws on GBV provide for the comprehensive testing, treatment, and care of survivors of sexual offenses;

---

[44] Mpani and Nsibande (2015), p. 33.

[45] The *Agreement Amending the SADC Protocol on Gender and Development, 2016*.

[46] The SADC Protocol documents promotes equal participation by both male and females in all electoral processes, decision making through putting in place policies, strategies and programmes through leadership, gender sensitivity training and mentoring. Providing structures for decision making positions, strengthening structures to enhance gender mainstreaming as well as changing discriminatory attitude and norms of decision-making structures and procedures. In terms of Implementation, Monitoring and Evaluation the State Parties would need to ensure the implementation of the Protocol document at a National Level and there are national action plans with measurable timeframes and evaluation mechanisms developed and implemented. The State parties should collect and analyze baseline data against progress in which through achieving targets it will be monitored. Reporting will be done every 2 years to the secretary of SADC.

- Review and reform criminal laws and procedures applicable to cases of sexual offenses and GBV;
- Enact and adopt specific legislative provisions to prevent trafficking in persons and provide holistic serviced to the victims, with the aim or re-integrating them into society;
- Enact legislative provisions, and adopt and implement policies, strategies, and programs which define and prohibit sexual harassment in all spheres, and provide deterrent sanctions for perpetrators of sexual harassment; and
- Adopt integrated approaches, including institutional cross sector structures, with the aim of eliminating gender-based violence.

Key provisions in the *SADC Protocol* include requiring the equal representation of women in all areas of decision-making, equal access to quality education and training for women and men, as well as their retention at all levels of education, and equal participation of women in economic policy formulation and implementation.

The *SADC Protocol* urges Member States to enact and enforce legislation prohibiting all forms of GBV. In addition, the SADC has developed the Regional Strategy and Framework of Action for Addressing GBV (2018–2030) and the Regional Strategy on Women, Peace and Security (2018–2022), all of which seek to harmonize and coordinate the regional response to GBV and to help Member States to effectively respond to GBV. Additionally, the SADC Strategy for Sexual and Reproductive Health and Rights (2019–2030)[47] (SRHR) and its corresponding scorecard includes indicators to measure progress to the SDG's targets related to SDG 5.1.[48] The SRHR SADC Scorecard is meant to be a high-level peer review accountability tool to track progress of the Region in achieving the SADC Regional Strategy for SRHR 2019–2030 and the SRHR targets of the SDGs.[49] It consists of twenty key indicators to track progress in meeting the ten outcomes of the strategy. Member States, including South Africa, are to report every 2 years on progress made against the SADC Scorecard.

As a SADC Community legal instrument, the *SADC Protocol*, has laid the basis for mainstreaming gender in all other SADC Community protocols and policies, thereby making it central to the agenda of achieving regional integration, development, and democracy. The *SADC Protocol* is therefore a critical instrument within the SADC Community as it brings together all the existing commitments made towards achieving gender equality into one sub-regional instrument. These include

[47] The SADC Regional Strategy on SRHR (2019–2030) builds on the progress made in the region, guided by the SADC Sexual and Reproductive Health Strategy (2006–2015), in improving sexual and reproductive health and rights (SRHR) during the period of the Millennium Development Goals.

[48] According to SDG Target 5.1 the goal is to end all forms of discrimination against women and girls everywhere.

[49] SDG Target 3.7 relates to Sexual and reproductive health and states that by 2030 the goals is to ensure universal access to sexual and reproductive health-care services, including for family planning, information and education, and the integration of reproductive health into national strategies.

the commitments made in the *CEDAW*, the *Beijing Platform for Action*, the *African Charter*, and the Development Goals.

7.3 South Africa's Obligations Under International, National, and Regional Instruments

South Africa is a signatory of the main international conventions relating to gender equality and the protection of women. In summary these include: *CEDAW* ratified in 1995, *DEVAW* ratified in 1996, *Beijing Platform for Action* which was ratified in 1995, Millennium Declaration and Millennium Development Goals (MDGs) ratified in 2000,[50] the SDGs,[51] and the *Protocol to Prevent, Suppress and Punishing of Trafficking in Persons Especially Women and Children* ratified in 2004,[52] which supplements the *UN Convention against Transnational Organized Crime* and was also ratified by South Africa in 2004.[53] South Africa has also ratified the following regional gender equality commitments: *Maputo Protocol* ratified in 2004, *SADC Protocol on Gender and Development* ratified in 2008 and the *Solemn Declaration on Gender Equality in Africa* ratified in 2004.[54]

Under these various instruments, South Africa is obliged to address persistent violations of human rights and take measures to prevent their occurrence. Through its ratification of *CEDAW*, South Africa has assumed the obligation to "pursue by all appropriate means and without delay a policy of eliminating discrimination against women 'by refraining' from engaging in any act or practice of discrimination against

[50] In September 2000, leaders of 189 countries gathered at the United Nations headquarters and signed the historic Millennium Declaration, in which they committed to achieving a set of eight measurable goals that range from halving extreme poverty and hunger to promoting gender equality and reducing child mortality, by the target date of 2015.

[51] After the MDGs came to an end in 2015, the UN developed the SDGs which saw 193 countries of the UN General Assembly adopt the 2030 Development Agenda titled "*Transforming our world: the 2030 Agenda for Sustainable Development.*" South Africa signed and ratified the *2030 Development Agenda* and agreed to this international commitment that seeks to promote development that meets the needs of the present without compromising the ability of future generations to meet their own needs.

[52] South Africa ratified the *Protocol to Prevent, Suppress and Punish Trafficking in Persons, Especially Women and Children* (commonly referred to as the "Palermo Protocol") which obliged Parliament to pass legislation that deals with all forms of Trafficking in Persons. Consequently, the *Prevention and Combating of Trafficking in Persons Act 7 of 2013* was passed and, except for section 15, 16 and 31(2)(b)(ii), came into operation on 9 August 2015. This Act is the first statute that comprehensively addresses Trafficking in Persons in South Africa.

[53] UN General Assembly, United Nations Convention against Transnational Organized Crime: Resolution/adopted by the General Assembly, 8 January 2001, A/RES/55/25.

[54] *The Solemn Declaration on Gender Equality in Africa*, was adopted in July 2004 in Addis Ababa, Ethiopia. The Solemn Declaration calls for member states' continual action toward achieving gender equality and reinforcing their commitment to international and regional women's rights instruments.

women."[55] States need to acknowledge their shortcomings and respond to recommendations in a positive way. Furthermore, by ratifying *CEDAW* without reservations South Africa has agreed to:

- incorporate the principle of equality between men and women in its legal system, abolish all discriminatory laws and adopt appropriate one prohibiting discrimination against women;
- to establish tribunals and other public institutions to ensure the effective protection of women against discrimination; and
- ensure the elimination of all acts of discrimination against women.

South also has obligations under *CEDAW* to report on its progress in eliminating various barriers to achieving equality. In addition, *CEDAW* provides the basis for realizing equality between men and women and in ensuring amongst others, that women have equal rights to family benefits and financial credit, rural women have the right to adequate living conditions, participate in development planning, and access to health care and education, and women have equal rights with men in matters related to marriage, inheritance, and family relations. *CEDAW* not only highlights the negative impact of discrimination on women, but it also stresses the need for behavioral and attitudinal change, through the education of both men and women to overcome prejudices and eliminate practices that discriminate against women.

To this end South Africa must ensure that public authorities and institutions act in conformity with the obligation not to discriminate against women, including by adopting legislative or other measures to prohibit discrimination, and by ensuring through competent national tribunals and other public institutions the effective protection of women against any act of discrimination.[56] Accordingly, States have a positive obligation to eliminate GBV. When states routinely fail to effectively respond to GBV it creates the impression that such attacks can be committed with impunity.[57] In so doing, states fail in their obligations under the various instruments.[58]

The international obligation to exercise due diligence requires States to establish effective measures to prevent, investigate and prosecute cases of violence against women. This includes effective means to respond to each case of violence, as well as to address the structural causes of violence by ensuring comprehensive legal and

[55] CEDAW, Article 2(d).

[56] Article 4 of the *DEVAW* calls on states to "pursue by all appropriate means and without delay a policy of eliminating violence against women" and, among other things, to "exercise due diligence to prevent, investigate and in accordance with national legislation, punish acts of violence against women, whether those acts are perpetrated by the State or by private persons." *DEVAW* is a non-binding resolution which sets out a common international standard that states should follow.

[57] For a more detailed discussion of South Africa's obligations under international law, see Human Rights Watch (2021), pp. 39–43.

[58] To the extent that this failure reflects discrimination on the basis of gender and/or race, it also constitutes a violation of the state's international obligation to guarantee equal protection of the law.

policy frameworks, gender sensitive justice systems and police, available health and social services and awareness raising activities. It is important to note that whilst States may and should be held liable for breach of its international obligations if it fails to take and provide appropriate measures for protection and judicial enforcement,[59] state responsibility does not always arise from all acts or omissions that take place within its territory.

However, the obligations in the various human rights instruments discussed above have two important implications. First, positive obligations are imposed on states to establish and maintain adequate legal and other measures through which the rights can be guaranteed. Second, and as mentioned above, states need to exercise due diligence to prevent the violation of human rights by private actors.[60] Therefore, the obligation to respect rights and to prevent its violations also requires positive government action to overcome the infringement of rights by private individuals. This view is consistent with *General Recommendation 19* which provides that "states may also be responsible for private acts if they fail to act with due diligence to prevent violations of rights or to investigate and punish acts of violence, and to provide compensation."[61] In accordance with international law, state responsibility arises when the conduct of the state breaches its international obligations, which arise from customary or treaty-based human rights law.[62] Therefore, states are not absolved from responsibility simply because they did not cause harm.[63]

In addition, the obligations enumerated by the *CEDAW* Committee extend beyond the justice system and encompass preventive and protective measures including counselling and support services.[64] This would include the provision of medical and psychological assistance to women and girls who are victims of violence.[65]

---

[59] Meyersfeld (2010).

[60] Combrinck (1998), p. 670.

[61] General Comments no. 9 of *General Recommendation 19*.

[62] Crawford (2013), p. 93.

[63] *Carmichele v Minister of Safety & Security & Another* 2001 (4) SA 938 (CC); 2001 (10) BCLR 995 (CC).

[64] In 1992, the CEDAW Committee adopted a general recommendation and comments on states' obligations under CEDAW that set forth the elements of potentially effective remedies to address the problem of violence against women as follows: "a. Effective legal measures, including penal sanctions, civil remedies and compensatory provisions to protect women against all kinds of violence, including, inter alia, violence and abuse in the family, sexual assault and sexual harassment in the workplace; b. Preventive measures, including public information and education programmes to change attitudes concerning the roles and status of men and women; c. Protective measures, including refuges, counselling, rehabilitation and support services for women who are the victims of violence or who are at risk of violence. *General Recommendation 19*."

[65] Also, in line with these principles would be the provision of medical assistance to victims of sexual violence consistent with the prevailing best practice on post HIV/AIDS-exposure prophylaxis to decrease the likelihood of contracting the virus.

Furthermore, the *Beijing Platform for Action* not only highlights critical areas of concerns that must be addressed to achieve gender equality and women's empowerment, but it also sets out detailed recommendations of action needed to address these areas. Countries that elected to sign the *Beijing Platform for Action* effectively committed themselves to implementing the detailed recommendations of action respective jurisdictions. Thus, as a signatory to the *Beijing Platform for Action*, South Africa committed itself to eradicating barriers hindering the empowerment and advancement of women and to advancing the goals of equality, development, and peace for women. It further requires dedicated efforts towards addressing the constraints and obstacles hindering the advancement and empowerment of women all over the world. It has been almost three decades since the Conference and South Africa has made some notable progress towards addressing the twelve critical areas of concern in terms of the *Beijing Platform for Action*. However, South Africa still needs to do more seeing as there are challenges in all twelve critical areas of concern. In addition, with regards to SDG 5 which focuses on gender equality, whilst good strides have been made by South Africa,[66] due to the high rates of GBV in the country, achieving same remains a major challenge.[67]

Furthermore, and in line with some of the above conventions, protocols, and treaties South Africa has developed, as discussed above, a range of legislation which addresses specific issues linked to gender equality.[68] Freedom from violence is specifically recognized as fundamental to the equal enjoyment of human rights and fundamental freedoms. Seeing that section 12(1) (c) of the *Constitution* provides that "everyone has the right to be free from all forms of violence from either public or private sources," the state is consequently required to protect individuals, both by refraining from such violations itself and by taking active steps to prevent violations by others. The subsection, read in conjunction with section 7(2) of the *Constitution*, places a positive duty on the state to protect everyone from violent crime.[69] Furthermore, section 12 imposes the correlative duties not to eliminate a person's security, to protect people against deprivation of security by others, and to provide for the security of those unable to provide for their own.[70] The constitutional mandate on gender equality is clear, and the legislative process is providing the building blocks for a gender equitable society. Looking at the rates of GBVF, the government does

---

[66] Stats SA (2019), p. 100.

[67] South Africa (2023).

[68] These include the *Constitution* and the *Bill of Rights*, *PEPUDA*, which gives the CGE powers to get involved in the equality court matters, *EEA*, *Recognition of Customary Marriages Act*, *Civil Union Act 17 of 2006* (South Africa is the fifth country in the world, the first in Africa and the second outside Europe to legislate on same sex marriages) the *DVA* and the *DVAA*, *SOA*, *Choice on Termination of Pregnancy Act 92 of 1996* and the *Amendment Act 1 of 2008* and the *Children's Act 38 of 2005* (As amended by the *Children's Act 41 of 2007*).

[69] *S v Baloyi* 2000 (2) SA 425 (CC), para 11.

[70] The *Carmichele v Minister of Safety and Security (Centre for Appeal Legal Studies Intervening)* 2001 (4) SA 938 (CC), case clearly outlines how these obligations have developed in relation to violence against women.

however face major challenges in ensuring that constitutional, legislative and policy imperative on gender equality and women's empowerment are translated into substantive improvements in the lives of women and girls.

7.4 Policy Framework and Interventions

In addition, South Africa has a National Gender Policy Framework that was created to ensure that all policies and laws at all levels of government incorporate gender equality and provide protections from GBV.[71] It therefore reflects South Africa's vision for gender equality and how it intends to realize this ideal. The policy stipulates the overarching principles, practices, and programs which will be integrated by all sectors of the South African government into their policies. This gender policy also details a strategy for gender mainstreaming and provides guiding principles for its implementation. Most importantly the policy details the long- and short-term mechanisms for determining the extent of gender justice and equality.[72] The National Gender Policy Framework is supported in its work by the CGE.[73] As mentioned previously, the CGE is responsible for advancing, promoting, and protecting gender equality in South Africa through undertaking research, public education, policy development, legislative initiatives, effective monitoring, and litigation. Its mandate is also to work towards the creation of a violence free society by significantly reducing GBV. In this regard, it developed a Gender Equality Strategic Plan (2008–2013) with a thematic area related to GBV.[74]

The 365 Day Action Plan to End Gender-Based Violence (2007), envisaged that each year the 16 Day Campaign on GBV would become a platform both to heighten awareness and take stock of gaps and achievements and to ensure sustained, measurable efforts to end GBV.

South Africa has also developed a National Strategic Framework on GBVF,[75] made possible by an Interim Steering Committee on GBVF. The Interim Steering Committee was established under Article 3 of the Declaration on GBVF,[76] with the mandate to draft a GBVF National Strategic Plan (NSP) framework and to establish a multi-sector GBVF Council, which is a coordinating body that will champion work

[71] Office on the Status of Women (2002).

[72] Some examples include the promotion of affirmative action in government; supporting government bodies to integrate a gender perspective in all policies and programmes; organising gender training for government departments and assisting different government departments to work together on issues, particularly pertaining to gender.

[73] Established in terms of Section 187 of the *Constitution* to promote respect for gender equality and the protection, development, and attainment of gender equality.

[74] South African Government (2007).

[75] Parliamentary Monitoring Group (2021).

[76] The Presidency: Republic of South Africa (2018).

around the national GBVF campaign.[77] The national GBVF campaign followed the adoption of the Declaration on GBVF during a Presidential Summit on GBVF held in November 2018.

The NSP aims to provide a multi-sectoral, coherent strategic policy and programming framework to strengthen a coordinated national response to the crisis of GBVF in the country. It seeks to address the needs and challenges faced by all. Included herein is everyone across age, sexual orientation, sexual and gender identities, and specific groups such as elderly women, women who live with disabilities, migrant women, and transgender women, who are affected and impacted by the GBV scourge in South Africa.[78] Furthermore, with the NSP, impetus is given to Priority Six (6) of Community Safety and Social Cohesion[79] and provides a coherent national framework to support South Africa in meeting its sustainable development goals and targets.[80]

7.5 GBV Services

In addition to what can only be termed a comprehensive legal framework, South Africa offers victims and survivors of GBVF various services. The states response to GBV can be analyzed through the lens of the programs and services directly provided by state institutions. The following discussion focuses on some of the most pertinent of services.

7.5.1 Thuthuzela Care Centers

One of the key responses of the South African government to provide care to rape victims and victims of sexual assault has been to establish the Thuthuzela Care

[77] Government of South Africa (2020).

[78] Hsiao et al. (2017).

[79] Department of Planning, Monitoring and Evaluation (2019), p. 4. The idea is that: "[a] socially cohesive and safe South Africa requires a series of intersecting interventions that unite our country. To achieve this vision, a democratic culture of participation and equality must be instilled, but it also requires dedicated interventions to address actions that undermine these values. Achieving social cohesion and safe communities requires strengthening criminal justice platforms, police services and community participation in public policing. This work cannot be done without improving trust in our public sector and its institutions," 2; and that sharing of common spaces enables people across race and class who had been separated for decades to get to know each other and appreciate each other's humanity as well as debunk stereotypes. Public interaction is important for building trusting societies.

[80] Specifically, SDG 5.1; 5.2; 5.3 and 16.1 and 16.2.

Centers (TCC).[81] The TCCs are a critical part of South Africa's anti-rape strategy and are located within a public hospital close to communities where the incidence of rape is particularly high. The Thuthuzela project is led by the National Prosecuting Authority's (NPA's) Sexual Offences and Community Affairs Unit (SOCA), in partnership with various departments and donors as a response to the urgent need for an integrated strategy for prevention, response and support for rape victims.[82] It operates as 24-hour one-stop centers that assist victims of sexual offenses by providing access to required services, including the police, counselling, doctors, assistance with court preparation and prosecution of the perpetrator.[83]

The centers also provide medical and psycho-social services to victims of GBV and is playing a significant role in advancing the fight against GBV crimes in the country. The TCCs are also linked to sexual offenses courts, which are staffed by skilled prosecutors, social workers, and magistrates. The goals of the TCCs are to reduce secondary victimization, reduce the cycle time to finalization of legal cases and improve the perpetrator conviction rate.[84]

Accountability by each stakeholder from the opening of the case to its conclusion has seen a considerable improvement of conviction rates. The conviction rates increased from an average of 7–60% among TCC clients who choose to open a case.[85] Since 2006, there are approximately 61 TCCs operating across South Africa. Overall, the TCC model in South Africa is regarded as a successful initiative as it is the most cohesive intervention to date that seeks to prevent and eradicate GBVF.

7.5.2 *Sexual Offenses Courts*

Internationally, South Africa is at the forefront of developments with respect to specialized sexual offenses courts that adopt a victim-centered approach. It has been found that most of the specifications of the blueprint for the Sexual Offences Courts are still recognized as an international best practice model.[86] Sexual Offences Courts were established to provide survivor-centered justice with specialized services, specialized infrastructure, and specialized personnel. The courts resulted in more efficient prosecution and adjudication in the various areas. First, the average conviction rate improved substantially to 62%, as opposed to 42% in the ordinary

[81] Details of operating TCCs are available at http://www.justice.gov.za/vg/TCCs-list.pdf.

[82] Dlamini (2023).

[83] African Commission on Human and Peoples' Right (2015).

[84] National Prosecuting Authority (2022).

[85] Segar (2023).

[86] The Model Guidelines for prosecutors in child sexual abuse cases require that, in assigning prosecutors to Sexual Offences Courts, emphasis must be placed on the individual prosecutor's experience with children and on any specialised training he or she might have. Müller and van der Merwe (2004).

courts.[87] The average conviction rate in some well-established Sexual Offences Courts increased to between 75% and 95%. The turnaround time in the finalization of proceedings for sex offenses was reduced to less than 6 months, although longer time frames were indicated in a study of the Bloemfontein court.[88] Secondary victimization was reduced as a result of the provision of separate waiting rooms for victims, counselling and other such services from other disciplines and intermediary and CCTV facilities. Finally, multidisciplinary training enhanced the skills of court personnel as well as other role-players.[89] The TCCs play an important role in the whole system of sexual assault prosecutions.[90] At their best, Sexual Offences Courts demonstrably improved conviction rates as part of a coordinated service system that looked after victims from the time of complaint through to trial.

Despite these many signs of success, the Sexual Offences Courts encountered opposition because they were better resourced than other courts, and this was perceived as a serious violation of the constitutional rights of other crime victims to equal protection under the law. In addition, the process of the establishment of the Sexual Offences Courts was inherently flawed and the implementation was not adequately structured and did not follow an all-inclusive consultative approach in certain areas, leading to its demise.[91] The evidence for the success of the Sexual Offences Courts in South Africa is considerable despite numerous difficulties, which are described in various evaluation reports. These include severe resource constraints, workload pressures, inadequate training of many prosecutors and differing levels of motivation, the stress of the work, the limitations of the courtroom facilities, and lack of support services.[92]

In 2013 the Department of Justice and Constitutional Development's Ministerial Advisory Task Team on the Adjudication of Sexual Offences Matters (MATTSO) recommended the re-establishment of Sexual Offences Courts which were scrapped in or around 2008.[93] The re-establishment of the Sexual Offences Courts will reinforce the establishment of a victim-centered court system that is prompt, responsive and effective. From the research studies, these courts were found to be successful in the establishment of a victim centered criminal justice system, reduction of secondary victimization, improvement of skills of court personnel, reduction of the cycle time in the finalization of sexual offenses cases and have generally contributed to the efficient prosecution and adjudication of these cases.[94]

---

[87] Reyneke and Kruger (2006).

[88] Walker and Louw (2005).

[89] Reyneke and Kruger (2006).

[90] Department of Justice and Constitutional Development (2013).

[91] Department of Justice (2021).

[92] Department of Justice and Constitutional Development (2013).

[93] Department of Justice and Constitutional Development (2013).

[94] Parkinson (2016).

7.5.3 One-Stop Centers

One-stop centers have also been established to provide sustainable and integrated services to victims and offenders of GBV. The project builds on work already done by UNODC Southern Africa.[95] The project was designed to offer multidisciplinary services to both the victims and the offenders of sexual and GBV in the communities of Vryburg in the North West province and Sunnyside in the Gauteng province.[96] Each center has provided a range of services (legal, counselling, medical) to the survivors of violence (specifically women and children) and rehabilitation services, including counselling and support groups for men who have been or who are seen to be potential perpetrators of violence in order to break the cycle of domestic violence.

The above discussion is in no way mean to be an exhaustive list of laws, polices, programs, and interventions adopted by the government and civil society to eliminate GBVF in the country. It is meant to merely provide an understanding and overview of the many interventions, polices and laws that are currently in place. This is done with the aim of highlighting that South Africa currently has a variety of policies, laws, and national strategies to ensure gender equality and to eliminate or curb GBV. These laws and policies are highly comprehensive and are aimed at fostering women's full participation in all spheres of life. In addition, South Africa's legislative and policy framework is aligned to international conventions that the country is a signatory to. As a signatory, the South African government is obliged to domesticate, implement, and ensure compliance with these international obligations, and attainment of their targets and principles.

What becomes clear is that South Africa does not need to implement more laws in its fight against GBVF. It has been said that:[97]

> South Africa is paper rich when it comes to dealing with sexual violence. It has ratified the leading international and regional human rights treaties and instruments seeking to address these problems, and enshrined a constitutional protection against privately perpetrated violence, applied and enforced through decisions of our highest courts. At a policy level, the South African government and the police service have identified violence against women as a critical policing priority and enacted institutional safeguards against inappropriate responses to rape complainants through National Instructions and Standing Orders. The problem is not with the law in the books but with criminal justice practice. It is in the practical realities of everyday policing and in the attendant discretionary choices, that police responses to rape crumble, reinforcing the pretext that rape is, essentially, a crime that is impervious to policing.

---

[95] United Nations (2008).

[96] UNODC Southern Africa is running additional one-stop centers in Mitchell's Plain (Western Cape), Vryburg (North-West), and Sunnyside (Gauteng).

[97] Smythe (2015).

7.6 Gaps and Challenges

Despite the major strides in law reform and political will, GBVF is still rampant in South Africa. The robust implementation of the various laws is required to efficiently eliminate GBVF. Furthermore, inadequate funding remains a major challenge.[98] The NSP attributes the high rates of GBV to South Africa's history of violence and apartheid, but particularly to the governments underinvestment in solving the problem. The CGEs March 2020 submission to the United Nations committee that oversees states' compliance with *CEDAW*[99] further highlighted that while there was "political willingness to lead national efforts to deal with gender-based violence," in practice, funding and implementation remained inadequate.[100] The CGE went on to highlight the major gaps and challenges in the area of combating GBVF. They reported that in particular, six departments responsible for carrying out specific government programs aimed at addressing GBV are restricted in various ways by resource limitations.

They are as follows:[101]

The South African Police Services

1. Inadequate training of SAPS officials to deal effectively with gender-based violence, including training on the relevant national strategic programs of action, as well as legislative and policy frameworks.
2. Lack of provisions for the establishment of adequate victim friendly rooms and specialized detectives (FCS Units) in police stations.
3. Shortages of rape kits.
4. Lack of vehicles to transport survivors to shelters, places of safety, and the medical facility for examination.

National Prosecuting Authority

1. Poorly resourced TCCs.
2. Lack of training of prosecutors.

Department of Justice and Constitutional Development

1. Inadequately resourced Sexual Offences Courts.
2. Lack of trained specialized staff (magistrates, intermediaries, and interpreters).

---

[98] For example, whilst the South African government has taken important steps in its fight against GBVF, it did not provide adequate funding for shelters and other services for GBV survivors during the COVID-19 pandemic. Many survivors have been made more vulnerable in the context of COVID-19. See Human Rights Watch (2021).

[99] In accordance with *General Recommendation 19.*

[100] Commission for Gender Equality (2020), pp. 5–6.

[101] Commission for Gender Equality (2020), pp. 5–6.

Department of Health

1. Limited number of trained Clinical Forensic Nurses.
2. Shortages of rape kits.

Department of Social Development

1. Shut down of shelters for survivors of violence due to cuts in government funding.
2. Lack of Department counsellors in police stations and TCCs.

Department of Correctional Services

1. Lack of support for survivors of violence against women, particularly when it comes to victim-offender dialogues and mediation by the parole boards.
2. Inadequate resources to track survivors to participate in the victim-offender dialogues and mediation processes.

In addition, there is a lack of cooperation among government departments.[102] It has also been identified that there are several instances in which the criminal justice system has not been supportive of survivors and low conviction rates are also a major problem.[103]

The limited resource allocations and ineffective implementation of existing policies and legislative frameworks, including weaknesses of some institutions and departments tasked with driving the country's fight against GBV must be addressed to effectively respond to GBVF in the country. Where services are being provided for survivors of GBVF, sufficient resources must be allocated to ensure sustainability of services. It has also been identified that the introduction of TCCs whilst it is a good initiative, the number of these centers per province is insufficient taking into consideration the vastness of the provinces. In summary it is clear that South Africa faces a plethora of challenges regarding gender equality and the elimination of GBV, however it has taken some very positive steps towards progress in this regard.

7.7 Concluding Remarks

South Africa has what can be labelled a comprehensive legal framework that has been put in place to combat GBV, yet despite these developments, GBV remains a grave issue. Additionally, the legislative framework on GBV in South Africa is in line with its international obligations to which the country is a signatory. While the law may not be the only panacea for what is now termed "a second pandemic" in South Africa it provides the legal foundation necessary to address this concern.

[102] Budoo-Scholtz (2022).

[103] National Prosecuting Authority (2018).

Although there appears to be political will at the national level to address the issue, challenges related to insufficient funding, budgetary limitations, and a lack of collaboration and effective coordination among government departments, have hindered progress in implementing initiatives aimed at the elimination of GBV. Funding has also affected shelters which are supposed to care for survivors of GBV. Training among police and government departments on the legislative changes has been inadequate.

Furthermore, there are too few GBV desks that have been established at police stations and too few rape kits have been provided. Addressing GBVF should remain a real priority. These failures, gaps and challenges question the commitment of government and the various institutions to addressing these issues. In addition, persistent implementation gaps and silo mentalities or tunnel vision within government departments stand in the way of a more integrated and coordinated approach. In summary, whilst the legislative and policy framework indicates that GBVF seems to be a priority in the country, the delivery of effective interventions and support is impeded by funding and consequently creates the unacceptable perception by its citizens that GBV is not considered an issue worthy of priority.

The next chapter will focus on the judicial responses to GBVF. This is an important discussion as the criminal justice system and particularly the prosecution of offenses remains one of the crucial ways in which the state protects, promotes, and fulfils constitutional rights and its various legal obligations.

References

African Commission on Human and Peoples' Rights (2015) South Africa: 2nd periodic report, 2003-2014. https://achpr.au.int/en/state-reports/south-africa-2nd-periodic-report-2003-2014. Accessed 8 Feb 2023

Budoo-Scholtz A (2022) South Africa needs to step up fight against gender based violence. https://www.hrw.org/news/2022/11/01/south-africa-needs-step-fight-against-gender-based-violence. Accessed 8 Aug 2023

Combrinck H (1998) Positive state duties to protect women from violence: recent South African developments. Hum Rights Q 670

Commission for Gender Equality (2020) Statement to the CEDAW Committee regarding South Africa's progress in the implementation of CEDAW Committee recommendations. https://tbinternet.ohchr.org/_layouts/15/treatybodyexternal/Download.aspx?symbolno=INT%2fCEDAW%2fIFS%2fZAF%2f41747&Lang=en. Accessed 15 Aug 2023

Crawford J (2013) Corollaries of breach of an international obligation. In: State responsibility: the general part. Cambridge University Press, pp 93–110

Deane T (2018) Sexual violence and the limits of laws' powers to alter behaviour: the case of South Africa. J Int Women's Stud 19(2):84–103

Department of Justice (2021) Sexual offences courts: National Strategic Plan 2016-2020. https://www.masiphephe.org.za/wp-content/uploads/2021/08/Sexual-Offences-Courts-NSP-Draft.pdf. Accessed 16 Mar 2023

Department of Justice and Constitutional Development (2013) Report on the re-establishment of sexual offences courts: ministerial advisory task team on the adjudication of sexual offence matters. https://www.polity.org.za/article/report-on-the-re-establishment-of-sexual-offences-

courts-ministerial-advisory-task-team-on-the-adjudication-of-sexual-offence-matters-2013-09-09. Accessed 24 Mar 2023
Department of Planning, Monitoring and Evaluation (2019) Priority 6: social cohesion and safer communities. https://www.dpme.gov.za/keyfocusareas/outcomesSite/MTSF_2019_2024/2019-2024%20MTSF%20PRIORITY%206.pdf. Accessed 10 Aug 2023
Dlamini J (2023) A case study on transdisciplinary approach to eradicating sexual violence: Thuthuzela Care Centres. IntechOpen. https://doi.org/10.5772/intechopen.110836
Government of South Africa (2020) National strategic plan on gender based violence and femicide. https://www.justice.gov.za/vg/gbv/nsp-gbvf-final-doc-04-05.pdf. Accessed 12 Aug 2023
Hsiao C et al (2017) Reducing violence in South Africa: from research to action. Policy Brief, Institute for Security Studies
Human Rights Watch (2021) South Africa: broken promises to aid gender-based violence survivors. https://www.hrw.org/news/2021/11/24/south-africa-broken-promises-aid-gender-based-violence-survivors. Accessed 14 Aug 2023
Kilkelly U, Liefaard T (eds) (2018) International human rights of children. Springer
Kilkelly U, Liefaard T (2019) Legal implementation of the UNCRC: lessons to be learned from the constitutional experience of South Africa. De Jure Law J 52(spe):521–539. https://doi.org/10.17159/2225-7160/2019/v52a30
Meyersfeld B (2010) Domestic violence and international law. Hart Publishers, Oxford
Mpani P, Nsibande N (2015) Understanding gender policy and gender-based violence in South Africa: a literature review. Tshwaranang Legal Advocacy Centre
Müller KD, van der Merwe IA (2004) The sexual offences prosecutor: a new specialisation? J Jurid Sci 29(1):135–151
National Prosecuting Authority (2018) Annual report 2017/18. https://www.npa.gov.za/sites/default/files/annual-reports/NDPP%20Annual%20Report-%202017-18.pdf. Accessed 24 Feb 2023
National Prosecuting Authority (2022) Thuthuzela Care Centres: turning victims into survivors. https://www.npa.gov.za/sites/default/files/human-trafficking/TCC%20Brochure%20sep%2020.pdf. Accessed 8 Aug 2023
Office on the Status of Women (2002) South Africa - South Africa's National Policy Framework for women's empowerment and gender equality. https://www.dffe.gov.za/sites/default/files/docs/national_policy_framework.pdf. Accessed 11 Mar 2023
Parkinson P (2016, March 29) Specialist prosecution units and courts: a review of the literature. https://ssrn.com/abstract=2756305. Accessed 3 Feb 2023
Parliamentary Monitoring Group (2021, August 25) National strategic plan on gender based violence: lead departments' report-back; 2021 women's parliament preparatory briefing; with ministers and deputy ministers. https://pmg.org.za/committee-meeting/33468/#:~:text=The%20National%20Strategic%20Plan%20(NSP. Accessed 4 Dec 2022
Pejan R et al (2007) The development of a framework for understanding human rights-based approaches and integrating them into water resources management in South Africa. Association for Water and Rural Development
People Opposing Women Abuse (POWA) (2010) Criminal injustice: violence against women in South Africa. https://www2.ohchr.org/english/bodies/cedaw/docs/ngos/powa_others_southafrica48.pdf. Accessed 9 Aug 2023
Rana B, Perrie V (2019) CEDAW: a tool for addressing violence against women. In: Aneel SS et al (eds) 70 Years of development: the way forward. Sustainable Development Policy Institute, pp 111–130
Reyneke JM, Kruger HB (2006) Sexual offences courts: better justice for children? J Jurid Sci 31(2):73–107
Ruck M et al (eds) (2017) Handbook of children's rights: global and multidisciplinary perspectives. Routledge
SADC (2023) Gender based violence. https://www.sadc.int/pillars/violence-basee-sur-le-genre-vbg. Accessed 22 Dec 2023

Segar S (2023) In-depth: Thuthuzela centres working well – experts say we need more of them. https://www.spotlightnsp.co.za/2023/07/24/in-depth-thuthuzela-centres-working-well-experts-say-we-need-more-of-them/. Accessed 14 Aug 2023
Skelton A (2015) South Africa. In: Liefaard T, Doek JE (eds) Litigating the rights of the child: the UN Convention on the rights of the child in domestic and international jurisprudence. Springer, pp 13–30
Smythe D (2015) Rape unresolved: policing sexual offences in South Africa. University of Cape Town, Cape Town
South Africa (2023) Sustainable development report: South Africa country profile. https://dashboards.sdgindex.org/profiles/south-africa. Accessed 23 Dec 2023
South African Government (2007) Commission for Gender Equality Strategic Plan 2008 – 2013. https://www.gov.za/sites/default/files/gcis_document/201409/cge-strategic-plan0.pdf. Accessed 9 Aug 2023
South African Government (2022, January 28) President Cyril Ramaphosa assents to laws that strengthen fight against gender-based violence. https://www.gov.za/speeches/president-cyril-ramaphosa-assents-laws-strengthen-fight-against-gender-based-violence-28#:~:text=The%20Criminal%20and%20Related%20Matters%20Amendment%20Bill%20aims%20to%20address. Accessed 4 Dec 2022
Stats SA (2019) Sustainable development goals: country report 2019. https://www.statssa.gov.za/MDG/SDGs_Country_Report_2019_South_Africa.pdf. Accessed 22 Dec 2023
The Presidency: Republic of South Africa (2018) Presidential Summit: declaration against gender-based violence and femicide. https://www.gov.za/sites/default/files/gcis_document/201903/summit-declaration.pdf. Accessed 13 Aug 2023
Tobin J (ed) (2019) The UN Convention on the rights of the child. A commentary. OUP
UN Office on Drugs and Crime (2017) South Africa: are we doing enough to end violence against women? https://www.unodc.org/southernafrica/en/vaw/index.html. Accessed 11 Aug 2023
UN Women (2015) Beijing declaration and platform for action, Beijing +5 political declaration and outcome. https://www.unwomen.org/en/digital-library/publications/2015/01/beijing-declaration. Accessed 23 Dec 2023
United Nations (2008) Establishment of one-stop centres to counteract violence against women. https://www.un.org/humansecurity/wp-content/uploads/2017/08/Programme-summary-105.pdf. Accessed 13 Mar 2023
Vandenhole W et al (eds) (2015) The Routledge international handbook of children's rights studies. Routledge
Walker SP, Louw D (2005) The court for sexual offences: perceptions of the victims of sexual offences. Int J Law Psychiatry 28(3):231–245. https://doi.org/10.1016/j.ijlp.2005.04.001

Chapter 8
Judicial Responses to Gender-Based Violence and Femicide

8.1 Overview

In recent years not only has the high rates of GBVF been of particular concern,[1] but it is also the progressively violent nature of these incidents that have caused outrage and alarm.[2] South Africa has a plethora of legislation, policies and plans to combat GBVF. Despite having some of the most sophisticated laws against discrimination and violence in the world GBV continues at an appallingly high rate in the country. This continued assault on women and girls hampers the fulfilment of South Africa's constitutional obligations.[3] One of the ways in which the state protects, promotes, and fulfils constitutional rights is through the criminal justice system and particularly the prosecution of offenses.[4]

However, the implementation of laws continues to be an area of concern, together with access or recourse to the law being limited for many, if not most, victims of GBVF. Various studies have pointed to high levels of dissatisfaction with the criminal justice system experienced by sexual offenses victims, accounting for many victims withdrawing from the process. It remains the responsibility of the criminal justice system to ensure that those responsible for committing crimes, specifically gender-based crimes are brought to account. The various relevant role-players such as the police and the prosecution, healthcare providers, social services, etc., are all required to combine their efforts to guarantee justice for victims of these crimes.[5] The Courts especially, play a crucial role in ensuring just outcomes in GBV cases and in alleviating the problem of GBVF. It is the court's duty to find the right

[1] TimesLive (2022, January 30).

[2] The Sunday World (2022, July 29).

[3] Sexual violence implicates several rights in the *Bill of Rights* including sections 9, 10, 11, 12 and 2.

[4] *S v Basson* 2005 (1) SA 171 (CC), para 31.

[5] The Judiciary (2018, November 1).

T. Deane, *Gender-Based Violence and Femicide in South Africa*, Gender, Justice and Legal Feminism 5, https://doi.org/10.1007/978-3-031-61053-0_8

balance between a just sentence on the one hand, and a clear message that will deter GBV in society on the other.

This section accordingly provides examples of a list, albeit not exhaustive, of some of the most horrendous crimes that were committed against women in the country. It evaluates the jurisprudence of the Constitutional Court over the past 20 years. Several significant decisions have also emerged from the Supreme Court of Appeal and High Courts in relation to the laws and aspects of the common law relevant to violence against women and girls. This chapter surveys the jurisprudence on GBV in assessing the Court's record in this area. While finding these decisions valuable in advancing the constitutional framework,[6] this section suggests that more resources are required to ensure that the legacy of economic vulnerability and violence perpetuated by discriminatory and prejudiced structures and institutions in the country's history, are not used as an excuse to keep women vulnerable and prone to incidents of GBVF.

In addition, it calls for a more robust implementation of laws and for harmonization of various instruments to address emerging gender issues and concerns, and to set realistic, measurable targets, time frames and indicators for achieving gender equality and equity. There is also a need to strengthen, monitor and evaluate the progress made to attain sustainable development, and strengthen community building.

8.1.1 Some Landmark Cases

8.1.1.1 *S v Chapman*[7]

The courts have played an instrumental role in fighting violence against women. Some Court decisions have informed a revision of the legislative and policy framework on GBV such as in *S v Chapman*[8] where the Supreme Court of Appeal (SCA) held that rape constituted "a humiliating, degrading and brutal invasion of the privacy, the dignity and the person of the victim. . . ."[9] and that women were entitled to the protection of these rights which were basic to the ethos of the *Constitution of the Republic of South Africa, 1996* (*Constitution*) and to any defensible civilization. The SCA went on to say that "the courts are under a duty to send a clear message to the accused and to other potential rapists and to the community that we are determined to protect equality, dignity and freedom of all women and we shall have no mercy to those who seek to invade those rights."[10]

[6] Dixon and Roux (2018), pp. 141–173.

[7] *S v Chapman* 1997 (3) SA 341 (SCA) (*S v Chapman*).

[8] *S v Chapman* supra.

[9] *S v Chapman* supra, 344J-345B.

[10] *S v Chapman* supra, 345D.

This approach was further emphasized in *DPP, North Gauteng v Thabethe*:[11]

> ... rape of women and young children has become cancerous in our society. It is a crime which threatens the very foundation of our nascent democracy, which is founded on protection and promotion of the values of human dignity, equality and advancements of human rights and freedoms. It is such a serious crime that it evokes strong feelings of revulsion and outrage amongst all right-thinking and self- respecting members of society. Our courts have an obligation to impose sentences in such crime—particularly where it involves young, innocent, defenseless, and vulnerable girls—of the kind which reflects the natural outrage and revulsion felt by the law-abiding members of the society. A failure to do so would regrettably have the effect of eroding the public confidence in the criminal justice system.

8.1.1.2 *Carmichele v Minister of Safety and Security and Another*[12]

This case dealt with the constitutional obligation of the courts to develop the common law to promote the spirit, purport, and objects of the *Bill of Rights*. The main issue in this case was the court's competency to broaden the common law concept of "wrongfulness" in the law of delict in light of the State's constitutional duty to safeguard the rights of women.

The applicant sued the Minister of Safety and Security and the Minister of Justice for damages resulting from a brutal attack by one Coetzee who was awaiting trial for having attempted to rape another woman. Coetzee had previously been convicted on charges of housebreaking and indecent assault for which he was sentenced to a fine and suspended period of imprisonment. At the time of the attack on the applicant, he was facing a charge of rape and had, despite his history of sexual violence, been released on his own recognizance by a magistrate, on the recommendation of the police and prosecutor. After his release Coetzee lived with his mother who worked for Gosling, a friend of the applicant, at her premises where the applicant frequently stayed. Upon learning of the charges against Coetzee and of his previous conviction for indecent assault, Gosling tried unsuccessfully to get the police and the prosecutor to incarcerate Coetzee to protect herself and the public. The public prosecutor did not provide assistance even when Gosling reported that the applicant had seen Coetzee snooping around Gosling's house. The prosecutor claimed that nothing could be done unless Coetzee committed another offense. Two months later the applicant and Gosling made another request to the public prosecutor for assistance but received the same response. A few days later Coetzee brutally attacked the applicant at Gosling's house.

Relying on the common-law duty of wrongfulness, the applicant brought a delictual action in the High Court against the two Ministers for the injuries she had sustained during the attack. The applicant's case was that the members of the police as well as the public prosecutors involved had owed her a legal duty to act in

[11] *DPP, North Gauteng v Thabethe* (2) SACR 567 (SCA), 577G-I.

[12] 2001 (4) SA 938 (CC); 2001 (10) BCLR 995 (CC). (*Carmichele*).

order to prevent Coetzee from causing her harm and that they had negligently failed to comply with this duty. She alleged that the release of Coetzee without bail had been an omission by the police and prosecutors. She also relied on the duties imposed on the police by the *Interim Constitution*[13] and on the State under the rights to life, equality, dignity, freedom and security of the person and privacy.[14]

The High Court dismissed the claim, finding that she had not established that the police or the prosecutor owed a legal duty of care to her specifically and had wrongfully failed to fulfil that legal duty. The applicant's appeal to the SCA was also unsuccessful.[15] The SCA held that the police and prosecution had no legal duty of care towards the applicant and could not, as a matter of law, be liable for damages to her. The applicant then sought a special appeal against the order of the SCA in the Constitutional Court, which was granted. In a unanimous decision the Constitutional Court granted the application for leave to appeal and upheld the appeal. The Court held that, although the major engine for law reform should be the legislature, courts are under a general duty to develop the common law when it deviates from the spirit, purport, and objects of the *Bill of Rights*.[16]

The Constitutional Court considered the potential liability of both police and prosecutors. It held that the State is obliged by the *Constitution* and international law to prevent gender-based discrimination and to protect the dignity, freedom, and security of women.[17] The Court held that the police service:[18]

> is one of the primary agencies of the State responsible for the protection of the public in general and women and children in particular against the invasion of their fundamental rights by perpetrators of violent crime.

It further held that in the circumstances of the present case, the police recommendation for the assailant's release could therefore amount to wrongful conduct giving rise to police liability for the harmful consequences. The Court went on to say that prosecutors, who are under a general duty to place before a court any information relevant to the refusal or grant of bail, might reasonably be held liable for negligent failure to fulfil that duty.[19]

---

[13] *Constitution of the Republic of South Africa, Act 200 of 1993* (*Interim Constitution*).

[14] Sections 11, 9, 10, and 12 of the *Constitution*, respectively.

[15] *Carmichele v Minister of Safety & Security & Another* 2000 (4) All SA 537 (A).

[16] *Carmichele v Minister of Safety and Security* 2002 (10) BCLR 1100 (C), 36.

[17] In *Carmichele* supra, at para 62 the Court stated that:

> South Africa ... has a duty under international law to prohibit all gender-based discrimination that has the effect or purpose of impairing the enjoyment by women of fundamental rights and freedoms and to take reasonable and appropriate measures to prevent the violation of those rights.

[18] *Carmichele v Minister of Safety and Security* 2002 (10) BCLR 1100 (C), para 62.

[19] See, also, *Van Eeden v Minister of Safety and Security (Women's Legal Centre Trust as Amicus Curiae)* 2003 (1) SA 389(SCA) where the SCA upheld an appeal by a young woman (appellant) who sought damages from the state (respondent). Her action was based on the state's breach of its duty of care towards her, following her sexual assault, rape and robbery by a known dangerous

The appeal was upheld, and the matter referred back to the High Court. The effect of the order was to have the case re-opened in the trial court on the basis that the appellant had made out a case which had to be met by the two Ministers. The trial recommenced in the Cape High Court and the matter was reconsidered in light of the judgment of the Constitutional Court. The court found in favor of the plaintiff, holding the defendants the Ministers of Safety and Security and Justice and Constitutional Development, liable. The Court ordered the two defendants to pay the plaintiff R177 000 and to cover all her legal costs. The state took the matter on appeal and lost.

This case constitutes a breakthrough for victims' rights and the fight to end violence against women. The decision set an important precedent with its recognition that sexual violence is not a private matter and that public officials have a duty to protect women. In some circumstances damages may be claimed against the state, in appropriate circumstances, when it fails to honor its duty to protect women against violence; and prosecutors and the police must think twice before setting dangerous criminals loose on the public.

Indeed, Justice Albie Sachs stated that:[20]

> The joint judgment between Justices Goldstone and Ackerman was very carefully crafted. What was significant was the weight given to the issue of violence in our society especially against women. Having two male judges steeped in the law giving this judgment showed the collegial character of the Court. It meant that the Court is taking gender rights seriously.

The decision sent a strong message to the governing bodies of the police that police personnel who abuse their positions of power remain the responsibility of the force. In a country where women live in fear of sexual violence, it is critical that they must be able to both expect protection from the police and feel confident that the police themselves will not abuse their authority and take criminal advantage of women.

In addition, the *Carmichele* decision of the Constitutional Court has been broadly applauded for its focus on the centrality of the values and rights within the constitution in shaping the development of the common law. *Carmichele* explicitly sets the precedent that SAPS has a duty to prevent violence against individuals, especially vulnerable ones (such as women and children). If SAPS and prosecutors do not meet this duty, then survivors have a right to claim damages against these bodies for failing in their duties towards the victim. The decision in *Carmichele* can be

---

criminal who had escaped from police custody. The Court held that it was the duty of the state to protect people against violent crime and that the police had a duty of care towards the victim. The Court further held that the state was obliged to protect individuals by taking active steps to prevent violations of the constitutional right to freedom and security of the person. The Court also held that the state was obliged by international law to protect women against violent crime and that in the light of these imperatives a special relationship between the plaintiff and the defendant was not required for the duty of care to exist. The Court declared that the conduct of the police was wrongful, and the state (as employer of the police) was liable to the plaintiff for such damages that she was able to prove.

[20] We, The People South Africa (2020, August 20).

considered a founding case wherein the principle of GBV victims' rights was entrenched.

8.1.1.3 *S v Baloyi* (Minister of Justice and Another Intervening)[21]

The seminal case of *Baloyi* concerned the predecessor to the *Domestic Violence Act 1998*, the *Prevention of Family Violence Act 1993*. The case related to whether a provision requiring a person charged with breaching a family violence interdict to prove that they were not guilty violated their right to be presumed innocent.[22] The Court found that the provision did not introduce a reverse onus and did not violate the rights of the person charged with breaching an interdict. The decision is significant in presenting an argument, informed by the feminist theory, for viewing domestic violence laws as different from other criminal law in the balancing of the rights of women to be safe from domestic violence against the rights of men accused of such crimes. In interpreting the section 12 right to be "free from all forms of violence from either public or private sources," Sachs J noted that:[23]

> The specific inclusion of private sources emphasises that serious threats to security of the person arise from private sources. Read with section 7(2), section 12(1) has to be understood as obliging the state directly to protect the right of everyone to be free from private or domestic violence. Indeed, the state is under a series of constitutional mandates which include the obligation to deal with domestic violence: to protect both the rights of everyone to enjoy freedom and security of the person and to bodily and psychological integrity, and the right to have their dignity respected and protected, as well as the defensive rights of everyone not to be subjected to torture in any way and not to be treated or punished in a cruel, inhuman or degrading way.

The right to be free from violence has thus been interpreted by the Court as placing a positive obligation on the state to protect women from domestic violence.[24] The right is read together with section 7(2) of the Constitution which requires the state to "respect, protect, promote, and fulfil the rights in the Bill of Rights." Sachs J suggested that there is a distinction in the wording of section 12 where the overall rights to freedom and security of the person[25] and to bodily and psychological integrity[26] are seen as essential features of personhood to which everyone is entitled

---

[21] 2000 (2) SA 425 CC; 2000 (1) BCLR 86 (CC); 2000 (1) SACR 8 (CC) (*S v Baloyi*).

[22] Section 3(5) of the *Prevention of Family Violence Act, 133 of 1993* had been declared invalid by the Pretoria High Court and referred to the Constitutional Court for confirmation in terms of section 172(2)(a) of the *Constitution*. Section 3(5) dealt with the procedure to be followed when a person is accused of breaching the terms of a family violence interdict.

[23] *S v Baloyi* supra, para 11.

[24] Bonthuys and Albertyn (2007), p. 295.

[25] Section 12(1) of the *Constitution*.

[26] Section 12(2) of the *Constitution*.

to receive protection.[27] The Judge went on to consider equality and reasoned that domestic violence "compels constitutional concern" because it is "gender-specific" and a product of a patriarchal society.[28] This, he noted, meant that "the non-sexist society promised in the foundational clauses of the Constitution, and the right to equality and non-discrimination guaranteed by section 9, are undermined when spouse-batterers enjoy impunity."[29]

The Judge then considered the issue of freedom when considering what autonomy means for women facing domestic violence. Drawing on feminist legal theory he noted that both autonomy and privacy have been used to shield men and prevent intervention to protect women in the home. He thus praised the idea behind domestic violence protection laws which are aimed at addressing the complexities of intimate partner abuse without immediate recourse to the criminal law. Sachs J pointed to the laudable purpose of protection legislation which "at its most optimistic ... seeks preventive rather than retributive justice, undertaken with a view ultimately to promoting restorative justice."[30] Sachs J came to the issue of freedom when considering what autonomy means for women facing domestic violence. Drawing on feminist legal theory he noted that both autonomy and privacy have been used to shield men and prevent intervention to protect women in the home. He thus praised the idea behind domestic violence protection laws which are aimed at addressing the complexities of intimate partner abuse without immediate recourse to the criminal law. Sachs J pointed to the laudable purpose of protection legislation which "at its most optimistic ... seeks preventive rather than retributive justice, undertaken with a view ultimately to promoting restorative justice."[31] The judgment has been rightfully lauded for its sensitive but firm elaboration of women's rights to be protected from domestic violence by the state.

The Court further held that the section in question most appropriately balances optimum protection of the complainant and the accused's right to a fair trial. The Court pointed out that:[32]

> [t]he non-sexist society promised in the foundational clauses of the Constitution and the right to equality and non-discrimination guaranteed by section 9, are undermined when spouse-batterers enjoy immunity.

The matter was consequently referred back to the High Court to be dealt with in accordance with the Constitutional Court's decision.

---

[27] Most of the sub-sections of ss. 12(1) and (2) contain the types of harms that people should not be subjected to what the judge refers to as "defensive rights." Thus, people must expect the state to defend them against such harms while protecting their freedom, security, and integrity. See Goldblatt (2016).

[28] *S v Baloyi* supra, paras 11–12.

[29] *S v Baloyi* supra, para 12.

[30] *S v Baloyi* supra, para 17.

[31] *S v Baloyi* supra, para 17.

[32] *S v Baloyi* supra, para 12.

This decision uses the *Constitution* to defend women's rights to freedom and security and affirm the state's obligations to protect them. They do not however consider how the *Constitution* might oblige the state to take measures to prevent violence against women from arising in the first place or to protect women by ensuring that they have access to the resources needed to avoid the violence that emerges in situations where poverty and disadvantage leave them defenseless.[33] What is clear though is that the Courts recognize the need to balance the rights of victims and perpetrators while appreciating the unique and illusive nature of domestic violence. It confirmed that the CEDAW imposes a positive duty on member states to pass legislation to punish violence against women, that domestic violence is viewed seriously by the courts and is no longer seen as a private matter; and that international human rights norms are important for strengthening the protection of women's rights at the domestic level.

8.1.1.4 *Tshabalala v S; Ntuli v S*[34]

In this case the Constitutional Court had to determine whether the common-law doctrine of common purpose is applicable to matters of common-law rape. Prior to its decision there was some uncertainty as to the application of the doctrine of common purpose to matters of common-law rape, resulting in conflicting applications of the doctrine. The judgment in *Tshabalala* ultimately takes a firm stand which protects the values of equality, human dignity, safety, and security for the women of South Africa.

The facts of the case saw a group of men who went on a late-night reign of terror through nine plots in Umthambeka in Tembisa. The group of men including Tshabalala and Ntuli, forced their way into numerous homes which were located on nine separate plots in a community where marginalized and vulnerable people, mostly women and children, lived. They forced their way into the homes on the plots where they ransacked, looted, robbed, assaulted, stabbed and gang raped the indigent and vulnerable people living there. The gang rapes included the rape of eight female occupants, some of whom were repeatedly raped, by several members of this group, the raping of a visibly pregnant woman and a 14-year-old girl.[35] It is important to note that while some of the men raped the female occupants, other members of the group were standing guard outside the homes in which these violent crimes were taking place. These individuals were essentially posted to act as "lookouts" or "guards" for the other members of the group.

On or about 13 August 1999, this matter was brought before the High Court on a charge of common-law rape mainly based on the common-purpose doctrine. The

[33] Goldblatt (2016).

[34] *Tshabalala v S; Ntuli v S* 2020 (5) SA 1 (CC) (*Tshabalala*).

[35] *Tshabalala* supra, para 6.

attacks brought into focus the applicability of the doctrine of common purpose on the common law crime of rape.[36]

The attacks were found by the High Court to be well orchestrated and meticulously calculated, with a preordained pattern of attack. The group was apprehended, charged, and were serving out their sentences. The SCA held differently. The SCA did not agree with the decision of the Full Court. The SCA held instead that to convict the appellant as an accomplice to the crime on the basis of his mere presence at the scene "would subvert the principles of participation and liability as an accomplice in our criminal law."[37] The SCA subsequently set aside all the convictions on common law rape on the basis that the appellant could not be convicted of rape on the basis of his mere presence at the rape scene because this undermined the principle of participation and liability. Furthermore, because the victims were blindfolded during their gangrape, there was no evidence to prove presence at the crime. The SCA concluded that it could therefore not establish common purpose with the actions of the gang.

As a result of the SCA's findings Tshabalala and Ntuli applied to the Constitutional Court to have their convictions overturned, on the basis that it was not possible for common purpose to apply to the crime of rape because rape could only be committed through the instrumentality of a person's own body and not through the instrumentality of another person or group of persons (the instrumentality argument). The Commission for Gender Equality (CGE)[38] intervened in the application because of the enormous ramifications that dispensing with the principle of common purpose would have on the successful prosecution of gang-rapes.

When the matter was before the Constitutional Court, the Court noted the scourge of rape against women in the country, more specifically incidents of group rape.[39] Mathopo AJ (Mogoeng CJ, Froneman J, Jafta J, Khampepe J, Madlanga J, Mhlantla J, Theron J, and Victor AJ concurring) stated that:[40]

> Rape is a very serious offence, constituting as it does a humiliating, degrading and brutal invasion of the privacy, the dignity and the person of the victim. The rights to dignity, to privacy, and the integrity of every person are basic to the ethos of the Constitution and to any defensible civilisation. Women in this country are entitled to the protection of these rights. They have a legitimate claim to walk peacefully on the streets, to enjoy their shopping and their entertainment, to go and come from work, and to enjoy the peace and tranquillity of their homes without the fear, the apprehension and the insecurity which constantly diminishes the quality and enjoyment of their lives.

---

[36] When two or more individuals engage in a joint criminal enterprise, the principle of common purpose allows—in certain circumstances—certain acts committed by one individual in the group to be at-tributed to others in the group. In other words, if a group of men agree to ensure that a woman is raped, the application of one element of common purpose will allow each individual involved to be convicted of rape, regardless of who ended up physically perpetrating the crime.

[37] *Tshabalala* supra, para 15.

[38] The Chapter 9 Institution empowered by the *Constitution* to protect gender equality.

[39] *Tshabalala* supra, para 31.

[40] *S v Chapman* supra, paras 3–4.

The Court went on to state that:[41]

> The facts of this case demonstrate that for far too long rape has been used as a tool to relegate the women of this country to second-class citizens, over whom men can exercise their power and control, and in so doing, strip them of their rights to equality, human dignity and bodily integrity. The high incidence of sexual violence suggests that male control over women and notions of sexual entitlement feature strongly in the social construction of masculinity in South Africa. Some men view sexual violence as a method of reasserting masculinity and controlling women.

The Constitutional Court noted that sexual violence committed against women is particularly prevalent and strips women of their rights to equality, human dignity, and bodily integrity. Importantly, the Court also acknowledged three aspects of GBV: first, that the incidence of sexual violence in South Africa is high; second, that incidents of sexual violence in South Africa are gendered; and third, that sexual GBV infringes many of women's rights, including the right to equality.[42] Indeed the crime of rape strips women of rights that are protected in the *Constitution*, national legislation and international and regional treaties.[43]

The Constitutional Court's main judgment by Mathopo J, and finding the CGE's argument on the issue helpful, found that rape is more about power than a sexual act; and held that the instrumentality argument by the applicants is flawed. There is no reason why the use of one's body should be determinative in the case of rape but not

[41] *Tshabalala v The State; Ntuli v The State* (2019) ZACC 48, para 1.

[42] *Tshabalala* supra, para 1.

[43] Equality and human dignity are provided for, first, as values and, second as justiciable human rights within ss 1(*a*), 7(1), 9, and 10 of the *Constitution* respectively; s 12 of the *Constitution* provides for the right to freedom and security of the person as violence constitutes a grave invasion of personal security; s 12(1)(*c*), in particular, provides for the right to be free from all forms of violence from either public or private sources; s 12(2) further provides for the right to bodily and psychological integrity, which includes the right to security in and control over a person's body; s 14 of the *Constitution* also provides for the right to privacy. When a person for example, invades someone's person or body without their permission, there is a violation of this right. Rape by its very nature constitutes an invasion of the right to privacy as consent or permission to access another person's body is lacking. However, this is not to reduce incidents of sexual GBV to a lack of mere consent. What is clear is that the rights to equality, human dignity, privacy, and bodily integrity are all linked in matters of sexual gender-based violence. With regard to national legislation, the *Domestic Violence Act 116 of 1998* provides for the issuing of protection orders in cases where domestic violence has taken place; *Criminal Law (Sexual Offences and Related Matters) Amendment Act 32 of 2007* provides for offences such as rape. The United Nations instruments that provide for the protection of the human rights of women are the: *Universal Declaration of Human Rights (UDHR), 1948*; *Convention on the Elimination of all forms of Discrimination Against Women (CEDAW), 1979*; and the Sustainable Development Goals (SDGs), 2015, specifically goal 5 and goal 5.2. South Africa ratified the *UDHR* on 7 November 1945 and CEDAW on 15 December 1995. At a regional level, the following instruments provide for the protection and promotion of the human rights of women: the *African Charter on Human and People's Rights (ACHPR), 1981*; and the *Protocol to the African Charter on Human and People's Rights on the Rights of Women in Africa (Maputo Protocol), 2003*. South Africa ratified the *ACHPR* in 1996. In the concurring judgment, Victor AJ also referred to the influence of international law in the present case in paras 93, 94, and 95.

in the case of other crimes such as murder and assault. The instrumentality argument perpetuates gender inequality, patriarchy and promotes discrimination—unconscionable in a society facing the social issues it does. The second judgment (concurring) noted that rape in this country is not rare, unusual, or deviant. It is structural and it would be irrational to not apply the doctrine of common purpose to the common law crime of rape. The third judgment also concurred and noted that historically, South Africa's jurisprudence demonstrates patriarchal gender norms in the law and the acceptance of common purpose in this case marks a removal of one of the remaining obstacles to rape convictions by infusing constitutional values to common law. There are various international instruments that South Africa is a party to, which places an obligation on the State to ensure domestic laws are developed to protect women from sexual violence.

Specifically in relation to international law the Court stated that:[44]

> These instruments illustrate the universal importance of protecting and enhancing domestic laws that protect the most vulnerable members of our society. The common law crime of rape is one that has to be developed to meet the obligations imposed by international law. These protocols place an obligation on the State, including this Court, to develop the domestic laws to ensure that women are protected from sexual violence.

In this case the Constitutional Court has sent out an unequivocal message of the judiciary's commitment to develop and implement the strongest laws to fight South Africa's scourge of GBV. As a milestone judgment, the *Tshabalala* case will have a significant impact on women's rights to bodily and psychological integrity, freedom and security of the person and dignity. It also allows for more effective prosecution of perpetrators involved in gang rape.

8.1.1.5 *S v Jackson*[45]

In the *S v Jackson* case the cautionary rule, which was an antiquated rule of evidence that encouraged courts to treat the evidence of rape victims with circumspection, was declared unconstitutional, leading to its abolition.

8.1.1.6 *Masiya v Director of Public Prosecutions*[46]

The *Masiya* case was an important one, as the Constitutional Court extended the definition of rape to include non-consensual anal penetration of the anus of females, which was until then not provided for in the statutory definition of rape. The complainant in the matter was a nine-year-old girl who alleged that she had been raped by a man who was known to her, Mr. Fanuel Sitakeni Masiya, on 16 March

[44] *Tshabalala* supra, para 98.
[45] 1998 (1) SALR 470 SCA.
[46] 2007 (8) BCLR 827 (hereinafter *Masiya*).

2004. She was medically examined one week later, on 23 March 2004. Mr. Masiya had initially appeared before the District Court at Sabie; later the case was referred to the Graskop Regional Court where he was charged with rape. The complainant stated that she had been both anally and vaginally penetrated. The observations of the medical professionals did not confirm these allegations entirely, but expert medical evidence satisfied the Regional Court that anal penetration had indeed taken place and that the accused was the perpetrator. Although the common law definition of rape did not include anal penetration, the magistrate convicted the accused of rape and committed him to the High Court for sentencing.

The High Court confirmed that Magistrates' Courts are not expressly precluded from developing the common law for purposes of passing the constitutionality test. The court, after much deliberation, concluded that the Magistrates' Court had been correct in its assessment that the definition of rape in the common law needed to be developed, that the definition of rape needed to be extended to include anal penetration, and that it needed to be applicable to males and female alike. The Court recognized that the accused had been convicted of an offense that did not exist at the time when he committed it (i.e., rape consisting of anal penetration) but accepted that his rights relative to retrospective criminalization[47] could, in the circumstances of the case, for various reasons be limited.

In its judgment the majority of the Constitutional Court confirmed that the definition of rape should be extended, but only to include female anal penetration. This finding was based on the notion that the common law needed to be developed in accordance with the "spirit, purport and objects of the Constitution" in terms of section 39(2) of the Constitution. Further, the Court referred *to Veldman v Director of Public Prosecutions, Witwatersrand Local Division*[48] in stating that the principle of legality was a "central to the rule of law under our constitution."[49] The Court found that it would be sufficient to develop the common law prospectively in this case and, furthermore, that the extended definition should not apply *in casu* and that Masiya should be charged with indecent assault as opposed to rape.

8.1.1.7 *Levenstein & Others v Estate of the Late Sidney Lewis Frankel & Others*[50]

In the *Levenstein* case, the High Court of South Africa (Gauteng Local Division, Johannesburg) (High Court) declared section 18 constitutionally invalid "to the extent that it bars, in all circumstances, the right to institute a prosecution for all sexual offences, other than those listed in section 18(f), (h) and (i), after the lapse of a

[47] Section 35(3)(l) and (n) of the *Constitution*.

[48] 2006 (2) SACR 319 (CC).

[49] *Masiya* supra, para 55.

[50] (CCT170/17) [2018] ZACC 16; 2018 (8) BCLR 921 (CC); 2018 (2) SACR 283 (CC) (14 June 2018) (*Levenstein*).

period of 20 years from the time when the offence was committed." The matter was referred to the Constitutional Court for confirmation proceedings in terms of section 172(2) of the *Constitution*.

On 14 June 2018, the Constitutional Court declared section 18 of the *Criminal Procedure Act 51 of 1977* (*CPA*) to be unconstitutional insofar as it bars the prosecution of sexual offenses after 20 years. The crux of the applicants' submission was that there was no rational basis for distinguishing rape or compelled rape from other forms of sexual offenses. In this regard, they contended that section 18 of the *CPA* was irrational and arbitrary, and therefore unconstitutional and invalid, in that the distinction it seeks to make is based on the perceived seriousness of the offenses and their impact on the survivors. They further contended that it unjustifiably violated their rights to human dignity, equality, and non-discrimination, to be protected from abuse as children, to be free from all forms of violence from both public and private sources, and access to courts. The Constitutional Court accordingly afforded Parliament 24 months to enact remedial legislation.

The facts and background to the case are as follows. Between 1970 and 1989, when the applicants were aged between 6 and 15 years old, Mr Frankel is alleged to have sexually assaulted them. When the applications sought to bring charges against Mr Frankel, the Director of Public Prosecutions declined to prosecute on the basis that the alleged crimes had occurred more than 20 years prior, and that section 18 of the *CPA* imposes a time bar of 20 years for the right to institute a prosecution for such crimes. The applicants submitted that they did not institute criminal proceedings against Mr Frankel within the prescribed period because of a lack of full appreciation of the nature and extent of the acts perpetrated on them.

When the matter was deliberated on by the Constitutional Court, the Court noted that the primary rationale for differentiation between sexual offenses in section 18 seemed to be based on a consideration that certain sexual offenses are more serious than others. The Constitutional Court held this to be irrational, stating that "the use of prescriptive periods in section 18 as a basis to distinguish between rape or compelled rape and other forms of sexual assault when the harm they all cause to their survivors is similar, is irrational."[51] The Constitutional Court stated further that by over-emphasizing the significance of the nature of the criminal act at the expense of the harm that it produces to the survivors, section 18 failed to serve as a tool to protect and advance the interests of survivors of sexual assault.

The Constitutional Court went on to explain its reasoning as follows:[52]

> Of pivotal importance to the case before us is this: that the systemic sexual exploitation of woman and children depends on secrecy, fear and shame. Too often, survivors are stifled by fear of their abusers and the possible responses from their communities if they disclose that they had been sexually assaulted. This is exacerbated by the fact that the sexual perpetrator, as the applicants allege Mr Frankel to have been, is in a position of authority and power over them. They are threatened and shamed into silence. These characteristics of sexual violence often make it feel and seem impossible for victims to report what happened to friends and

[51] *Levenstein* supra, para 52.

[52] *Levenstein* supra, paras 56–57.

> loved ones – let alone state officials. Combined with this is the frequent impact of deeply-located self-blame, which . . . disables the victim from appreciating that a crime has been committed against her for which the perpetrator, and not she, is responsible.
>
> All these features of survival of sexual trauma make it rational to be reluctant to report and to avoid reporting. And this is before even considering the effect of rape trauma syndrome, the now recognised patterns of emotional, physical, cognitive and behavioural disturbances that approximately one in three survivors of sexual assault develop. Even if a survivor is fully aware that she was abused, she naturally weighs up the possibility of reprisals from the perpetrator together with the possible lack of support from the police and statistically small eventuality that reporting will actually, eventually, result in a conviction in a criminal court.

The Constitutional Court further stated that section 18 of the *CPA* undermined the state's efforts to comply with its international obligations, including in terms of the *CEDAW*, the *CRC*, and the P*rotocol to the African Charter on Human and People's Rights on the Rights of Women in Africa*. As noted in the judgment, these instruments impose a duty on the state to prohibit all gender-based discrimination that has the effect or purpose of impairing the enjoyment by women of fundamental rights and freedoms, and to take reasonable and appropriate measures to prevent the violation of these rights.

The Constitutional Court therefore concluded that "it is clear from the preceding analysis that there is no rational basis for the right to prosecute to lapse after 20 years in respect of other forms of sexual offences, and not for rape or compelled rape. Sexual offences may differ in form but the psychological harm they all produce may be similar" and consequently upheld a confirmation case of the High Court.

The decision has been lauded as a significant and progressive development in South African law. It also brings this decision in line with the provisions on criminal law prescription of the African Commission on Human and Peoples' Rights' Guidelines on Combating Sexual Violence and its Consequences in Africa.[53] Indeed, this decision saw the *Prescription in Civil and Criminal Matters (Sexual Offences) Amendment Act 15 of 2020* being passed into law. This *Prescription in Civil and Criminal Matters (Sexual Offences) Amendment Act* intends to: first; amend the *Prescription Act, 1969*, so as to extend the list of sexual offenses in respect of which prescription does not commence to run under certain circumstances regarding a debt that is based on the alleged commission of any of those sexual offenses; second; amend the *Criminal Procedure Act, 1977*, so as to extend the list of sexual offenses in respect of which a prosecution may be instituted after a period of 20 years has lapsed since the date of the alleged commission of the sexual offense; and third; it provides for matters connected therewith.

In the *Levenstein* matter, the victims of the sexual assault alleged that they did not institute criminal proceedings against the perpetrator within the period prescribed by section 18 because of a lack of full appreciation of the nature and extent of the criminal acts allegedly perpetrated on them. The amendment therefore seeks to correct a situation where a sexual assault takes place when the victim is a child,

---

[53] African Commission on Human and People's Right (2017).

and the victim reaches majority but is still not in a position to institute their claim based on some kind of mental incapacity. It therefore broadens the basis on which prescription can be interrupted once the victim has become an adult. The judgment is a progressive step in the protection of the rights of children, in protecting their right to freedom and security of the person, human dignity and equality. The ruling serves to empower survivors of sexual assault to come forward. It gives many victims the choice to come forward and seek justice, where before, a timer was put on their access to justice.

8.1.1.8 *AK v The Minister of Police*[54]

The judgement in *AK v The Minister of Police* or *Kawa* relates to police treatment of victims of abuse. On 5 April 2022, the Constitutional Court handed down its precedent-setting judgment in the case of activist and author Andy Kawa. Kawa has battled for more than a decade to get justice for the rape and abduction she endured at King's Beach in Gqeberha (formerly Port Elizabeth) in 2010. Kawa's claim was made against the Minister of Police and focused on the trauma she endured due to SAPS alleged inefficient and negligent handling of the investigation into her rape and abduction. Kawa's principal argument, with which the majority of the Constitutional Court agreed, was that the failure of the police to conduct a reasonably skilled and diligent search for her when she was being held by her captor for about 15 h, and subsequently a reasonably effective investigation, made her suffer "serious psychological and psychiatric trauma."[55]

In brief the background to this case is that on or about 9 December 2010 at 14:30, the applicant was attacked, robbed, and held captive between bushes and sand dunes on King's beach, Gqeberha. She was repeatedly raped until she escaped during the early hours of the next morning. SAPS launched four searches on the day she went missing; first, a SAPS officer searched for her by driving along the coastline with a 4×4 vehicle; second, a foot search was conducted on the beach; third, a dog search by the K9 Search and Rescue Unit and fourth, a helicopter searched for the applicant for 20 min. The searches excluded the specific area where the applicant was held, and her attackers have until today not been captured.

Following proceedings in the High Court and the SCA, the Constitutional Court found that the negligent search and investigation of SAPS, which had caused the applicant harm, was unlawful. SAPS violated their statutory and constitutional duty to keep citizens safe and therefore, the Minister of Police could be held liable in delict for the applicant's damage. SAPS's four searches were negligent because reasonable police officers in the same position would have included the area where the applicant was held captive. During the investigation, SAPS committed two negligent omissions: they failed to interrogate "bush sleepers" in the area and failed

---

[54] [2022] ZACC 14.

[55] *AK v Minister of Police*, para 4.

to study CCTV footage promptly. It was also found that SAPS's negligent omissions were the factual and lawful cause of the applicant's damage. If she had been found earlier, she would have been spared from hours of rape.

This judgement proves that South African courts understand the seriousness of the protection against GBV. It encourages victims of GBV to report and hold SAPS accountable for their failures. The majority of the Judges found that this ruling would not hinder SAPS in carrying out their duties, but that victims of GBV would be protected if they chose to litigate. Writing on behalf of the majority, Justice Pule Tlaletsi, citing *Carmichele*,[56] acknowledged that "truly, few things can be more important to women than freedom from the threat of sexual violence."[57] He further found that "the state has a duty to protect women against all forms of gender-based violence that impair their enjoyment of fundamental rights and freedoms" and that it has to "take reasonable and appropriate measures to prevent the violation of those rights."[58]

Indeed, the principle of a positive obligation on the state, and thus SAPS, to actively protect women from GBV was confirmed in the landmark *Carmichele* case almost 21 years ago. *Carmichele* explicitly sets the precedent that SAPS has a duty to prevent violence against individuals, especially vulnerable ones (such as women and children). If SAPS and the prosecutors do not meet this duty, then survivors have a right to claim damages against these bodies for failing in their duties towards the victim. Kawa's case builds on this, and it is now very clear that the law also holds that SAPS has a duty to investigate cases of gender-based violence in a way that is reasonably effective. Thus, SAPS do not only have duties around prevention of GBV but has a duty to reasonably assist in the criminal justice process of securing sanctions against perpetrators of this violence.

An alleged problem with this duty to investigate reasonably, as expressed by the Minister of Police, is that holding SAPS to a reasonable duty of effectiveness "would have a chilling effect on its (SAPS's) ability to conduct investigations and carry out its constitutional mandate." This is because, the Minister argued, the police might adopt "defensive policing"—where they may refuse to take risks in case it attracts liability. The minister relied heavily on this "floodgates" argument which was based on the case of *Hill v Chief Constable of West Yorkshire* in the UK.[59] In response to this argument, Justice Tlaletsi stated that, "if anything, not imposing liability would have a 'chilling effect' on the ability of survivors of gender-based violence to vindicate their rights and hold SAPS liable for any secondary victimization it has caused."[60] Justice Leona Theron, concurring with Justice Tlaletsi, said the case of *Hill*, which denounced police liability in shoddy investigations, was both

[56] *Carmichele* supra, para 62.

[57] *AK v Minister of Police* supra, para 1 pg. 3.

[58] *AK v Minister of Police* supra, para 3.

[59] See *Hill v Chief Constable of West Yorkshire [1987] 1 All ER 1173 (CA) and Commissioner of Police of the Metropolis v DSD* [2018] UKSC 11 (DSD) (*Hill*).

[60] *Hill* supra, para 27.

counterintuitive and speculative. Both these judgments reiterated that South African law is different from UK law in that in South Africa various state organs have positive duties towards citizens.

Overall, what is important from Justice Tlaletsi's judgment is that when SAPS fails to investigate GBV crimes to a reasonable threshold, secondary trauma can manifest in the survivor. This inaction of SAPS can exacerbate the trauma of the initial violation, and our courts explicitly acknowledge now that survivors may have a claim against SAPS for this further trauma. It is noted that the idea of the rights of the victim is underexplored in South African law and jurisprudence. Section 35 of the *Bill of Rights* establishes the rights of arrested, detained and accused persons, yet, arguably, a similar class of rights does not currently exist for victims of any crimes, let alone offenses involving GBV. However, the judgment in Kawa makes some progress in this regard. The ruling of the Constitutional Court further advanced the protection of women and ruled for further relief. It confirms that police services have a duty not only around preventing GBV, but also in reasonably assisting in securing sanctions against the perpetrators, failing which, they can be held liable for the secondary trauma that manifests.

8.1.2 What Does the Jurisprudence Tell Us

It is clear that the state has a duty to protect women against all forms of GBV that impair their enjoyment of fundamental rights and freedoms. It must take reasonable and appropriate measures to prevent the violation of those rights. The South African Police Service is one of the primary state agencies responsible for the protection of the public in general, in particular women and children, against the invasion of their fundamental rights by perpetrators of violent crimes.[61] The courts are also under a duty to send a clear message to perpetrators of GBV that they are determined to protect the equality, dignity, and freedom of all women.[62] They have attempted to do so and have even developed the law to protect these rights. It is also clear that the prevention of GBV is still an issue 25 years into constitutional democracy. While the country cannot solve the issue overnight, judgments like these mean that small steps can be made towards victims attaining justice.

Currently, there is low confidence in SAPS to battle GBV. Specifically, regarding the *Kawa* decision, holding SAPS to account for below par investigations and their effect on victims, however, is a notable step forward. Hopefully, this could lead to SAPS improving their quality of work and increasing public confidence in the police. An evaluation of the jurisprudence indicates that the Constitutional Court sees violence against women as an extremely serious infringement of human rights that is at odds with the values that underlie the *Constitution*. The Courts have shown

[61] *AK v Minister of Police* supra, para 3.

[62] *S v Chapman* supra, para 345C-D.

a willingness to develop the common law and require the improvement of statutes where these are failing to appropriately tackle this urgent social crisis. The Courts have also made it clear that the state has positive obligations in terms of the *Constitution* and international law to protect women from violence. The cases also point to the Court's preparedness to use its remedial jurisdiction to order remedies that require the state to expend resources and take actions to meet its obligations under the law.

Most of the decisions are contextual in approach and situate legal development within an understanding of the extent, nature, and impact of violence against women. This ensures that the decisions avoid conservative, inappropriate or formalistic approaches to law. The combination of a progressive court and a strong constitutional text has resulted in jurisprudence and a constitutional model worth emulating. The judgments discussed demonstrate an engagement with the rights to freedom and security of the person alongside dignity and equality as key rights contravened by acts of violence against women and children. The values of human dignity, equality and freedom have been given prominence in some of the leading decisions set out above.

The South African constitutional experience on violence against women reflects some important successes but these must be taken further to expand the legal frameworks and the state's obligations in this area. There are real questions about the ability of the Court to address lack of state capacity in implementing its laws in the face of massive social and economic problems, including the epidemic of violence against women. Clearly, the *Constitution* alone is not sufficient to solve this issue. Nevertheless, it is a text with the capacity to contribute further, in tandem with a range of other mechanisms and actors to tackle this major challenge.

8.1.3 *Review of Some Alarming Case Studies of South Africa's Femicide Epidemic*

Whilst the discussion above focused on some seminal judgments it becomes important at this juncture to highlight some cases of GBVF that have been reported in the media and that have caused outrage from the public. It is important as despite the successes discussed above, the cases highlighted below continue to fuel perceptions about the protection accorded to women and the adequacy of the enforcement mechanisms in the fulfilment of their rights. It also looks at the sentences that have been handed down in those cases. The cases highlighted are just some cases in point chosen from a spate of femicide incidents over the past few years.

In April 2017, a 22-year-old, was gruesomely murdered by her partner.[63] What was particularly heinous about this crime was that the perpetrator after murdering her, burnt her body beyond recognition. Throughout his trial, the accused denied

[63] BBC News (2018, May 2).

having killed his former partner but claimed she had committed suicide. With no remorse shown or responsibility taken for his actions, the Court was scathing in the sentencing of the convicted murderer and was called the "devil in disguise."[64] He was handed a three-decade-long jail term for assault and murder as well as disposing of his former partner's body. Whilst the 32-year prison sentence handed-down will not bring the victim back to her loved ones, it is a step in the right direction in allowing her family time to heal and gain closure.

In *S v Rhode*,[65] the accused, Jason Rohde, was the CEO of a prestigious international realty company convicted for the murder of his wife and defeating or obstructing the administration of justice. The state pathologist determined that the cause of death of deceased was consistent with asphyxia following manual strangulation and external airway obstruction. The deceased sustained substantial and distinct injuries before her death. The Court found that the manner, cause of death and nature of injuries sustained showed that the accused had the direct intention to kill Susan Rohde. During the sentencing proceedings, the Court found that the crimes the accused were convicted of a very serious in nature and accepted the evidence on intimate femicide.[66] The accused was sentenced to 18 years direct imprisonment for the murder of his wife and five years direct imprisonment for defeating or obstructing the administration of justice.[67] He was sentenced effectively to a term of 20 years direct imprisonment. However, in October 2021, Rohde's sentence was reduced by the SCA after the bench took the decision to shorten his sentence to 15 years. The presiding judges accepted the arguments set out in the appeal, rejecting claims that Mrs. Rohde was "viciously assaulted."[68]

Additional cases worth mentioning that highlight the scourge of GBVF in the country includes the murder of a 34-year-old mother of three who was axed to death by the father of her children while attending a cultural function,[69] the murder of a mother to a 9-year-old, murdered by her partner, and father of her child, in May 2020,[70] the murder of a Cape Town theology student at the hands of a relative,[71] and the rape and murder of a 22-year-old female whose body was found in her bedroom

---

[64] TimesLive (2018, June 3).

[65] *S v Rohde* (SS43/2017) [2018] ZAWCHC 146; [2019] 1 All SA 740 (WCC) (*Rhode*).

[66] *Rohde* supra, para 24.

[67] IOL News (2018, May 4).

[68] *Rohde v S* (815/2019) [2021] ZASCA 134; 2021 (2) SACR 565 (SCA); [2021] 4 All SA 710 (SCA). The Court went on to add that "the SCA found that the court erred in finding that the deceased had been smothered. There was also no evidential basis for finding that the appellant [Jason Rohde] had punched Susan with his ring bearing first. It's also reasonably possible that the deceased was not smothered, and the fractured ribs were caused by a CPR attempt. . . . Accordingly, the suspect did not assault the victim in a way that has been previously described. No substantial or compelling arguments can justify a departure from anything other than 15 years in prison."

[69] News24 (2020a, June 9).

[70] Sowetan Live (2020a, May 7).

[71] IOL News (2022, February 8).

in Welkom.[72] When she was found, her hands were bound and she had ligature marks around her neck. There was also a written message next to her: "STOP ASSAULTING INMATES." It is alleged that the student was raped and murdered in her bedroom by a suspect who waited for her father to leave the house before he broke in and attacked her.[73] Many more cases go unreported, but the scourge remains.

An emblematic case was the brutal murder of a 28-year-old female in 2020.[74] The victim in this case went missing on 4 June 2020 and was found four days later, on 8 June, stabbed and hanging from a tree in Johannesburg while she was eight months pregnant. In June 2020, a man was charged with premeditated murder for the killing.[75] Her family had initially expressed frustration with the criminal justice system after the suspected perpetrator did not to appear in court physically due to COVID-19 related risks.[76] When the suspect did appear, the victim's then-boyfriend was singled out as the mastermind behind the murder after the hitman he hired testified against him. The former boyfriend and prime suspect has been convicted for masterminding the murder of the 28-year-old. In 2022 he was found guilty of premeditated murder for ordering the hit on her. This case once again saw an outcry against this murder and on 17 June 2020, in his address to the nation President Cyril Ramaphosa referred to GBV as:[77]

> Another pandemic that is raging in our country—the killing of women and children by the men of our country... As a man, as a husband and as a father, I am appalled at what is no less than a war being waged against the women and children of our country.

In August 2020, another case that caused a major uproar involved the killing of a first-year University of Cape Town (UCT) student.[78] She was raped and killed, by a 42-year-old employee, who had a known criminal record, at a post office in Cape Town. The perpetrator admitted to raping her before bludgeoning her to death on the same day at his place of work. The post-office employee left her body overnight in the safe of the Post Office, collected it the next day and set it alight at a field in Lingelethu West, Khayelitsha. He was sentenced to a life sentence for murder, two life sentences on two counts of rape, and five years for defeating the

---

[72] Netwerk 24 (2019, December 12).

[73] OFM News (2019, December 10).

[74] *S v Shoba* (SS36/2021) [2022] ZAGPJHC 174.

[75] Sowetan Live (2020b, July 9).

[76] With the COVID-19 pandemic causing the world to come to a standstill, many operations and services in the country came to a halt, including the judiciary. During the hard lockdown, only urgent cases were heard, which meant inevitable delays in many other matters. See Sowetan Live (2020b, July 9). According to the National Prosecution Authority (25 September 2020), the accused would have appeared through video link due to the national lockdown. This explains why the media reported that he never appeared in court.

[77] The Presidency of South Africa (2020, June 17).

[78] News24 (2020b, August 10).

course of justice. The five-year sentence will run concurrently, he will also not be eligible for parole before the first 25 years.

Prior to news of the UCT students death, a prominent South African boxer and karate champion died at the hands of her then boyfriend, who shot and killed her, whilst she was on her way to the gym.[79] This despite the victim having taken out a protection order against her former boyfriend.[80] The UCT students killing while running a mundane errand, as well as the killing of the renowned sports personality, the epitome of what a "physically strong" woman is meant to be, led to women taking to the street in massive numbers asking "Am I Next?"[81] and calls for a national shutdown against GBVF amplified. These deaths were "a potent reminder of the psychosis of violence"[82] and it represented a bigger problem that cannot be ignored, that woman, no matter who they may be, were unsafe to go wherever and do whatever they wanted.

Among the other cases that have confirmed the gravity of violence against women in South Africa are *S v Pistorius*,[83] *S v Dewani*,[84] and *Panayiotou v S*.[85] In these cases, which attracted unprecedented publicity in the trial courts, all the accused persons were found responsible for the brutal killing of their deceased partners. For example, the *S v Pistorius*[86] case involved a human tragedy where an Olympian who became an international celebrity, began a romantic relationship with a young woman, Reeva Steenkamp who was a law graduate and a successful model. Ironically, on Valentine's Day 2013, Oscar Pistorius, shot and brutally killed Reeva at his home in a secured complex alleging that he had believed she was an intruder.[87]

Another case that shocked the country included one in May of 2022, when the country woke to the sad news of the death of the daughter of politician.[88] Her body was found next to a pine plantation 40 km outside Mbombela in Mpumalanga on May 2, with visible wounds to her head. She was kidnapped in the town on April 29 while travelling home with her adopted three-year-old daughter. Three suspects were arrested and charged with murder, rape, conspiracy to commit murder, kidnapping, defeating the ends of justice and possession of an unlicensed firearm and ammunition. However, the charges were later dropped for various reasons and the family of the victim has still not found any closure.[89]

---

[79] IOL News (2019, September 8).

[80] IOL News (2019, September 8).

[81] In reaction to the killings, South Africans, mostly women, took to the streets calling on everyone to take a stand against women abuse and femicide. News24 (2020b, August 10).

[82] IOL News (2019, September 8).

[83] *S v Pistorius* (CC113/2013) [2014] ZAGPPHC 793 (*S v Pistorius*).

[84] *S v Dewani* (CC15/2014) [2014] ZAWCHC 188.

[85] *Panayiotou and Others v S* (CC26/2016) [2018] ZAECPEHC 21.

[86] *S v Pistorius* supra.

[87] *Director of Public Prosecutions, Gauteng v Pistorius* (96/2015) [2015] ZASCA 204, para 2.

[88] Times Live (2022, August 8).

[89] Sunday World News (2023, October 9).

The killing of women by intimate partners and non-intimate partners is alarmingly common.[90] In July 2022, eight women were raped and robbed by a gang of armed men, believed to be illegal miners, while shooting a video at an abandoned mine dump in West Village, Krugersdorp. The news of this incident triggered a massive public uproar and saw police descend on the area in a series of raids over several days.[91] Despite many arrests being made, the NPA in October withdrew these charges after DNA testing failed to link them to the crime.[92] This has unsurprisingly created more distrust and anger towards SAPS and NPA. At the time of the writing of this chapter, justice continues to remain elusive for the victims.

These cases indicate the urgent need for the criminal justice system to effectively address the issue of violence against women. In many of these cases the survivors of GBVF together with their loved ones blame authorities for the prevalence of impunity amid the rise in cases. It has been stated that "the system is failing victims which is why most people who have been through this don't speak out; they are too scared,"[93] whilst human rights defenders attribute institutional failures to poorly trained police force and justice system officials on GBVF.[94]

8.1.4 Harmful Practices and GBVF

Harmful cultural practices and customs remain barriers to women's rights protection and is one of the major reasons for the high rates and the escalation of GBV. It is widely acknowledged that traditional cultural practices reflect the values and beliefs held by members of a community for generations.[95] Whilst some traditional cultural practices and beliefs may be beneficial to its members, others are harmful to a specific group, such as women. Examples of these harmful traditional practices include female genital mutilation (FGM), forced feeding of women, early marriage, the various taboos or practices which prevent women from controlling their own fertility, nutritional taboos and traditional birth practices, son preference and its implications for the status of the girl child, female infanticide, early pregnancy, and dowry price. However, despite their harmful nature and their violation of international human rights laws, such practices persist because they and is associated with a sense of morality by those practicing them.

One cultural practice that deserves mentioning and that was identified as a particular harmful practice by the *Constitution* is forced marriage through

[90] Mail & Guardian (2017, May 22).

[91] EWN (2022b, December 29).

[92] EWN (2022a, October 27).

[93] Amnesty International (2020).

[94] Amnesty International (2020).

[95] UN Office of the High Commissioner for Human Rights (1995).

ukuthwala.[96] *Ukuthwala* is a form of abduction that involves the kidnapping of a girl or a young woman by a man and his friends or peers with the intention of compelling the girl or young woman's family to endorse marriage negotiations. Historically in ancient Africa, *ukuthwala* was condoned as a path to marriage targeted at certain girls or women of marriageable age. This was a particular practice of the Nguni people. The traditional practice however did not involve raping or having consensual sex with the girl until marriage requirements had been concluded.

This practice of *ukuthwala* was thrust into the spotlight by the criminal appeal case of *Jezile v S and Others.*[97] In this case, the Court took judicial notice of a public debate on the practice of *ukuthwala* that "its current practice is regarded as an abuse of traditional custom and a cloak for the commission of violent acts of assault, abduction and rape of not only women but children as young as eleven years by older men."[98] The Court went on to say that "these practices—under the guise of custom—have been described by several organizations as a '*harmful cultural practice'*."[99] This is an important ruling because the Court balanced its constitutional duty to respect and give effect to customary law while remaining sensitive and mindful to the vulnerability of the girl-child. The Court found that Jezile relied on an aberrant form of *ukuthwala* that involved unlawful sexual coercion to subdue an underage girl who did not consent to the marriage. Jezile's belief that he lawfully concluded a customary marriage under the practice of *ukuthwala* was determined insufficient grounds to reverse his conviction of human trafficking and rape of a child. The order recognizes that men cannot interpret customary law to abduct and rape young women and girls. The Court acknowledged that customary law is part of our law and can be aligned with the constitutional framework.

The Court accordingly considered the legal framework regulating customary marriages, including constitutional provisions,[100] legislation, and human rights treaties to which South Africa is a signatory. Section 28 of the *Constitution* provides that protection of the child from harm and the best interests of the child are paramount in matters concerning children. Section 28 further defines a child as a person under the age of 18 years. The *Constitution* also provides guidance for interpreting the constitutional rights in the *Bill of Rights* (section 39). The Court reviewed the *Children's Act, 2005* (*Children's Act*), and referred amongst others to section 1 on the definition of trafficking, Section 12(1) which prohibits subjecting children to cultural practices that are detrimental to their wellbeing, and section

---

[96] The *Constitution* is clear that cultural rights are protected subject to the provisions of the *Constitution*. Section 31 of the *Constitution* recognises cultural rights of communities and groups provided that such rights are not exercised in a manner inconsistent with any of the provisions of the *Bill of Rights*. See Department of Justice and Constitutional Development (2021).

[97] *Jezile v S and Others* (A 127/2014) [2015] ZAWCHC 31; 2015 (2) SACR 452 (WCC); 2016 (2) SA 62 (WCC); [2015] 3 All SA 201 (WCC) (23 March 2015) (*Jezile*).

[98] *Jezile* supra, para 56.

[99] *Jezile* supra, para 56.

[100] Section 211(3) of the *Constitution* requires courts to apply customary laws subject to the *Constitution* and relevant legislation.

284(1) which prohibits child trafficking. Section 284(2) provides that it is no defense that the child or the person having control over the child consents to trafficking.

The Court referred to provisions of the *Criminal Law Sexual Offences and Related Matters Amendment Act 32 of 2007* (*Sexual Offences Act*) on rape and called attention to section 56(1) which provides that it is not a defense to the charge of rape to rely on a marital or existing relationship. It also referred to sections 70 to 72 of the *Sexual Offences Act*, which prohibit trafficking in persons for sexual purposes. The Court also noted that the *Sexual Offences Act* defined trafficking in a similar manner to the definition in the *Children's Act*, and that the *Sexual Offences Act* makes trafficking of any person without their consent an offense as consent can only be voluntary or uncoerced. The Court referred to the South African *Prevention and Combatting of Trafficking in Persons Act*, which at the time of the judgment had been passed but had not yet entered into force (it has since been signed into effect).[101] However, the Court stated that the *Act's* various provisions pointed to the intention of the Legislature to comply with its obligations under international human rights law. The Court then made reference to the *Recognition of Customary Marriages Act 120 of 1998* (*RCMA*) which provides for recognition of customary marriages under the *Constitution* and stipulates the requirements for contracting a valid customary marriage.[102]

The Court also referred to section 8 of the *PEPUDA*, which prohibits discrimination on the grounds of gender and includes any cultural practice that impairs the dignity of women or undermines the dignity and welfare of female children. Finally, the Court reviewed several international human rights treaties and South Africa's obligations in relation to them, including the *CRC*, which stipulates that member states take measures to abolish traditional practices prejudicial to the wellbeing of children and also protect children from exploitation and the *African Charter on the Rights and Welfare of the Child, 1990* (*ACRWC*) which prohibits child marriage and betrothal. The Court determined that there was clear authority that child trafficking and child abuse or exploitation for sexual purposes was "not to be tolerated in [its] constitutional dispensation."[103]

The Court subsequently reviewed information provided by the parties and *amici curiae* regarding the practice of *ukuthwala*. The *amici* indicated that *ukuthwala* is one of several alternative ways under customary law to bring about marriage negotiations, and that it generally requires:[104]

---

[101] *Prevention and Combating of Trafficking in Persons Act, 2013* Act No. 7 of 2013.

[102] Section 3(1) of the *RCMA* lists the following requirements: (a) prospective spouses should be over the age of 18 years; (b) both must consent to the customary marriage; and (c) the process must be in accordance with customary law. Sections 3(3)(a) and 3(4)(a) provide for conditions under which a person below the age of 18 can enter into a customary marriage with the consent of parents or guardians.

[103] *Jezile* supra, para 69.

[104] *Jezile* supra, para 72.

(a) the woman to be of marriageable age, typically childbearing age;
(b) the consent of both parties, though there are instances in which the women's acquiescence in the process occurs after the fact;
(c) a mock abduction of the woman at dusk, during which the woman would feign protest but would have agreed beforehand;
(d) a smuggling of the woman to the man's homestead; and
(e) an invitation sent to the woman's homestead to inform the woman's family that she was with the man's family, which was supposed to signal the desire of the man's family to enter into marriage negotiations.

The *amici* argued that, based on the record, *ukuthwala* was not properly performed in the matter due to the Complainant's young age, her lack of consent, and the payment of the bride fee before the *ukuthwala* occurred. After evaluating the legal framework and the information provided on the practice of *ukuthwala*, the Court then turned to the facts of the case. The Court determined that the offenses for which the Appellant was charged had taken place after a traditional *ukuthwala* would ordinarily have happened, as the trafficking and sexual assaults occurred after the customary marriage. Therefore, the Court held that the Appellant could not rely on the traditional practice of *ukuthwala* to justify his criminal conduct.

Further, the Court was persuaded largely by the views on the distinction between the traditional and the aberrant forms of *ukuthwala*. The aberrant form did not have the same requirements of consent and age. The Court found that the Appellant had relied on an aberrant form of *ukuthwala* and held that the Appellant could not rely on the misapplied form of *ukuthwala*, which did not comply with the requirements of the *RCMA*, to justify commission of the offenses of trafficking and rape. On the second issue, the Court concluded that the Appellant's two convictions of assault both arose out of the same incident. The Court therefore concluded that the two counts should be treated as a single offense in order to prevent a duplication of punishment and the appeal against the convictions for trafficking and rape was dismissed, and the Appellant's convictions on the counts of assault were set aside.

This case has raised various questions around issues that were not determined by the Court. First is *ukuthwala*, even in its innocuous form cloaked in patriarchal values which is contrary to gender equality and human rights. For example, it cannot be acceptable for a mock-abduction to be a feature for girls only and not boys. This flies in the face of gender equality laws and further reinforces the subjugated position of a girl in relation to that of a man. Second, regarding the consent of families rather than the person's consent. This shines light on the ambiguity of consent which the practice of mock-abduction poses. This is an important observation because it has been argued that "mock-abduction mystifies the process of consent and obscures whether it does in fact take place, or whether the girl succumbs to pressure or merely acquiesces after being coerced."[105] The whole practice of *ukuthwala* is clearly based

[105] Kangaude (2017), p. 27.

on patriarchal notions about the place of women in society. Due to the entrenched practice, it will be difficult to dissuade communities from continuing such practices.

Third, and of particular concern is why those family members who were party to the abduction, even if it was a "mock abduction" were not prosecuted. The evidence showed that the complainant's uncle and other family members of the complainant as well as family members of the Appellant, were accomplices to the abduction. The brother of the Appellant had also allegedly held the Complainant down while the Appellant raped her but was never charged for any criminal conduct. The Court, however, agreed, without explaining its reasoning, with the trial court in the view that "the involvement of the complainant's male family members and grandmother was nothing more than a neutral factor insofar as the Appellant's own blameworthiness was concerned."[106] The Court agreed with the trial court's reasoning even though it was evident that family members played key roles in the commission of various offenses. Whatever the reason may be for not following thought with prosecution, it raises questions about the adequacy of the criminal justice systems response to harmful traditional practices. It is a barrier and fails in its duty where it does not, without justification, prosecute those who are involved, either directly, indirectly or as accomplices to harmful practices in activity that can be perceived as criminal or have criminal aspects to it. The failure to address such issues constitute barriers for women and girl survivors seeking justice from competent authorities.

8.1.5 Concluding Remarks

South Africa's legal framework and jurisprudence is indeed pioneering. The various jurisprudence highlights how a functioning criminal justice system can play an important role in ensuring that victims of GBV are able to access justice. As the final arbiters in matters involving GBV, the judiciary has the power to protect abused women and to effectively punish the offenders, and in so doing declare that such conduct will not be condoned. The judiciary also has the inherent ability to ensure that courtroom policies and procedures are sensitive to the victims, and that the victims who go through the legal system are not subjected to secondary trauma in the form of harsh, humiliating, and unnecessary cross-examination when they present themselves to testify.

There has been a marked ideological shift in the way matters relating to GBVF are currently adjudicated, including the abolition of the cautionary rule in respect of sexual offenses, and the conduct of many judicial officers can be commended, as can be seen from some of the judgments. However, all judges hearing such cases must be attuned to the sensitivities of cases concerning GBVF. For example, they should consider how survivors of GBV may face intersecting power dynamics and inequality, whether it is on the basis of their gender, class, race and sexuality. To this end,

[106] *Jezile* supra, para 104.

continuous training of judges and practitioners must be accelerated. Every member of the criminal justice system must be cognizant of how to conduct themselves efficiently as their actions will affect the victims who seek justice. A humane and just approach is necessary for the survivors to retain hope and faith in the system.

The next chapter will consider some of the cases involving GBVF in institutions of higher learning. This is an important consideration because the negative repercussions of GBV on students' ability to learn, not only has a detrimental effect on their academics and career potential but it has a negative impact on the university and more broadly on the society, through lost potential.

References

African Commission on Human and People's Right (2017) The guidelines on combating sexual violence and its consequences in Africa. https://achpr.au.int/en/node/848. Accessed on 11 Apr 2023

Amnesty International (2020) "Treated like furniture": Gender-based violence and Covid-19 response in Southern Africa. https://www.amnesty.org/en/wp-content/uploads/2021/05/AFR0334182021ENGLISH.pdf. Accessed on 4 Feb 2023

BBC News (2018, May 2) South Africa's Sandile Mantsoe guilty of Karabo Mokoena murder. https://www.bbc.com/news/world-africa-43979207. Accessed on 28 Feb 2024

Bonthuys E, Albertyn C (2007) Gender, law and justice. Cape Town, Juta

Department of Justice and Constitutional Development (2021) Justice/resources/publications/ukuthwala. https://www.justice.gov.za/brochure/ukuthwala/ukuthwala.html. Accessed on 22 Dec 2022

Dixon R, Roux T (2018) Constitutional triumphs, constitutional disappointments: a critical assessment of the 1996 South African Constitution's local and international influence. Cambridge University Press, UK

EWN (2022a, October 27) Rape charges withdrawn against 14 suspects in Krugersdorp gang rape case. https://ewn.co.za/2022/10/27/rape-charges-withdrawn-against-14-suspects-in-krugersdorp-gang-rape-case. Accessed on 16 Mar 2023

EWN (2022b, December 29) Justice proving to be illusive for Krugersdorp gang rape victims. https://ewn.co.za/2022/12/29/justice-proving-to-be-illusive-for-krugersdorp-gang-rape-victims. Accessed on 16 Mar 2023

Goldblatt B (2016) Violence against women in South Africa: constitutional responses and opportunities. At https://papers.ssrn.com/sol3/papers.cfm?abstract_id=2872478. Accessed on 7 Aug 2023

IOL News (2018, May 4) Femicide, a South African curse. https://www.iol.co.za/news/opinion/femicide-a-south-african-curse-14780746. Accessed on 4 Apr 2023

IOL News (2019, September 8) "Baby Lee": such a sad, tragic, violent loss. https://www.iol.co.za/Sport/Opinion/Baby-Lee-Such-a-Sad-Tragic-Violent-Loss-32553068. Accessed on 17 Mar 2023

IOL News (2022, February 8) Shocking details emerge of how Jesse Hess and her grandfather were attacked and murdered. https://www.iol.co.za/news/south-africa/western-cape/shocking-details-emerge-of-how-jesse-hess-and-her-grandfather-were-attacked-and-murdered-7bdf8860-b01d-414b-8d38-97669525cced. Accessed on 17 Mar 2023

Kangaude GD (ed) (2017) Legal grounds: reproductive and sexual rights in Sub-Saharan African Courts, vol III. Pretoria University Law Press, Pretoria

Mail & Guardian (2017, May 22) Government action on femicide goes wrong from the bottom up. https://mg.co.za/article/2017-05-22-00-government-action-on-femicide-goes-wrong-from-the-bottom-up/. Accessed on 10 Apr 2023

Netwerk 24 (2019, December 12) Goldfields student found dead at home with hands tied. At https://www.netwerk24.com/Netwerk24/goldfields-student-found-dead-at-home-with-hands-tied-20191211-2. Accessed on 17 Mar 2023

News24 (2020a, June 9) Man hands himself over for brutal murder of Naledi Phangindawo. https://www.news24.com/news24/southafrica/news/man-hands-himself-over-for-brutal-murder-of-naledi-phangindawo-20200609. Accessed on 17 Mar 2023

News24 (2020b, August 10) Femicide: Uyinene Mrwetyana's mother: We are gripped by hurt, sadness, anger and frustration. https://www.news24.com/news24/SouthAfrica/News/femicide-uyinene-mrwetyanas-mother-we-are-gripped-by-hurt-sadness-anger-and-frustration-20200810. Accessed on 23 Jan 2023

OFM News (2019, December 10) No arrests yet after Welkom woman's murder. https://www.ofm.co.za/article/centralsa/282597/no-arrests-yet-after-welkom-woman-s-murder. Accessed on 1 Mar 2024

Sowetan Live (2020a, May 7) Mom fights in vain to stop her daughter's murder. https://www.sowetanlive.co.za/news/south-africa/2020-05-07-mom-fights-in-vain-to-stop-her-daughters-murder/. Accessed on 17 Mar 2023

Sowetan Live (2020b, July 9). Tshegofatso Pule's family left frustrated by court delay. At https://www.sowetanlive.co.za/news/south-africa/2020-07-09-tshegofatso-pules-family-left-frustrated-by-court-delay. Accessed on 11 Apr 2023

Sunday World News (Oct 9, 2023) The R300m Hillary Gardee lawsuit in numbers. https://sundayworld.co.za/news/the-r300m-hillary-gardee-lawsuit-in-numbers/. Accessed on 1 Mar 2024

The Judiciary (2018, November 1) Judicial and legal responses to gender-based violence and femicide: Justice Mandisa Maya President: Supreme Court of Appeal. https://www.judiciary.org.za/images/speeches_from_the_judiciary/Gender_Based_Violence_and_Femicide_Summit_Speech.pdf. Accessed on 3 Jan 2023

The Presidency of South Africa (2020, June 17) Speeches: The Presidency. https://www.thepresidency.gov.za/speeches/address-president-cyril-ramaphosa-south-africa%E2%80%99s-response-coronavirus-pandemic%2C-union-buildings%2C-tshwane-4. Accessed on 11 Apr 2023

The Sunday World (2022, July 29) Ntuthuki Shoba sentenced to life for the murder of Tshegofatso Pule. https://sundayworld.co.za/news/ntuthuko-shoba-sentenced-to-life-for-murder-of-tshegofatso-pule/. Accessed on 8 Jan 2023

Times Live (2022, August 8) Women's Month: 5 gender-based violence cases that have made headlines in 2022. https://www.timeslive.co.za/news/south-africa/2022-08-08-womens-month-5-gender-based-violence-cases-that-have-made-headlines-in-2022/. Accessed on 16 Mar 2023

TimesLive (2018, June 3) "You're the devil in disguise": 8 quotes from Sandile Mantsoe's sentencing. https://www.timeslive.co.za/news/south-africa/2018-05-03-watch%2D%2Dyoure-the-devil-in-disguise-8-quotes-from-sandile-mantsoes-sentencing/. Accessed on 15 Mar 2023

TimesLive (2022, January 30) Violence against women is endemic and the pandemic has made it worse. https://www.timeslive.co.za/sunday-times/opinion-and-analysis/insight/2022-01-30-violence-against-women-is-endemic-and-the-pandemic-has-made-it-worse/. Accessed on 7 Jan 2023

UN Office of the High Commissioner for Human Rights (1995) Fact sheet no. 23, harmful traditional practices affecting the health of women and children. https://www.ohchr.org/sites/default/files/Documents/Publications/FactSheet23en.pdf. Accessed on 22 Mar 2023

We, The People South Africa (2020, August 20) A duty to protect women: Carmichele v Minister of Safety and Security and Minister of Justice (2001). https://ourconstitution.wethepeoplesa.org/a-duty-to-protect-women/. Accessed on 13 Jan 2023

Chapter 9
Gender-Based Violence and Femicide in Institutions of Higher Learning

9.1 Overview

Security and education are fundamental human rights protected in both the *UDHR* and the *Constitution* of SA. There is an expectation that educational institutions constitute safe places. Higher education campuses are among those that had traditionally been viewed as sanctuaries that were immune to the crimes faced by the larger society that surrounded them.[1] However, "with the wall between academe and the world outside disintegrating, inevitably the problems of the larger culture have begun to intrude upon the academy."[2] Higher education institutions (HEIs) of learning do not exist in a vacuum, nor are they immune to the larger social issues experienced in the contexts wherein they exist.[3] These environments mirror the reality of society at large, including the culture of GBVF that is seemingly permeating society, while at the same time holding the potential to address societal problems.

GBV is indeed a complex, persistent, and often unspoken force in many organizations, and institutions of higher learning are no exception.[4] GBVF at HEIs remains an ongoing issue that urgently needs to be addressed and researched.[5] For South Africa, the struggle for equality remains a challenge and GBV remains one of the greatest barriers to achieving equality. The *Constitution* of South Africa promises all South Africans a society founded on democratic values and social justice amongst others. Focusing on social justice, gender equality is one of the

---

[1] Jacobsen (2017).

[2] Smith (1988), p. 8.

[3] Committee for Gender Equality (2019).

[4] Makhaye et al. (2023), p. 40.

[5] Makhaye et al. (2023), p. 41; Council on Higher Education (2019), p. 5.

T. Deane, *Gender-Based Violence and Femicide in South Africa*, Gender, Justice and Legal Feminism 5, https://doi.org/10.1007/978-3-031-61053-0_9

fundamental principles enshrined in the *Bill of Rights* of the *Constitution*.[6] Likewise, the issue of gender inequality remains a present and persistent challenge in South African higher education.[7] Higher Education Institutions (HEIs) have a social obligation to equip people with the intellectual dimensions necessary to pursue national development plans.[8] Research has indicated that GBV in HEIs create a public health and safety concern because of the host of physiological, psychological, and academic outcomes associated with student victimization.[9] GBV disrupts students' education and social lives, and potentially results in lower grades, dropped classes, or withdrawal from the institution.[10] Such consequences for GBV at HEIs translates to lost potential, inequality in education and a failure to achieve a country's development goals. This is especially serious for a developing country like South Africa who has international, national, and regional obligations to eliminate discrimination and violence and commitments towards development goals.[11] This chapter therefore looks at GBV in HEIs as a challenge that needs to be addressed.

9.1.1 GBVF in South African Higher Education Institutions

University students' experiences of sexual assault on university campuses have been documented by scholars around the world as a matter of grave concern.[12] For example, studies in the US have shown that university campuses are places conducive to rape, and places where rape often occurs.[13] In South African HEIs GBVF is an escalating problem, where nearly 50% of these assaults are committed by someone close to the victim.[14] Between 2011 and 2014, approximately 247 cases of sexual violence, partner violence, and rape were reported at 15 universities across the country.[15] The wave of GBV that has infiltrated institutions of higher learning in

[6] Section 9 of the Constitution speaks to the principle of equality and this section not only upholds and protects women's rights, but it also unambiguously forbids discrimination on the premise of gender.

[7] Council on Higher Education (2019), p. 8.

[8] Forum for African Women Educationalists (2015), p. 2.

[9] Banyard et al. (2020), p. 4375.

[10] Krebs et al. (2007, 2016); Mengo and Black (2016), pp. 234–248.

[11] The Sustainable Development Goals (SDG) have clearly been articulated to highlight the need to address gender inequality and empowerment through SDG 5 and, specifically, to address gender disparities in education in SDG 4. SDG 4 is the education goal that aims to ensure inclusivity and equity in education. On the other hand, SDG 5 aims to promote gender equality and empowerment of women.

[12] Anderson and Naidu (2022).

[13] The Sexual Assault Response Team (2016).

[14] Siebritz (2022, October 21).

[15] Boonzaier et al. (2019).

the country warrants immediate and sustained action[16] as this untenable situation continues to threaten social cohesion and deepens the erosion of a human rights culture as articulated in the *Bill of Rights*.[17]

Furthermore, from 2016 to date, Rhodes University, University of Cape Town, Nelson Mandela University, University of the Witwatersrand and Tshwane University of Technology have all been affected by highly publicized protests by students against GBV.[18] However, scholars agree that incidents of GBV are underreported.[19] The impact of under-reporting was reiterated by the UNODC where the UN data reveals that in the majority of countries with available data, less than 40% of the women who experience violence seek help of any sort, that among women who do, most look to family and friends and very few look to formal institutions and mechanisms, and less than 10% of those women seeking help after having experienced violence sought help by appealing to the police.[20]

It is widely documented that like statistics on GBV in general, the challenges of GBV in HEIs is also related to the lack of sufficient information to provide a comprehensive picture of the extent of the scourge therein. The problem can be attributed to the fact that for many years, Universities did not have a system in place that collected rape and sexual violence statistics, nor did it have any reporting mechanisms that would allow them to report back to the Department of Higher Education and Training.

Indeed, the Higher Education and Training Minister Dr Blade Nzimande has indicated that for 2019 and 2020 the lack of a standardized tool impacted on reporting of data, consequently impacting data collection, which is needed to enable the effective implementation of GBVF interventions. What is important to note is that the previous minister Naledi Pandor, who formerly held Nzimande's position, indicated that notwithstanding this deficiency in collecting data, in 2018, she elicited the requisite data from universities by requesting same.[21] Her reply revealed the shocking statistic that in 2017 there were 47 cases of rape and sexual assault on students reported on campuses across South Africa. The University of Cape Town had recorded nine rape incidents, making it the institution with the highest number of cases. This was followed by the Walter Sisulu University with seven, the Tshwane University of Technology reported six rapes, five rapes were reported at the Nelson Mandela University and four at the University of Johannesburg.[22]

Despite the issue with the collection of data using standardized tools, during the 2019 year, when HEIs were requested to provide details thereof, it was reported that fifteen cases of rape were recorded and fifteen of physical assault. Data collected in

---

[16] Brink et al. (2022).

[17] Department of Higher Education and Training (2020).

[18] The Sexual Assault Response Team (2016).

[19] Swartz et al. (2017).

[20] UN Office on Drugs and Crime (2017).

[21] Orth et al. (2020).

[22] IOL News (2022, March 11).

2020 recorded 26 rape cases on campuses and a further sixteen cases of sexual assault, nine of touching and innuendo/insinuation, nine of incest, eleven of unwanted sexual touching and fifteen of physical assault.[23]

In 2021 HEIs started reporting online through the Survey Hub,[24] a new reporting system for GBV cases. Nzimande has acknowledged that data collated from HEIs responses to the Survey Hub, indicated that 88 alleged campus rape cases were reported in 2021.[25] Nzimande further acknowledged that these statistics would not include other incidents like sexual or physical assault. He said, "the reports from colleges varied (and) as such this cannot be taken as a true reflection of what transpires in colleges."[26] The reporting of sexual offences cases by individuals remains low in all HEIs because of several factors such as the fear of stigmatization, the unwillingness of survivors to expose perpetrators (especially in cases of intimate partners) and the fear of possible further victimization and harassment.[27]

9.1.2 HEI-Related GBVF Cases

Whilst only a few of the HEI-related rape cases were reported in newspapers over the years one of the most publicized cases in 2017 involved the alleged rapes of numerous students on the University of Cape Town campus. The main suspect a 43-year-old male was apprehended and charged[28] with the kidnapping, rape, assault, and robbery of the women. He was subsequently handed nine life sentences by the Western Cape High Court.[29] It is expected that since the convicted rapist and killer was handed nine life sentences and that it will not run concurrently, he will therefore remain in jail for the rest of his life. However, the serial rapist's conviction and sentencing has failed to stem the sex attacks on University of Cape Town students.[30] Less than a year after the suspect was given nine life sentences, sixteen cases were

[23] IOL News (2022, March 11).

[24] SurveyHub is a bespoke online survey platform that makes it easier for directorates and branches of the DHET to publish survey questionnaires. These questionnaires are developed to collect valuable data and information from stakeholders and entities of the DHET in support of the DHET's monitoring and evaluation activities. See Department of Higher Education and Training (n.d.).

[25] IOL News (2022, March 11), para 4.

[26] IOL News (2022, March 11), para 8.

[27] IOL News (2022, March 11), para 11.

[28] The 43-year-old suspect entered a plea agreement with the State after being charged with twelve counts of rape, six of aggravated robbery, and one of assault with intent to inflict grievous bodily harm.

[29] News24 (2016, November 14).

[30] TimesLive (2017, August 29).

reported in the first half of 2017 alone. This was approximately three case of sexual violence a month and correlates with the numbers during the same period in 2016.[31]

Another disturbing case reported during October 2017 was that of the rape of one student and the stabbing and sexual assaulted of another student at a computer laboratory on the premises in Nelson Mandela University.[32] The suspect herein pleaded guilty to raping a 25-year-old student and sexually assaulting her 30-year-old friend in the computer labs of the fashion design department. In his explanation, the accused admitted he went to the university premises with the intention of stealing valuable items and while there he saw the two women students in the computer labs. He at that stage decided to rob the two females of their belongings. Having no weapons on him he said that he then left to go to one of the rooms in the building and found a pair of scissors. The man then later returned to the computer laboratory wearing yellow rubber gloves. After robbing the victims of their belongings and stabbing one of the women in the back "with the intention of forcing her to give me her cellular phone,"[33] the accused forced the women to strip. Thereafter, he raped the younger woman and sexually assaulted her friend.

According to the indictment, the accused had scaled the perimeter fence of Nelson Mandela University's Second Avenue campus before making his way into the fashion design building. Shortly after the attack, Nelson Mandela University students staged a number of protests.[34] They called for increased security on the institution's campuses across the city.[35] The accused was later found guilty of the rapes.[36] What was particularly concerning about this case, is that like many others it was a crime of opportunity but this had occurred on premises that was meant to educate and that should have afforded students not only a sense of safety and security, but actual safety and security. The leadership and management of health and safety in higher education is an integral part of achieving effective health and safety in institutions.

In 2018 another case that made headlines included the murder of a female student killed in her room at the Mangosuthu University of Technology off-campus residency.[37] The female student was killed by her then boyfriend who was later sentenced to life imprisonment in the KwaZulu-Natal High Court in Durban, having been found guilty of her murder. In addition to the life sentence handed down by the court, the perpetrator was further sentenced to 28 years for the possession of an illegal firearm and three live rounds of ammunition. During the trial the motivation

---

[31] TimesLive (2017, August 29). See also, The South African (2017, August 29).

[32] SowetanLive (2018, August 29). The testimony of two of his victims and CCTV footage from the Nelson Mandela University computer labs captured on the night of 2 October 2017, when the accused assaulted and raped the two female students, sealed his fate.

[33] TimesLive (2017, August 29).

[34] eNCA (2017, October 13).

[35] Nelson Mandela University News (2020).

[36] TimesLive (2018, August 29).

[37] IOL News (2020, March 4).

behind the murder become known. Both the former boyfriend and victim were students at the Mangosuthu University of Technology and were in a relationship that ended in April 2018. Angered by this, the accused, on 1 May 2018, entered the former girlfriend's student residence armed with a semi-automatic firearm. He confronted her in her room, reprimanded her for making a fool out of him, and shot her in the head and chest. The accused's defense in court was that the firearm went off during a struggle with his former girlfriend. However, this version did not correlate with the testimony of two witnesses who were in the room at the time of the shooting. Furthermore, the voice recordings on the accused's cell phone from shortly after the shooting contained a confession that he had intentionally killed his ex-girlfriend. In mitigation of sentence, the accused's legal representative said that he was remorseful and had apologized to the girl's family.

However, the State Advocate refuted this, indicating that the apology only came 18 months after the crime was committed, and that the accused had believed he had a right to take the victims life because she had the "audacity" to end their relationship. These kinds of cases are disturbing as it points to the reality that if a woman is to be murdered, there is a high probability that it would be by an intimate partner or an ex-intimate partner. The State Advocate further argued that the evidence revealed the accused to be a ruthless and cold-hearted killer. Very shortly after the girl's death, the accused "calmly and unemotionally" reported the crime to his friends on Facebook while her body lay meters away from him. It was additionally argued that in a crime of this nature, which was planned and calculated, the focus ought to be on retribution and punitive punishment.

In handing down sentence, Judge Nompumelelo Radebe said that "violence by men towards women in South Africa is escalating at alarming proportions. This calls for harsh sentences to be imposed."[38] In recognition of the scourge of GBVF when handing down judgement, the Judge said that the accused planned the murder, adding that the brutality used by the accused shows that he has no value for other people's lives:[39]

> The accused by killing the deceased in the manner he did has shown that he has no value for other people's lives or their physical integrity, or for that matter their dignity. The prevalence of femicide is worrying. Women are no longer free to pursue their lives and to choose their romantic relationship in the manner they would have loved to. It is not an offence for a woman to reject a man; there is no law that says a woman must not reject a man. Women have become the scapegoat for some of the weak man. I emphasise the word 'some' because it's not all men who behave like the accused.

Another case of GBVF that was particularly disconcerting related to the death of a final year business management student at Capricorn TVET college. The student was stabbed multiple times[40] inside her rented room in Mokomene, Botlokwa, in December 2019. The chilling confession by the 29-year-old suspect at the time on

---

[38] National Prosecuting Authority (2020).

[39] SABC News (2020, March 5).

[40] News24 (2021, January 10).

how and why he killed the student has exacerbated the struggle of women and young girls in the country in their fight against GBVF. The accused, through his lawyer, gave the Polokwane High Court in Limpopo a detailed account of why he had abruptly ended the young woman's life. According to him, he went to the girls home in the early hours of the morning on November 24 and told the 21-year-old that he had feelings for her. When she would not open the door, he forcefully gained entry through the window and spoke to her. When she rejected him once again, he raped her and then stabbed her multiple times. In his evidence-in-chief in mitigation of sentence, the accused admitted that he had stabbed the deceased several times and then raped her while she was bleeding. After raping her, he then stabbed her again multiple times. The court heard that the victim was stabbed ninety times. The accused, was handed two life sentences in June 2021.[41]

Although this disturbing confession has by a small measure assisted the family to gain some closure on events that transpired that fateful morning, it also raised the question for them on why a grown man would bluntly refuse to accept their daughter's "no."[42] The most reasonable conclusion that can be reached is that of the objectification of women and the belief of a man's right to sex. This case, like the others who have been sexually assaulted or experience various forms of GBV reflects the continuous crisis facing female citizens in the country. It communicates a particularly sinister message to women and girls and that is that they remain unsafe in public as well as in private spaces.[43]

In 2021, one of the cases highly and widely reported on included a 21-year-old Vhembe TVET college student kidnapped, raped, stabbed multiple times, and left for dead.[44] The student was kidnapped by two men from her room at Makwarela Location, Thohoyandou, on June 27, 2021. The suspects, aged 25 and 27, of which one is the victim's former partner, are said to have gone to her rented room and then forced her into the boot of their vehicle and drove off to a nearby village. She was later raped by her former partner whereafter both men used sharp objects to hack at her body until she lost consciousness.[45] Once again this case highlights the serious reality of intimate partner violence.

In 2022, approximately 10% of rape cases reported in South Africa were from institutions of higher learning.[46] Whilst some reports indicate that South African public universities were affected by students' protests against "rape culture" from 2016 to date,[47] others report that students protesting across the country, began

[41] SABC News (2021, June).
[42] IOL News (2021, June 11).
[43] Sibanda-Moyo et al. (2017, April 28).
[44] SAPS (2020, June 30).
[45] SAPS (2020, June 30).
[46] RSA Media Releases (2022, September 13).
[47] RSA Media Releases (2022, September 13). See also BBC News (2016, April 20).

between 2015 and 2016.[48] However, there have been students actively challenging this violence from as early as the 1980s.[49] These protests have centered around the issue of institutional responses to sexual violence, by claiming that a "rape culture"[50] has been allowed to develop on campuses.[51] Whilst the numerous protests around the country have brought the issue of GBV at HEIs to the media's attention as well as to the attention of the general South African public, sexual violence on campuses in South Africa has been a long-standing issue. The responses to GBV have been reactive, rather than proactive. The positive development is that these protests have allowed most institutions to develop or adopt systems for the reporting, as well as ratifying of various policies on such violations.[52]

It would also seem that the country is becoming more aware of and responsive to the issue of GBV at HEIs. However, there is still a lack of a nationally representative research which can give a clearer understanding of the nature and extent of this phenomenon. Further, the under-reporting of this type of violence, particularly sexual violence, makes it difficult to determine the true prevalence of the different forms of it at HEIs.[53] The anger over GBV on and around university campuses is because of the few incidents reported in the media, both local and national. As one can ascertain from the statistics, many others do not make it into the national news and that only a small portion of the incidents of GBV on and around campuses in the country is reported.[54]

9.1.3 Perceptions of Safety and Fear of Crime on Campus

Young women remain under the threat and fear of GBVF while attending colleges and universities. The Minister of Higher Education stated that "the post-school education and training sector is home to over 2,5 million youth, where more than 51 percent of these are adolescent girls and young women between the ages of 15–24

[48] In April 2016, the #Endrapeculture protests spread across South African university campuses. These protests raised awareness of university policies regarding rape and sexual assault cases on campus. The protesters accused the university management of perpetuating a rape culture through policies which reinforced victim-blaming and protected perpetrators of sexual assault. Using hashtag campaigns and public demonstrations, the movement quickly gained momentum across social and mainstream media.

[49] Klerk et al. (2007).

[50] A term developed by feminists referring to a set of general cultural beliefs supporting men's violence against women, including the idea that this violence is an unpleasant fact, and that that men have a right to sexual intercourse. Phipps et al. (2017).

[51] Boonzaier et al. (2019).

[52] In the 1990s, through the development of policies, some gains were made in the transformation of institutional cultures in higher education, especially in relation to issues of sexual harassment.

[53] Safer Spaces (2018).

[54] Mutinta (2022).

years old, with statistics from the MRC indicating that 10 percent of all reported rape cases come from the higher education sector…… Female students fall directly under this 10 percent, and run the risk of experiencing sexual violence (and other forms of GBV) while on campus, often at the hands of their male peers."[55]

While the number of studies related to the fear of crime in communities has been increasing, only a few studies to date have focused on the fear of crime among university students. This is disconcerting as university students may be more vulnerable to a greater risk[56] of some crimes, such as sexual assault, violence and threatening behavior due to their greater involvement in social activities.[57] The existing evidence highlights gender differences in perceptions of safety and fear of crime at tertiary institutions.[58] International literature indicates that in many tertiary institutions, women are more fearful of crime and violence than men.[59] This reflects findings from the general public where fear of crime is more prevalent among women than men.[60] Sex is one of the most important parameters in the fear of crime, according to the literature.[61]

The main reason for this disparity between females and males with respect to fear of crime concerns the sense of vulnerability to sexual assault for females. Another reason for the higher level of fear of crime among women concerns gender roles.[62] South African literature affirms a similar trend domestically.[63] Statistics South Africa has reported that, "in general, crime impedes the activities of women more than it does those of men, though marginally in some cases."[64]

Inevitably, fear of crime and being victimized can lead to avoidance behaviors, as well as resulting in the psychological stress associated with feeling intimidated. Such pressures impact on educational attainment as well as restrict participation in all aspects of college/university life.[65] Research demonstrates that women's fears can increase perceptions of risk and result in women engaging in behaviors that restrict their social freedom.[66] It further leads to social isolation, feelings of humiliation, shame and guilt.[67] In one study it was shown how students also mentioned the

---

[55] South African Government (2022, August).

[56] Lee and Hilinski-Rosick (2012).

[57] Köseoglu (2021); Forbes-Mewett et al. (2015).

[58] Tomsich et al. (2011).

[59] Britto et al. (2017).

[60] Ross and Rasool (2019).

[61] Chih-Ping (2018).

[62] Williams et al. (2018).

[63] Sexual Violence Task Team (2016).

[64] Stats SA (2020), p. 12.

[65] Apart from potential physical harm, the emotional and psychological trauma that victims typically experience seriously hamper their ability to concentrate on their studies. GBV also limits the ability of students to contribute to the campus community.

[66] European Commission (2012).

[67] Sloane (2011).

stigma associated with sexual attacks: "the worst thing that can happen to you in this world is being raped, and therefore if it happens to you, your integrity, your dignity as a person fails,"[68] and it therefore restricts their choices made at university. The fear and perception of crimes unfairly limits the lifestyle of female students and impacts their rights to a quality of life and the right to be free from all forms of discrimination and violence.

9.1.4 HEIs Role in GBVF

South African HEIs have the opportunity and a significant role to play in tackling gender equality, empowering women and reducing GBV. This can be achieved through their pedagogies, research, and innovation, and through their public outreach and engaged scholarships programs. Importantly, the policies that are adopted by institutions can also advocate for a change in norms and culture and institutional practices.

In acknowledgment of the specific roles that HEIs can play in the fight against GBVF, as well as the fact that HEIs do not have sufficient means to deal with GBV, that survivors are not sufficiently supported and that there are insufficient mechanisms in place to monitor and report on GBV, on 31 July 2020, the Minister of Higher Education, Science and Innovation released the Policy Framework to address Gender-Based Violence in the Post School Education and Training System (PSET) in South African HEIs.[69] This policy aims to create an enabling environment for the eradication of GBV and instill respect, protection, promotion and fulfilment of human rights as enshrined in the *Bill of Rights*:[70]

> The Policy Framework compels PSET institutions to both create awareness of GBV policies and prevent incidents of GBV; as well as to assist PSET institutions to address the occurrence of GBV. It also provides a monitoring instrument to the Department to assess the implementation of the Policy Framework.

The Department developed this Policy Framework with the aim to serve as a guide to the entire HEI system. The intention is that the Policy Framework will not only address GBV occurrence in institutions, but also compel the creation of awareness programs to prevent the occurrence of GBV and to support survivors. This Policy Framework is composed of measures that involve the strengthening of the application of national legislation through improved collaboration between HEIs,

[68] European Commission (2012), p. 167.

[69] Department of Higher Education and Training (2020).

[70] Department of Higher Education and Training (2020).

civil society and sister departments.[71] This Policy Framework also addresses safety and security and contains monitoring and reporting mechanisms.[72]

These provisions regarding monitoring and reporting mechanisms are extremely important. On its own policies have limited utility to change embedded institutional cultures. This is more so with policies considered "politically symbolic." HEIs are "confined spaces where people from different socio-economic backgrounds meet and interact at different levels and on many different aspects, and therefore there is an urgent need for the democratic values of human dignity, equality and freedom to be affirmed and promoted."[73] Consequently, HEIs must be wary and resist falling into the trap of thinking of policy formulation as having little to do with praxis. HEIs should focus on the effective implementation of those policies, together with monitoring of the efficacies of such policies and interventions and simultaneously interrogate the reasons why these are necessary for a particular institution.

GBVF is not going to disappear by itself, commitment towards the elimination thereof is key. The importance of having a steadfast commitment on the part of each university towards eliminating GBVF cannot be overemphasized. This political commitment must be part of each universities legal commitment to protect and promote gender equality, fight all types of crime, and promote a respectful and safe learning and working environment. A possibly good way to formalize and make public this political commitment would be through an official declaration by the highest university authorities of "zero tolerance" towards any form of gender violence and this political statement should be made public, be easily visible on all university web pages, via leaflets and brochures and be available to all new students and staff members arriving at the university.[74]

---

[71] In partnership with Higher Health (Higher Health is a branch of the Department of Higher Education, Innovation and Technology (DHET), is working towards combating the escalating situation GBVF on university and college campuses across South Africa), various interventions have been put in place across the country's universities, Technical and Vocational Educational Training (TVET) colleges, as well as Community Education and Training (CET) Colleges. See South African Government News Agency (2023, January 24).

[72] Department of Higher Education and Training (2020), p. 3. The Policy Framework intends to assist PSET institutions address the occurrence of GBV and to provide a monitoring instrument to the Department to assess the implementation of the Policy Framework.

The Policy Framework aims to:

i. Conceptualise GBV and define its manifestation in terms of existing laws and policies;
ii. Detail the international and national regulatory framework compelling institutional and departmental responses to GBV;
iii. Provide guidance around the structures, mechanisms and processes that PSET institutions must put in place to address GBV;
iv. Compel PSET institutions to both create awareness of GBV policies and prevent incidents of GBV; and
v. Set out a framework for oversight of the Department and PSET institutions' development and implementation of policy.

[73] Department of Higher Education and Training (2020), p. 1.

[74] European Commission (2012), p. 180.

It is imperative that each University develop and adopt a specific protocol/ procedure to prevent and respond to GBV on campuses. These protocols/procedures, to be effective, should facilitate a permanent collaboration between university authorities, police forces, and existing resources and services outside the university. The protocol/procedures should aim to serve as a tool to all students and staff members working in the university to enable them to respond to cases of GBV and to raise awareness about these issues amongst students. Where HEIs do offer a range of services and resources for students who had experienced GBV, there still needs to be more effective coordination of policies. The co-ordination of policies should be done in a way that ensures that victims are at the core of the policy. Indeed, victims' needs must be protected and taken as the starting point for promulgating effective intervention and prevention measures.

9.1.5 Expressions of Outrage and Media Reporting and Its Impact on GBVF

Studies conducted on the fear of crime have shown the effect that the media has on fear.[75] For example, Heath and Gilbert[76] determined that the media influences people's fear of crime, but that effect is influenced by a variety of factors, including the sensationalism or randomness of the crime and the characteristics[77] of the audience. If people are predisposed to fear, like the fear of sexual assault and rape then sensationalizing reporting thereof will likely increase people's fears and it will impact how they live their lives, through, for example, restricting their movements and options.

Furthermore, one must caution against sporadic expressions of outrage as whilst it may lead to some short-term gains, empirical studies argue that for the long term the prevention of rape and GBV require the addressing of community and collective cultures.[78] Whilst it is important to have a zero-tolerance attitude towards GBVF, by responding with outrage there is a failure to acknowledge the everyday, systemic nature of misogyny, patriarchy, and male entitlement. Scholars have acknowledged that GBV can be tackled effectively if measures are taken to change the underlying social norms and overall institutional cultures of organizations like HEIs.[79] It therefore becomes pertinent to interrogate and understand how an issue such as GBVF is represented and made collective sense of in challenging embedded norms and cultures. Various scholars have argued that the ways in which rape is

[75] Fleming and Muzzatti (2006), p. 837; Dolliver et al. (2018).

[76] Heath and Gilbert (1996).

[77] Characteristics such as race, age, sex, class schedule, participating in campus activities, academic classification, and hometown size. See, del Carmen et al. (2000).

[78] Boonzaier (2018).

[79] Boonzaier et al. (2019); Walsh (2015).

communicated through the media,[80] involve attention to victims and victimization, the silencing of the issue of perpetration, the construction of rape as exceptional and "othered," all of which produce a context in which rape can be seen as apolitical and not a manifestation and assertion of patriarchal domination.[81] "Sensationalist reporting" and expressions of outrage serves to distract and detract from the important societal factors which have led South Africa to have such high rates of sexual violence.[82] Studies have highlighted how media representations have been shown to be important for drawing upon and shaping public discourse, especially in relation to topics such as GBV.[83] The media plays a significant role in the construction of public belief and attitudes and is, therefore, a critical tool in shifting and shaping public consciousness about violence, patriarchy, misogyny and sexual entitlement. Media representations are additionally important, not only for collective sense-making but also for their potential to shape policy and legal opinion. Accordingly, the ways in which they challenge or reinforce existing stereotypes is a crucial factor in the reporting of GBVF.[84]

It has been argued that on the one hand, one of the dangers of expressions of outrage in particular cases are that there is a tendency to distance oneself from the problem,[85] thereby neglecting to question those beliefs and practices in the environments which forms a part of South Africa's "rape and violence culture." On the other hand, one must note that the way in which the rapist is positioned as "other" must be read within a context of South Africa's history of colonization and apartheid.[86] Research has illustrated that the "othering" of violence to black men and black communities is frequently at work in academic, media and lay discourse.[87] Moffett argues that in the post-apartheid context, rape is "fuelled by justificatory narratives that are rooted in apartheid practices that legitimated violence by the dominant group against the disempowered."[88] Hegemonic masculinities[89] across color lines are deeply patriarchal and normalize violence.

Expressions of outrage, shock and surprise are not particularly beneficial in tackling deeply racist, sexist, and misogynistic views that clearly form part of the daily life in South Africa. What it does do is allow citizens to show anger and shock

---

[80] Boonzaier et al. (2019).

[81] Boonzaier (2017, 2018).

[82] Deane (2018).

[83] van Niekerk et al. (2015); Boonzaier (2017); Deane (2018).

[84] Ross (2019).

[85] Hirji (2022), p. 2.

[86] Daily Maverick (2013, February 9).

[87] van Niekerk (2018).

[88] Moffett (2006), p. 129.

[89] In numerous studies, young men have identified violence as an important way to display power and to prove their masculinity in their communities. Among youth in South Africa there is also a prevalent need for young men to control women in intimate relationships because this is considered essential in affirming their masculinity. Reardon and Govender (2011); Salter (2016); Morrell et al. (2012).

for a period of time and by so doing give them permission to deflect responsibility for the crisis related to GBVF. Thereafter there is a sense that something has been done and it allows people to go back to the pretense of normality until the next shocking incident. This does not in reality contribute to the elimination of GBV but acts as a vindication for the context of violence, in which it operates.

As mentioned, the media plays a significant role in the construction of public belief and attitudes. To begin to shape and shift consciousness about violence on a large scale, there needs to be a move away from episodic reporting, that merely elicits outrage. Instead of sensationalizing crimes against women as and when they occur, there needs to be sustained media campaigns on GBVF, not only during women's month[90] or 16 days of activism or when a woman is brutally murdered. The Minister has also noted that the "condemnation of gender-based violence needs to be constant and consistent, and perpetrators need to be prosecuted. It requires that we address societal issues of patriarchy, economic relations and changing the way of thinking about gender relations. Preconceived notions of how women and men should behave must be addressed as no person has the right to treat anyone as inferior, or to harm them in any way."[91]

The reporting on violence against women needs to be thematic reporting that includes detailed, contextualized, grounded stories on GBV. This will go a long way towards promoting public understanding and to shift consciousness about violence. Shifting media narratives on GBV will allow society to talk about the root causes of the prominent levels of GBV in the country. It will allow one to challenge the shame, stigma and blame for the violence that is usually allocated to women and girls. These conversations may lead to greater awareness and changes to normative ways of doing and being, which ultimately must shift the consciousness of society.

9.1.6 *Observations*

Sexual assault on the campuses of HEIs is a critical concern not only for the students themselves but for policy makers, college administrators, and loved ones of current and prospective students. The current GBVF scourge has infiltrated HEIs and the rates and prevalence of GBV reflects the growing problem in the country. The literature has identified areas of sexual violence prevention policy and practice that

[90] Women's Day marks the anniversary of the women's march of 1956, where women marched to the Union Buildings to protest the carrying of passbooks. There were significant perils that came with protesting during this time, demonstrating the solidarity and unfaltering courage of the 20,000 women that marched. At the centre of the march was the resistance to a system that controlled women and reduced women to passive beings, at the mercy of men. Over six decades have passed since this ground-breaking march, and the legacy and persistence of the marginalisation of women remains a key area of reflection.

[91] Department of Higher Education and Training (2020).

is of major concern and which is prevalent in the wider social context.[92] Like the current context of GBV in the country, patriarchal cultures within institutions of higher learning continue to create an enabling environment for the continued perpetration of sexual assault and violence. Both masculinist and sexist cultures of institutions have been found to perpetuate ideas around women's subordination alongside ideas that sanction violence against them. These include an emphasis on the sexualization of women and the positioning of women as potential sexual conquests.[93]

In addition, HEI's have not been as proactive as they should have been in dealing with GBVF,[94] leading to a culture of silence amongst students. It has been reported that on campuses, students have little faith that perpetrators will be punished, they do not have confidence in the authorities to whom such crimes ought to be reported and they are afraid of stigma or gossip against them, leading them to be "silenced due to power relations in society." For GBV to be effectively addressed measures must be taken to change the underlying social norms and overall institutional cultures.[95] Interrogating and understanding how an issue such as sexual violence is represented and made collective sense of are important. Further, it is crucial to challenge embedded norms and cultures within HEIs.[96] Institutions should adopt practices that are reflective of the values and norms to which the *Constitution* and the institution aspires.[97]

Profound transformations are urgently needed to guarantee freedom from GBVF in HEIs. Overall, researchers and activists have pointed out that HEIs interventions and their responses to sexual violence seem to concentrate on preserving their brands and reputations rather than reversing the institutional cultures that allow a "rape culture"[98] to fester. A comprehensive campus sexual assault policy will go a long way towards reducing the prevalence of campus sexual assault. Policies must also be adaptable to address contemporary manifestations of sexual violence and harassment such as online harassment and revenge pornography. However, by themselves, policies have limited utility to change embedded institutional cultures.[99] This is more so with policies considered "politically symbolic." In addition, HEIs need to

---

[92] Boonzaier et al. (2019).

[93] Boonzaier et al. (2019).

[94] Students especially have argued that the systems that are set up to deal with the issue of sexual violence on campuses put the burden of addressing sexual violence almost exclusively on women survivors themselves. See DeLong et al. (2018).

[95] Phipps et al. (2017).

[96] Boonzaier et al. (2019).

[97] DeLong et al. (2018).

[98] Rape culture refers to the trend in which violence against women is normalized and prevalent due to patriarchal domination of women and conceptions about the role and status of women within a society.

[99] Boonzaier et al. (2019).

equip students with knowledge on how to respond to survivors of GBV, and where these survivors can seek support and redress. University resources must be designated for GBV services and support programs for survivors and students and staff should have easy access to information about campus-based and external services and support for GBV survivors.

An effective agenda for inclusivity in higher education necessitates "the duty of using 'the powers conferred by academic freedom' to substantively decolonise, deracialise, demasculinise and de-gender inherited 'intellectual spaces'." Consequently, a critique of institutional responses to the material conditions of its communities must be seen as part of the national imperative as outlined in the Constitution as well as the Higher Education Act[100] to transform HEIs. Institutions must therefore formulate policy by acknowledging the importance of praxis and theory.

The implementation of policies based on an apposite theoretical basis for a specific institution must be critically interrogated. Simultaneously the central reasons for the why the policies are necessary for that institution must be probed. This can be done through open and sustained dialogues and discussions. Combating a culture of silence around sexual violence in HEIs demand that every member of university community be allowed and encouraged to participate in conversations about the internal and external manifestations of the culture of silence around rape and sexual violence.[101] Constructive conversations of every kind, including those related to the curriculum, or not, formal, informal, challenging, or uncomfortable, must be encouraged.

Strong leadership, be it in politics or institutions, investments and comprehensive policy reforms are needed to dismantle systemic barriers to achieving gender equality and end GBVF. The goal of ending GBVF must therefore be an overarching objective and a key focus of national policies, budgets, and institutions.

9.1.7 Concluding Remarks

Over the past few years, several incidents of GBV on campuses in South Africa made national headlines, despite a transformative constitution and legislation that protect human rights and prohibits human rights abuses. In addition, South Africa has ratified and adopted regional and international conventions and protocols focused on the eradication of GBV, but this has had little impact on the problem. It therefore becomes imperative to better contextualize GBV in institutions of higher learning. Currently there is a lack of understanding and awareness of how GBV manifests in HEIs, its intersectional nature and the intersectionality of the identities of victims and offenders, prevalence patterns, root causes, or the conditions that

[100] *Higher Education Act of 1997.*

[101] Sexual Violence Task Team (2016).

perpetuate it. Addressing GBV remains an important issue as the students themselves hold the key to change approaches and attitudes towards gender inequality in their intimate relationships, families, communities, universities and eventually their workplaces.

One of the greatest concerns of GBV, particularly non-physical forms of violence, is that it is normalized in families and societies. Structural and systemic GBV is often not identified as forms of violence because it is so deeply entrenched and accepted in social, economic, and legal systems and institutions. When HEIs fail to identify and effectively address gender inequality and the direct and indirect promotion of patriarchy and toxic masculinities in their teaching, policies, practices, and responses to GBV, these institutions contribute to normalizing and reproducing gender inequality and all its manifestations including GBVF. HEIs therefore have a crucial role to play in combatting all forms of violence against women. Failure to do so would be tantamount to perpetuating the normalization of the scourge of GBVF.

References

Anderson B, Naidu C (2022) "Fresh meat": first year female students negotiating sexual violence on campus residences. S Afr J High Educ 36(1). https://doi.org/10.20853/36-1-4800

Banyard V et al (2020) Academic correlates of unwanted sexual contact, intercourse, stalking, and intimate partner violence: an understudied but important consequence for college students. J Interpers Violence 35(21–22):4375–4392. https://doi.org/10.1177/0886260517715022

BBC News (2016, April 20) South Africa anti-rape protests: Rhodes University students arrested. https://www.bbc.com/news/world-africa-36090431. Accessed on 20 Jan 2023

Boonzaier F (2017) The life and death of Anene Booysen: colonial discourse, gender-based violence and media representations. S Afr J Psychol 47(4):470–481. https://doi.org/10.1177/0081246317737916

Boonzaier F (2018) Challenging risk: the production of knowledge on gendered violence in South Africa. In: Fitz-Gibbon K et al (eds) Intimate partner violence, risk and security. Routledge, Taylor and Francis Group. https://doi.org/10.4324/9781315204765

Boonzaier FA et al (2019) Communicating about sexual violence on campus: a university case study. Afr Saf Promot: J Inj Violence Prev 17(1):17–31

Brink JG et al (2022) Practitioner's perspectives on a national South African higher education institution policy framework mitigating gender-based violence at a South African university. Int J Crit Divers Stud 4(2). https://doi.org/10.13169/intecritdivestud.4.2.0047

Britto S et al (2017) Perceptually contemporaneous offenses: gender and fear of crime among African-American university students. J Ethn Crim Justice 16(2):117–136. https://doi.org/10.1080/15377938.2017.1354117

Chih-Ping L (2018) Exploring the gender difference in fear of crime among older people. J Manag Econ Soc Sci 7(Special Issue):26–39

Committee for Gender Equality (2019) Report on gender transformation in tertiary institutions 2018/19. https://cge.org.za/wp-content/uploads/2021/01/report-on-gender-transformation-in-tertiary-institutions-2018-2019.pdf. Accessed on 21 Jan 2023

Council on Higher Education (2019) Gender-based violence in South African universities: an institutional challenge. https://www.che.ac.za/file/6459/download?token=XT7N1ToO. Accessed on 24 Dec 2023

Daily Maverick (2013, February 9) SA's rape epidemic: the limitations of outrage. https://www.dailymaverick.co.za/opinionista/2013-02-09-sas-rape-epidemic-the-limitations-of-outrage/. Accessed on 14 Apr 2023

Deane T (2018) Sexual violence and the limits of laws' powers to alter behaviour: the case of South Africa. J Int Women's Stud 19(2):84–103

del Carmen AO et al (2000) Fear of crime on campus: examining fear variables of CRCJ majors and nonmajors in pre- and post-serious crime environments. J Secur Adm 23:21–36

DeLong SM et al (2018) Starting the conversation: are campus sexual assault policies related to the prevalence of campus sexual assault? J Interpers Violence 33(21):3315–3343. https://doi.org/10.1177/0886260518798352

Department of Higher Education and Training (2020) Policy framework to address gender-based violence in the post-school education and training system. https://www.dhet.gov.za/Social%20Inclusion/Gazette%20Z95_1221889%20Policy%20Framework%20to%20Address%20GBV%20in%20the%20PSET%2. Accessed on 23 Jan 2023

Department of Higher Education and Training (n.d.) Login: Welcome to SurveyHub. https://dhetwebapps.dhet.gov.za/SurveyHub/Home/Login. Accessed on 17 Jan 2023

Dolliver MJ et al (2018) Examining the relationship between media consumption, fear of crime, and support for controversial criminal. J Contemp Crim Justice 34(4):399–420. https://doi.org/10.1177/1043986218787734

eNCA (2017, October 13) Protests break out at NMU after student raped. https://www.enca.com/south-africa/protests-break-out-at-nmmu-after-student-raped. Accessed on 20 Jan 2023

European Commission (2012) What is gender-based violence? Bochum, Directorate – General Justice, Freedom and Security

Fleming T, Muzzatti S (2006) Constructing crime: media, crime, and popular culture. Can J Criminol Crim Justice 48(6):837–865

Forbes-Mewett H et al (2015) International students as victims of crime. Int Stud Crime 44–69. https://doi.org/10.1057/9781137034977_3

Forum for African Women Educationalists (2015) Tackling gender inequality in higher education institutions in Africa: from affirmative action to holistic approaches. Senegal, Policy Brief, Dakar

Heath L, Gilbert K (1996) Mass media and fear of crime. Am Behav Sci 39(4):379–386

Hirji S (2022) Outrage and the bounds of empathy. Philos Impr 22(16):1–20. https://doi.org/10.3998/phimp.1296

IOL News (2020, Mar 4) MUT student Zolile Khumalo's ex-boyfriend found guilty of her murder. https://www.iol.co.za/dailynews/news/mut-student-zolile-khumalos-ex-boyfriend-found-guilty-of-her-murder-44101307. Accessed on 29 Feb 2024

IOL News (2021, June 11) Precious Ramabulana murder: we need to teach boys that NO means NO. https://www.iol.co.za/news/opinion/precious-ramabulana-murder-we-need-to-teach-boys-that-no-means-no-1a8fe75c-1948-4a77-9091-9d140d704ece. Accessed on 21 Jan 2022

IOL News (2022, March 11) 88 alleged rapes reported on campus last year. https://www.iol.co.za/the-star/news/88-alleged-rapes-reported-on-campus-last-year-7597dc61-225d-49c3-b3b5-85230ec0d395. Accessed on 20 Jan 2023

Jacobsen SK (2017) Examining crime on campus: the influence of institutional factors on reports of crime at colleges and universities. J Crim Justice Educ 28:559–579

Klerk V et al (2007) The habitus of the dominant: addressing rape and sexual assault at Rhodes University. Agenda: Empower Women Gender Equity 21(74):115–124

Köseoglu M (2021) Fear of crime perceptions of university students. Sociologia, Problemas E Práticas 96:41–57. https://journals.openedition.org/spp/9017

Krebs CP et al (2007) The Campus Sexual Assault (CSA) Study. National Institute of Justice, U.S. Department of Justice, Washington, DC

Krebs C et al (2016) Campus climate survey validation study. Final technical report. Bureau of Justice Statistics, US, Washington, DC

Lee DR, Hilinski-Rosick CM (2012) Role of lifestyle and personal characteristics on fear of victimization among university students. Am J Crim Justice 37:647–668

Makhaye MS et al (2023) Female students as victims of sexual abuse at institutions of higher learning: insights from Kwazulu-Natal, South Africa. SN Soc Sci 3:40. https://doi.org/10.1007/s43545-023-00611-z

Mengo C, Black BM (2016) Violence victimization on a college campus: impact on GPA and school dropout. J Coll Stud Retent: Res Theory Pract 18(2):234–248

Moffett H (2006) "These women, they force us to rape them": rape as narrative of social control in post-apartheid South Africa. J South Afr Stud 32(1):129–144. https://doi.org/10.1080/03057070500493845

Morrell R et al (2012) Hegemonic masculinity/masculinities in South Africa. Men Masc 15(1): 11–30. https://doi.org/10.1177/1097184x12438001

Mutinta G (2022) Gender-based violence among female students and implications for health intervention programmes in public universities in Eastern Cape, South Africa. Cogent Soc Sci 8(1). https://doi.org/10.1080/23311886.2022.2079212

National Prosecuting Authority (2020) Annual report 2019/2020. https://www.npa.gov.za/sites/default/files/annualreports/NPA%20Annual%20Report%202019-2020_0.pdf. Accessed on 5 Jan 2023

Nelson Mandela University News (2020) NMU rapist pleads guilty on seven counts. https://news.mandela.ac.za/Mandela-University-in-the-NEWS/Mandela-University-in-the-NEWS-Archive/NMU-rapist-pleads-guilty-on-seven-counts. Accessed on 18 Jan 2023

News24 (2016, November 14) Waiter jailed for 9 life terms for Rhodes Memorial rapes. https://www.news24.com/news24/waiter-jailed-for-9-life-terms-for-rhodes-memorial-rapes-20161114 . Accessed on 13 Jan 2023

News24 (2021, January 10) Precious Ramabulana was stabbed 90 times, court hears. https://www.news24.com/news24/southafrica/news/precious-ramabulana-was-stabbed-90-times-court-hears-20210610. Accessed on 21 Jan 2023

Orth Z et al (2020) "What does the University have to do with it?": Perceptions of rape culture on campus and the role of university authorities. S Afr J High Educ 34(2). https://doi.org/10.20853/34-2-3620

Phipps A et al (2017) Rape culture, lad culture and everyday sexism: researching, conceptualizing and politicizing new mediations of gender and sexual violence. J Gend Stud 27(1):1–8. https://doi.org/10.1080/09589236.2016.1266792

Reardon CA, Govender K (2011) "Shaping up": the relationship between traditional masculinity, conflict resolution and body image among adolescent boys in South Africa. Vulnerable Child Youth Stud 6(1):78–87. https://doi.org/10.1080/17450128.2011.554578

Ross T (2019) Media and stereotypes. The Palgrave handbook of ethnicity 1–17. https://doi.org/10.1007/978-981-13-0242-8_26-1

Ross E, Rasool S (2019) "You go to campus with fear and come back with fear." University students' experiences of crime. SA Crime Q 68:7–20. https://doi.org/10.17159/2413-3108/2019/i68a4895

RSA Media Releases (2022, September 13) Minister Blade Nzimande on progress in addressing gender based violence in the post school education and training institutions. https://www.gov.za/speeches/minister-nzimande-statement-progress-addressing-gender-based-violence-post-school-education. Accessed on 19 Jan 2023

SABC News (2020, March 5) MUT student's murderer sentenced to life in prison. https://www.sabcnews.com/sabcnews/mut-students-murderer-sentenced-to-life-in-prison/. Accessed on 21 Jan 2023

SABC News (2021, June) Gender-based violence: Aubrey Manaka sentenced to two life terms for murdering Precious Ramabulana. https://www.youtube.com/watch?v=9H9k0Sb5Jac. Accessed on 21 Jan 2023

Safer Spaces (2018) Gender-based violence at higher education institutions in South Africa. https://www.saferspaces.org.za/understand/entry/gender-based-violence-at-higher-education-institutions-in-south-africa1. Accessed on 19 Jan 2023

Salter M (2016) "Real men don't hit women": constructing masculinity in the prevention of violence against women. Aust N Z J Criminol 49(4):463–479. https://doi.org/10.1177/0004865815587031

SAPS (2020, June 30) Media statement: second suspect in the kidnapping, rape and attempted murder of TVET college student arrested. https://www.saps.gov.za/newsroom/msspeechdetail.php?nid=33455. Accessed on 19 Jan 2023

Sexual Violence Task Team (2016) "We Will Not Be Silenced": a three–pronged justice approach to sexual offences and rape culture at Rhodes University/UCKAR. Grahamstown: South Africa, Critical Studies in Sexualities and Reproduction

Sibanda-Moyo N et al. (2017, April 28) Violence against women in South Africa: a country in crisis 2017. At https://www.africaportal.org/publications/violence-against-women-south-africa-country-crisis-2017/. Accessed on 13 Apr 2023

Siebritz G (2022, October 21) Department of Higher Education tackles violence on campuses. https://www.careersportal.co.za/news/department-of-higher-education-tackles-violence-on-campuses. Accessed on 21 Jan 2023

Sloane C (2011) Talk about its survey: results and recommendations. http://www.whiteribbon.org.au/uploads/media/talk-about-it-survey-results-andrecommendations.pdf. Accessed on 22 Mar 2023

Smith MC (1988) Coping with Crime on Campus. Simon & Schuster Books for Young Readers

South African Government (2022, August) Minister Blade Nzimande hosts roundtable on Youth Health and Wellness in the Post School Education and Training Sector. https://www.gov.za/speeches/minister-blade-nzimande-hosts-roundtable-youth-health-and-wellness-post-school-education. Accessed on 21 Mar 2023

South African Government News Agency (2023, January 24) Addressing gender-based violence at institutions of higher learning. https://www.sanews.gov.za/south-africa/addressing-gender-based-violence-institutions-higher-learning. Accessed on 21 Mar 2023

SowetanLive (2018, August 2018) Man found guilty of raping NMU student on campus. https://www.sowetanlive.co.za/news/south-africa/2018-08-29-man-found-guilty-of-raping-nmu-student-on-campus/. Accessed on 29 Feb 2024

Stats SA (2020) Crimes against women in South Africa: an analysis of the phenomenon of GBV and femicide. https://www.parliament.gov.za/storage/app/media/1_Stock/Events_Institutional/2020/womens_charter_2020/docs/30-07-2020/A_Statistical_Overview_R_Maluleke.pdf. Accessed on 23 Dec 2022

Swartz S et al. (2017) Ready or not! Race, education and emancipation: a five-year longitudinal, qualitative study of agency and impasses to success amongst higher education students in a sample of South African universities. https://repository.hsrc.ac.za/handle/20.500.11910/11305. Accessed on 6 Mar 2023

The Sexual Assault Response Team (2016) Sexual Assault Response Team end of year report for 2016. http://www.ceuhealth.uct.ac.za/sites/default/files/image_tool/images/388/Get_Information/Quarterly_Reports/2016-12-14_UCT_SART_YearEndReport_December2016.pdf. Accessed on 2 Feb 2023

The South African (2017, August 29) UCT may have arrested serial rapist but sexual attacks are still common. https://www.thesouthafrican.com/news/uct-may-have-arrested-serial-rapist-but-sexual-attacks-are-still-common/. Accessed on 14 Jan 2023

TimesLive (2017, August 29) Serial rapist's imprisonment fails to stem UCT sex attacks. https://www.timeslive.co.za/news/south-africa/2017-08-29-serial-rapists-imprisonment-fails-to-stem-uct-sex-attacks/. Accessed on 14 Jan 2023

TimesLive (2018, August 29) Man found guilty of raping NMU student on campus. https://www.timeslive.co.za/news/south-africa/2018-08-29-man-found-guilty-of-raping-nmu-student-on-campus/. Accessed on 20 Jan 2023

Tomsich EA et al (2011) Examining the role of gender in the prevalence of campus victimization, perceptions of fear and risk of crime, and the use of constrained behaviors among college students attending a large urban university. J Crim Justice Educ 22(2):181–202. https://doi.org/10.1080/10511253.2010.517772
UN Office on Drugs and Crime (2017) South African Department of Justice launches national dialogue to address gender-based and sexual violence in South Africa. https://www.unodc.org/documents/southernafrica//press/GBV_Round_Table_Press_Release_FINAL.pdf. Accessed on 11 Aug 2023
van Niekerk T (2018) Respectability and reputation: tracing intersections of race, class and gender in news discourses of violence against women. Psychol Soc 56:1–22. https://doi.org/10.17159/2309-8708/2018/n56a1
van Niekerk A et al (2015) The invisibility of men in South African violence prevention policy: national prioritization, male vulnerability, and framing prevention. Glob Health Action 8(1): 27649. https://doi.org/10.3402/gha.v8.27649
Walsh S (2015) Addressing sexual violence and rape culture: issues and interventions targeting boys and men. Agenda 29(3):134–141. https://doi.org/10.1080/10130950.2015.1050817
Williams NE et al (2018) Fear of violence during armed conflict: social roles and responsibilities as determinants of fear. Soc Sci Res 71:145–159. https://doi.org/10.1016/j.ssresearch.2018.01.004

Chapter 10
Conclusion

10.1 Conclusions

Gender-based violence (GBV) remains systemic and persistent on a global scale. It knows no borders, affecting women and girls of all ages and can happen anywhere, from the domestic setting to public places including in educational institutions and within the home. GBV has been recognized as an increasing problem in today's society, a violation of human rights and a public health problem. In its entirety, GBV is a barrier to economic development and is a threat to society and humanity. It creates emotional, social, and economic unrest that prohibits the growth and success of individuals, families, communities, and society as a whole.

In the quest to achieve economic development, the government of South Africa faces the incredible task of eradicating GBV and restructuring a historically unequal economy that continues to marginalize women and girls. The achievement of gender equality is a key component for achieving sustainable development in South Africa and globally. The SDGs and its Agenda require countries to vigorously pursue gender equality by eliminating all forms of discrimination against women and to eliminate all forms of violence against women and girls by 2030. The Sustainable Development Agenda is squarely rooted in the principle of "leave no one behind." With less than seven years to go to 2030, achieving these goals will require significant and concerted interventions to eliminate GBVF and inequality in South Africa. Both GBVF and inequality have a deep-rooted history and legacy that is ingrained in the patriarchal and misogynist practices, traditions, and systems within South Africa.

GBV comprises a wide range of acts, from verbal harassment and other forms of emotional abuse to daily physical or sexual abuse. At the far end of the spectrum is femicide, the murder of a woman and the most extreme consequence of violence. Despite enjoying high priority on the political agenda GBV and femicide (GBVF) remains the most predominant form of abuse in contemporary South Africa. Regardless of the constitutional endorsement for gender equality and legislation that

T. Deane, *Gender-Based Violence and Femicide in South Africa*, Gender, Justice and Legal Feminism 5, https://doi.org/10.1007/978-3-031-61053-0_10

protects the physical and emotional well-being of all people, violence against women and girls and specifically intimate partner violence continues at a disturbing rate in South Africa. While ones understanding of femicide can be improved upon,[1] what is known is that a considerable proportion of femicides are of women in violent relationships and are committed by current or former partners.

Several factors continue to exacerbate the rates of violence and include, inter alia, the legacy of apartheid and colonialism, high forms of unemployment, patriarchy, and other factors. It is further important to highlight the fact that the COVID-19 pandemic and subsequent lockdown measures that were implemented exacerbated GBV in the home environment. During this period homes increasingly become an enclave of cruelty, rape and violence for women and girls who were effectively trapped with abusive family members. They had nowhere to report such incidents to or even anywhere to go to, to escape the danger, seriously impacting the rates of GBV. This book has highlighted that even before the COVID-19 pandemic women and girls are subjected to elevated levels of rape, sexual offences, femicide, domestic violence and intimate partner violence. It has been reported on more than one occasion that the alarmingly high rates of GBV make being a woman in South Africa more dangerous than being in some of the world's war-torn areas.[2] This is a particularly frightening thought, seeing that worn-torn areas are characterized by violence, lawlessness, damage, destruction, looting and where rape is used as a weapon of war.[3]

The costs of such violence on victims and survivors of violence are severe. However, this is not just a problem for women. Gender-based inequality and GBV has many negative consequences for families, communities, and societies. For example, the research has highlighted how GBVF negatively effects economic activity and a country's GDP.[4] Studies have indicated that the cost of violence against women (public, private, and social) amounts to US$1.5 trillion at the global level[5] and that violence against women can cost up to 3.7% of GDP in some countries.[6] Gender inequality is also interconnected with other systems of oppressions. The research evidence has highlighted that violence against women is more detrimental to economic development in countries without protective laws against domestic violence, where women are deprived of decision-making power and during

[1] As discussed above, collecting correct data on femicide is challenging, largely because in most countries, police and medical data-collection systems that document cases of homicide often do not have the necessary information or do not report the victim-perpetrator relationship or the motives for the homicide, let alone gender-related motivations for murder.

[2] South African Human Rights Commission (2021).

[3] Meger (2016), p. 94.

[4] Ouedraogo and Stenzel (2021); KPMG (2017).

[5] UN Women (2016).

[6] World Bank (2020).

economic downturns such as the COVID-19 pandemic crisis.[7] Indeed, the outbreak of the coronavirus disease greatly exacerbated many of the risk factors associated with GBV.[8] In particular, domestic violence had intensified.[9] Furthermore, dropout rates for girls were higher for girls than it was for boys.[10] The research has highlighted how the economic cost of violence against women is higher in countries where the gender gap in education between partners is high, and increased gender inequality.[11] The pursuance of gender equality is both an international legal obligation and necessary to achieve national development goals. The elimination of GBVF is therefore not only an objective in itself and an aspect of achieving gender equality, which is one of the Goals of the 2030 Agenda for Sustainable Development, but it is also crucial to the achievement of other SDGs, such as poverty eradication, access to health care and education, decent work, and the building of a just and peaceful society.[12]

The previous chapters have highlighted that interventions to eliminate GBV should be targeted towards various forms of violent behaviors and those factors that continue to leave women susceptible to perpetual violence. In addition, the government of South Africa has instituted sweeping legislation and policies regarding GBV. However, there are major concerns around the lack of effective implementation thereof rendering these policies largely ineffective. In addition, many of the policies seemingly focus on aftercare and other services for women who have already experienced GBV, rather than focusing on the prevention of violence. The intrinsic importance of prevention is obvious. However, the failures to expand interventions that ensure efficacious practices, the allocation of resources and inefficient attention to developing integrated and multi-pronged best practice approaches in different sectors, remains problematic. Additionally, the failures of the justice system to administer justice for women and girls have been well documented despite the existence of the strong legal and policy frameworks.[13]

Limited awareness, discriminatory attitudes, and harmful gender bias inherent in law enforcement and justice sector institutions are some of the most challenging issues identified in effectively responding to GBV. There is a need to strengthen the justice sectors response, particularly that of law enforcement. A positive-first contact experience and high quality, survivor-centered police and justice responses have been identified as fundamental to preventing and eliminating GBV[14] and is crucial to

---

[7] As health, police, and justice service providers have been overburdened with COVID-19 cases and related consequences, clinical management of rape, mental health assessment and care for survivors of violence, as well as access to justice, were disrupted. United Nations Population Fund (2020).

[8] United Nations (2020).

[9] Böök et al. (2020), p. 22.

[10] Deane (2021).

[11] Ouedraogo and Stenzel (2021).

[12] United Nations (2020).

[13] South African Human Rights Commission (2021).

[14] UNODC (2020).

ensuring that the violence experienced does not escalate to femicide/gender-related killings. Ensuring a positive first contact experience including gender-sensitive responses throughout the criminal proceedings will significantly contribute to increasing trust in the system and lead to an improvement in the reporting of violence over time.

The credibility of any government's response to GBV can be sourced not only to the strength of its laws, policies, and interventions, but the way it is both implemented and prioritized.[15] As mentioned, the South African government has enacted legislative reforms, approved progressive policies, and implemented programs that give expression to the constitutional rights of women and girls to equality, human dignity, freedom, and security of the person. The problem is with the implementation of these progressive laws and regulations. Accordingly, the elevated levels of violence and gender-based crimes remain a matter of critical concern and the resolution thereof must be prioritized. Additionally, even though it is not yet clear to what extent GBV increased during the COVID-19 lockdowns,[16] emerging reports have shown that several types of violence against women and girls have intensified. It is very clear though, that the disruptive nature of the virus played out in several ways, directly impacting GBVF. The response efforts of the government to the COVID-19 crisis focused primarily on a combination of containment and mitigation measures to delay a surge in cases that could overwhelm the health sector. This prioritization, however, entirely neglected the disproportionate effect that it has had on vulnerable women and girls.[17] South Africa failed to deal with the escalations of GBV during this period, effectively creating a breeding ground for the continuation and intensification of violence against women and girls. It therefore becomes even more crucial to further prioritize GBVF during times of crisis and pandemics, in both policy and program development.

Outside of times of crisis, an important legislative measure includes the implementation of what can be described as a comprehensive legislative framework that looks at addressing violence against women and girls in all its manifestations and in its myriad of forms. Priority has been accorded to sexual offences and domestic violence. Some specific areas targeted by the law include issues of victim empowerment and integrated responses to GBV. A critical component of South Africa's response to sexual violence is the support offered to the victims of such crimes. In this regard, the *Criminal Law (Sexual Offences and Related Matters) Amendment Act, 2007*[18] establishes the legal framework for the adequate and effective protection of victims of sexual violence. In terms of the *Act*, victims of sexual offences are entitled to HIV/AIDS Post Exposure Prophylaxis (PEP).[19] They are also entitled to apply for an order that the alleged offender be tested for HIV and that the results

[15] Mpani and Nsibande (2015), p. 30.

[16] Human Rights Watch (2021, November 24).

[17] Deane (2021), p. 12.

[18] Act No. 32 of 2007.

[19] Meel (2005).

thereof be disclosed to the victim. The *Domestic Violence Act, 1998*[20] imposes a duty on SAPS to render such assistance as may be required by victims of domestic violence. Such assistance may include finding suitable shelter and obtaining medical treatment for victims. The Independent Police Investigative Directorate (IPID)[21] is mandated to monitor whether members of SAPS discharge this duty as required by law. These are just some of the progressive legislations aimed at empowering women and eliminating GBVF. In addition, South Africa has ratified a plethora of international human rights instruments directly aimed at protecting the rights of women and girls.

Moreover, the courts have also played a critical role in transforming societal beliefs and attitudes through some of their landmark decisions that have fundamentally changed customary and religious practices that violate women's rights. Important judgments include *Carmichele v Minister of Safety and Security*, where the Constitutional Court held that the state is obliged in terms of the *Constitution* and international law to prevent violence against women and to protect the dignity, freedom, and security of women. The judgment of *Tshabalala v S* takes a firm stand which protects the values of equality, human dignity, safety, and security for the women of South Africa. Indeed, it was recognized in *Tshabalala* that the South African "jurisprudence in the context of rape has moved in an inexorable direction consonant with our constitutional norms and values."[22] In this regard, in *Masiya v Director of Public Prosecutions* the Constitutional Court extended the definition of rape to include non-consensual anal penetration of females, which was previously not included in the definition. Courts have also taken heed of the warning by Sachs J, albeit in the context of domestic violence that[23] "the ineffectiveness of the criminal justice system ... sends an unmistakable message to the whole of society that the daily trauma of vast numbers of women counts for little."[24]

Decisions like the *Levenstein* case is also a sign of progress and development for some of the most vulnerable in society. It is however important to note that the amendment to the statutory provisions relating to the prescription of civil claims and criminal prosecutions arising out of sexual offences does not cure the disease of violence against women and children but rather treats its symptoms by ensuring that survivors can be appropriately compensated and that offenders can still be prosecuted despite lengthy lapses in time. It provides protection to children who have been victims of any sexual offence by allowing them to come forward many years after the offence took place. Whilst the *Prescription in Civil and Criminal Matters*

[20] Act No. 116 of 1998.

[21] The mission of IPID is to be an effective, independent, and impartial investigating and oversight body that is committed to justice and acting in the public interest, while maintaining the highest standards of integrity and excellence. See National Government of South Africa (2023).

[22] *Tshabalala v S; Ntuli v S* 2020 (5) SA 1 (CC). (*Tshabalala*), para 48.

[23] *Tshabalala* supra, para 48.

[24] *S V Baloyi* 2000 (2) SA 425 CC; 2000 (1) BCLR 86 (CC); 2000 (1) SACR 8 (CC) (*Baloyi*), para 12.

(Sexual Offences) Amendment Act 15 of 2020 is a step in the right direction, it is unfortunately reactive in nature. This judgment therefore highlights that South Africa needs to have proactive solutions and legislative frameworks which deal with the root cause of violence against women and children.

The effects of the *AK v The Minister of Police* or *Kawa* judgement will be felt, inevitably, beyond GBV and into all areas where the police fail in their duties towards society. It is important for women to see positive changes are happening in South African courts. Victims now have better odds when choosing to hold the SAPS accountable for their poor service delivery. Women and any other victims need to know the measures that are available to protect themselves and to act against SAPS. This may assist to a significant extent in addressing South Africa's GBV statistics.

It therefore begs the question why despite the international conventions, progressive decisions and plethora of local legislation enacted to prevent it, is GBV so widespread in South Africa. The legal reforms promoted in recent decades to address GBV, particularly the adoption of comprehensive laws on violence and the promulgation of laws criminalizing GBVF, play a key role in encouraging cultural changes that advance the transition towards societies in which such violence is no longer socially tolerated. However, the enforcement of laws to protect women's and girls' right to live a life free from violence faces various interlinked challenges, including in relation to women's access to justice and the capacity of justice administration systems to implement an intersectional and gender perspective that is also culturally relevant.

By looking towards an understanding of GBVF, this book seeks to address a fraction of the many complex questions that arise when studying an issue like GBVF. This study remains uniquely positioned to shed light on the complex issues of sex, gender, race, power, politics, and their intersections with GBV. It advocates for the reframing of conversations and initiatives on GBV from individual actions to the broader context in which GBVF is allowed to persist.

In detailing the extent and root causes of the scourge of GBVF in the country what has become obvious from the various studies highlighted in the chapters is that South Africa's high rates of GBVF cannot be attributed to a single factor. There are several contributing factors which are drivers of this "pandemic."[25] GBVF occurs within a complex interplay of individual, family, community, and social factors. Even though all women are at risk of violence in every society in the world, not all women are equally vulnerable to acts and structures of violence. Accordingly, researchers investigating GBVF should aim to do so within an ecological framework using an intersectional perspective. This approach will allow for an appreciation of the different and overlapping forms of oppressions faced by women and girls across societies. It will also guarantee that South Africa's impressive gender equality architecture delivers on its obligation to achieve human rights.

---

[25] Centre for the Study of Violence and Reconciliation (2016).

An intersectional and/or integrated ecological framework is extremely important in acknowledging and validating the unique experiences of differently situated women[26] in South Africa. The reality is that many of the people affected by GBVF are subject to intersecting forms of oppression. The multiplicative effects of intersecting factors are however often overlooked by researchers.[27] Failing to consider the way that various forms of oppression intersect prevents an effective understanding of the root causes of GBV, the complex reasons for which survivors may choose not to report abuse, and the relationship between marginalized people and the state, including all members in the criminal justice system. An integrative and intersectional approach will heighten awareness on the different intersecting oppressions, such as individual or interpersonal conflicts within intimate and non-intimate relationships, cultural norms or traditions that justifies GBVF or the different levels of institutionalized gender inequality across societies, and how these factors magnify the risk of GBVF.[28]

Basically, such an approach acknowledges the intersections between the different levels of structural (e.g., economic, social, and political systems), institutional (e.g., formal and informal social and professional networks), interpersonal (e.g., personal, family, and community relationships) and individual (e.g., personality, psychological state, personal attitudes towards violence) factors that intersect to exacerbate the vulnerabilities of women and girls.[29] An understanding of the feminist and ecological theories is urgently required to appreciate the overlapping and mutually constructed systems of discrimination and oppression that lead to non-inclusive policies and practices putting certain individuals and groups at a disadvantage.[30] A failure to look at GBVF through a holistic feminist lens and not utilizing the theoretical frameworks relating to gender and violence or failing to acknowledge the intersectionality of many GBV survivors and the vulnerability of people with intersecting identities to GBV will negatively impact the development of effective and targeted interventions and services[31] and consequently the implementation of any truly meaningful solutions towards the elimination of GBVF.[32]

Furthermore, the effective prevention and elimination of GBVF requires an in-depth understanding of the full dimension of this crime through accurate and comprehensive data. This book has identified various limitations with measuring gender-related killings of women and girls. Various stakeholders including, researchers, policymakers and data producers must work on developing an effective data analysis toolkit for data collection to overcome the current limitations and to ensure improved data collection efforts are made to cover all gender-related killings

[26] Crenshaw (1991), p. 1241.

[27] Rogers and Kelly (2011), p. 397.

[28] United Nations Women Europe and Central Asia (2019).

[29] United Nations General Assembly (2012).

[30] United Nations Women Europe and Central Asia (2019).

[31] Crenshaw (1991).

[32] Jayasinghe and Ward (2018).

of women and girls in both the public and private sphere. The acquiring of accurate and comprehensive data is therefore crucial and requires, in addition to the current methods of gathering data through Stats SA, medico-legal reports and surveys etc., the conducting of participatory research in affected communities. The information gathered should then be analyzed to realize the most appropriate solutions, as there can never be a one size fits all model for a country like South Africa.

For example, the results from participatory research will involve data analysis that can inform specific community interventions such as looking at specific needs for community police stations and the requirements for other support services that may have been identified. It can also assist in developing an understanding around the specific causes underlying GBVF and how it can be addressed, to find ways of creating social cohesion and better conversations around gender equality and different sexual orientations. If properly developed such an analysis toolkit and data can change the paradigm of how women are viewed and treated. For example, one of the root causes of GBVF is patriarchy. The patriarchal system is so entrenched in all communities for various reasons that it will take deliberate and consistent effort and support to eliminate GBVF and gender inequality. With the right data and analysis, it will be possible to predict and prevent GBVF, influence policy, appropriate interventions and crucially, resource allocations.

The goal must be to develop a tool with an intersectional lens that can analyze those social identities that tend to be ignored and the different contexts for different communities, so that any solution developed will truly address the issues that provide an enabling environment for GBVF. Such an approach would enable a more comprehensive measurement and understanding of the real magnitude of this phenomenon and enable monitoring of patterns and trends over time. To achieve same, a collaborative approach to ending GBVF is required. Collaboration across sectors, academic disciplines, civil society, and government hold the key to finding a sustainable solution.

Finally, the increasing prevalence of GBVF at HEIs in South Africa is a major concern to all. The high rates of violence in HEIs is indicative of fundamental challenges in the institutional cultures, the curricula and the management and governance of the universities. Profound transformations are urgently required to guarantee freedom from GBVF in HEIs and to transform higher education so that it should be focused on promoting social justice and human rights. It is therefore crucial that GBVF becomes an important area of research and discourse in higher education, much as decolonization and the alienation of students from the spaces and cultures of HEIs are.

This is an important proposal as HEIs play a key role in the developmental agenda of the country. These spaces cannot be conducive or be seen to be conducive to the different acts of GBV. Indeed, HEIs should be at the forefront of international, national, and regional efforts to curb social injustices and human rights violations. The students of these institutions must be inculcated with values and teachings that encourages them to be agents of change in stereotypes and social biases and in denormalizing GBV. One of the best ways to "reduce the risk of violence is to empower women and maximize their role in society."[33] Reducing the risk of violence to women through empowerment and social participation prevents more than just individual cases of GBV. Peace, equality, and social justice prevail when women are empowered to participate in society and act against gender-based injustices.[34]

In this regard, HEIs must be proactive in ensuring that students are initiated and facilitated into educational spaces and programs, which challenge deeply embedded inequalities and social norms, that on the one hand, sustain patriarchal control and power, and on the other hand, tolerates and encourages violence against those who are perceived to be weak.[35] Management of universities need to be proactive in GBVF resolutions. They must continuously review their initiatives, programs, etc., and ensure that there are robust policies that are reflective of the changing climate to effectively address GBV directly. They must actively ensure that relevant knowledge on how students and members must respond to survivors of GBV is imparted and provide information on spaces where these survivors can seek support and redress. Universities must invest in awareness trainings, GBV services and support programs for survivors. Every member of the university community must have access to information about campus-based and external services and support for GBV related matters and for the survivors.

Ultimately it is clear that that more research is required to better understand what is driving increases in GBVF in certain contexts and what the enabling factors and pathways to prevention are in contexts where there have been decreases in GBVF.

References

Böök B et al (2020) Gendering the COVID-19 crisis: a mapping of its impact and call for action in light of EU gender equality law and policy. Eur Equal Law Rev 2020(2):22–44

Centre for the Study of Violence and Reconciliation (2016) Gender-based violence (GBV) in South Africa: a brief review. https://www.csvr.org.za/pdf/Gender%20Based%20Violence%20in%20South%20Africa%20-%20A%20Brief%20Review.pdf. Accessed on 26 Jan 2023

Crenshaw K (1991) Mapping the margins: intersectionality, identity politics, and violence against women of color. Stanford Law Rev 43(6):1241–1299

Deane T (2021) Marrying young: limiting the impact of a crisis on the high prevalence of child marriages in Niger. Laws 10(3):61. https://doi.org/10.3390/laws10030061

Hudson V et al (2012) Sex and world peace. Columbia University Press, New York

Human Rights Watch (2021, November 24) South Africa: broken promises to aid gender-based violence survivors. https://www.hrw.org/news/2021/11/24/south-africa-broken-promises-aid-gender-based-violence-survivors. Accessed on 8 Feb 2023

Jayasinghe T, Ward E (2018) Responding to violence, restoring justice. https://bcrw.barnard.edu/publications/responding-to-violence-restoring-justice/. Accessed on 19 Nov 2023

[33] Hudson et al. (2012).

[34] Women's International League for Peace and Freedom (2014).

[35] Mendes et al. (2019).

KPMG (2017) Too costly to ignore – the economic impact of gender-based violence in South Africa. https://assets.kpmg.com/content/dam/kpmg/za/pdf/2017/01/za-Too-costly-to-ignore.pdf. Accessed on 14 Apr 2023

Meel BL (2005) HIV/AIDS Post-Exposure Prophylaxis (PEP) for victims of sexual assault in South Africa. Med Sci Law 45(3):219–224. https://doi.org/10.1258/rsmmsl.45.3.219

Meger S (2016) Rape loot pillage: the political economy of sexual violence in armed conflict. Oxford Academic, New York. https://doi.org/10.1093/acprof:oso/9780190277666.003.0006

Mendes K et al (2019) Digital feminist activism: girls and women fight back against rape culture. Oxford University Press, New York

Mpani P, Nsibande N (2015) Understanding gender policy and gender- based violence in South Africa: a literature review. Tshwaranang Legal Advocacy Centre

National Government of South Africa (2023) Independent Police Investigative Directorate. https://nationalgovernment.co.za/units/view/20/independent-police-investigative-directorate-ipid#:~:text=The%20mission%20of%20the%20Independent,standards%20of%20integrity%20and%20excellence. Accessed on 10 Aug 2023

Ouedraogo R, Stenzel D (2021) The heavy economic toll of gender-based violence: evidence from Sub-Saharan Africa. International Monetary Fund

Rogers J, Kelly UA (2011) Feminist intersectionality: bringing social justice to health disparities research. Nurs Ethics 18(3):397–407

South African Human Rights Commission (2021) Action on gender equality: the past, present and future are weighted against women. https://www.sahrc.org.za/index.php/sahrc-media/opinion-pieces/item/2769-action-on-gender-equality-the-past-present-and-future-are-weighted-against-women. Accessed on 21 Mar 2023

UN Women (2016) The economic costs of violence against women', Remarks by UN Assistant Secretary-General and Deputy Executive Director of UN Women, Lakshmi Puri, at the High-level discussion on the 'Economic Cost of Violence against Women'. https://www.unwomen.org/en/news/stories/2016/9/speech-by-lakshmi-puri-on-economic-costs-of-violence-againstwomen. Accessed on 27 Dec 2023

United Nations (2020) Report of the Secretary-General on the intensification of efforts to eliminate all forms of violence against women and girls. https://undocs.org/en/A/75/274. Accessed on 24 Dec 2023

United Nations General Assembly (2012) Report of the Special Rapporteur on Violence against Women. https://www.ohchr.org/Documents/Issues/Women/A.HRC.20.16_En.pdf. Accessed on 2 Dec 2023

United Nations Office on Drugs and Crime (2020) The handbook on gender-responsive police services for women and girls subject to violence. https://www.unodc.org/documents/middleeastandnorthafrica/2021/handbook-on-gender-responsive-police-services-en.pdf. Accessed on 23 Dec 2023

United Nations Population Fund (2020) Impact of COVID-19 pandemic on family planning and ending gender-based violence, female genital mutilation and child marriage. https://www.unfpa.org/sites/default/files/resource-pdf/COVID-19_impact_brief_for_UNFPA_24_April_2020_1.pdf. Accessed on 26 Dec 2023

United Nations Women Europe and Central Asia (2019) The value of intersectionality in understanding violence against women and girls (VAWG) July 2019. https://eca.unwomen.org/en/digital-library/publications/2019/10/the-value-of-intersectionality-in-understanding-violence-against-women-and-girls#view. Accessed on 12 Dec 2023

Women's International League for Peace and Freedom (2014) Does gender equality lead to peace? Fact sheet building on the global study on 1325. https://www.peacewomen.org/sites/default/files/Fact%20Sheet%20Gender%20Equality.pdf. Accessed on 2 Dec 2023

World Bank (2020) Women, business and the law 2020. The World Bank Group, Washington DC

GPSR Compliance

The European Union's (EU) General Product Safety Regulation (GPSR) is a set of rules that requires consumer products to be safe and our obligations to ensure this.

If you have any concerns about our products, you can contact us on ProductSafety@springernature.com

In case Publisher is established outside the EU, the EU authorized representative is:

Springer Nature Customer Service Center GmbH
Europaplatz 3
69115 Heidelberg, Germany

The manufacturer's authorised representative in the EU is Springer Nature Customer Service Centre GmbH, Europaplatz 3, 69115 Heidelberg, Germany. If you have any concerns regarding our products, please contact ProductSafety@springernature.com

Printed and bound by CPI Group (UK) Ltd, Croydon, CR0 4YY
01/10/2026
02225865-0006